History vs Hollywood

"Never let the truth stand in the way of a good story." For decades this famous maxim could have served as the motto of countless Hollywood filmmakers. Though for centuries writers and artists have been selective with the facts in order to dazzle an audience, some of tinseltown's biggest blockbusters have taken a pickaxe to the past, and torn up timelines in the name of entertainment. From *Gladiator* to *Apollo 13*, over the following pages *History vs Hollywood* uncovers the real-life characters and stories behind some of cinema's all-time classics. Will they turn out to be factual flops, or take the Academy Award for accuracy? Read on to find out.

Contents

Timeline of Key Events 6
The Birth of Hollywood 8
Golden Age Tours and Sites 14
Hollywood Influencers 16
Inside a Golden Age Film Set 18
Hollywood Goes to War 20

★ **HISTORY VS HOLLYWOOD SCORE** ★

We have dug up the real history behind Hollywood's biggest flops and blockbusters. Each gets a score based on its tinseltown dazzle, combined with its faithfulness to the facts.

ANCIENT

The Fall of the Roman Empire (1964)	28
Cleopatra (1963)	30
300 (2006)	34
Ben-Hur (1959)	36
Gladiator (2000)	38
Spartacus (1960)	42
Troy (2004)	44
Pompeii (2014)	46
Alexander (2004)	48

DRAMA

Titanic (1997)	52
Gangs of New York (2002)	56
The Untouchables (1987)	57
Lincoln (2012)	58
Robin Hood - Prince of Thieves (1991)	60
Amistad (1997)	61
All The President's Men (1976)	62
Apollo 13 (1995)	63
Lawrence Of Arabia (1962)	64
The King (2019)	66
The Other Boleyn Girl (2008)	68
JFK (1991)	70

WAR

Das Boot (1981)	76
The Great Escape (1963)	78
Fury (2014)	82
The Patriot (2000)	83
Braveheart (1995)	84
Dunkirk (2017)	88
Pearl Harbor (2001)	90
The Killing Fields (1984)	91
Kingdom of Heaven (2005)	92
Downfall (2004)	94
Enemy at the Gates (2001)	98

BIOPIC

The Aviator (2004)	102
12 Years A Slave (2013)	103
The Young Victoria (2009)	104
Amadeus (1984)	108
Casanova (2005)	109
Marie Antoinette (2006)	110
The Last Emperor (1987)	112
Becoming Jane (2007)	113
Joan Of Arc (1948)	114
First Man (2018)	118
Elizabeth: The Golden Age (2007)	122
Selma (2014)	124
Malcolm X (1992)	126

KEY EVENTS

Take a look at some of the groundbreaking moments in the history of Tinseltown

The Golden Age of Hollywood lasted until the 1950s/1960s.

1915 THE BIRTH OF A NATION
The controversial silent film *The Birth Of A Nation*, directed by DW Griffith, marks the beginning of Hollywood's Golden Age thanks to its advanced production techniques. However, it also includes racist depictions of African Americans and makes the KKK into heroes.

1927 THE JAZZ SINGER
The Jazz Singer starring Al Jolson and Warner Oland becomes the first feature length film to have a synchronised vocal track as well as music. It sparks the popularity of movies with sound, and a couple of years later most Hollywood films are 'talkies'.

FILMMAKERS ATTRACTED TO CALIFORNIA c. 1908
The varied scenery and good climate of Southern California attracts people from the film industry who had previously been making movies in Chicago and New York.

WARNER BROS. ESTABLISHED 1923
One of the big five film studios, Warner Brothers Inc is founded by Harry, Jack, Albert and Samuel Warner. They produce the first talkie.

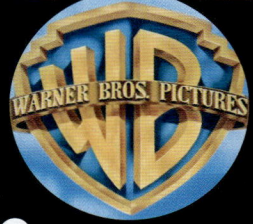

HAYS CODE 1934
The Hays Code is imposed by the film industry to regulate Hollywood movies. It features rules on violence and profanities and remains in place until 1968.

1915 — 1923 — 1927 — 1939

HOLLYWOOD THRIVES c. 1918
Due to the events of World War I in Europe, Hollywood productions begin to overtake the success of European film, dominating the landscape of international cinema.

THE KING OF HOLLYWOOD 1931
The charismatic Clark Gable, commonly known as the King of Hollywood, is credited with a main role in a film for the first time.

SNOW WHITE AND THE SEVEN DWARFS 1937
Disney's first feature length film *Snow White And The Seven Dwarfs* is released. Its advanced animation marks the beginning of a plethora of animated movies.

1923 HOLLYWOOD SIGN FIRST BUILT
The iconic Hollywood sign is first constructed as an advertisement for a new housing estate that had been built in the hills. Originally reading 'Hollywoodland', the sign eventually loses the 'land' and becomes an integral and infamous landmark of Hollywood, Los Angeles.

The Hollywood sign was rebuilt in 1978 thanks to donations from wealthy benefactors including Hugh Hefner and Alice Cooper.

1939 GONE WITH THE WIND
Based on the hugely popular novel by Margaret Mitchell, Victor Fleming's *Gone With The Wind* breaks box office records. Starring Clark Gable and Vivien Leigh, it is believed by some to be the highest grossing movie of all time. The film wins ten Academy Awards.

Key Events

1972 — THE GODFATHER
Combining the epic storytelling of old Hollywood with the grounded performances of New Hollywood, Francis Ford Coppola's *The Godfather* is released after a period of great anticipation. Widely regarded as one of the greatest films of all time, it stars Hollywood icons including Marlon Brando and Al Pacino.

The portrayal of Italian-Americans in The Godfather transformed how Italians were traditionally depicted in Hollywood films.

THE WIZARD OF OZ — 1939
An iconic film in Hollywood's history and a moment in American popular culture, *The Wizard Of Oz* delights audiences with its use of colour and music.

THE SEVEN YEAR ITCH — 1955
The Seven Year Itch is released, with its star Marilyn Monroe providing one of the most emblematic images of Hollywood glamour from the 1950s.

JAWS — 1975
Widely considered the first blockbuster, Steven Spielberg's *Jaws*, a movie about a monstrous shark, is released. The film paves the way for expensive action movies.

CASABLANCA — 1942
A film about love and sacrifice, *Casablanca* is still considered one of the best movies to have come out of old Hollywood. It stars Humphrey Bogart and Ingrid Bergman.

SIDNEY POITIER WINS OSCAR — 1964
Sidney Poitier becomes the first Black winner of the Best Actor Academy Award for his role in *Lilies Of The Field* in 1963.

STAR WARS — 1977
The first film of the *Star Wars* series is released, presenting a new form of escapism and adventure to audiences. It also marks the beginning of huge Hollywood franchises.

1952 — SINGIN' IN THE RAIN
Epitomising the best of Hollywood musicals, *Singin' In The Rain* starring Gene Kelly and Debbie Reynolds is released. The musical is set in Hollywood itself, with the plot revolving around the transition from silent films to talkies in the 1920s.

1967 — BONNIE AND CLYDE
Centred on the real American criminals Bonnie Parker and Clyde Barrow, the movie *Bonnie And Clyde* starring Warren Beatty and Faye Dunaway is released. The film marks the beginning of the New Hollywood phase, where movies become cheaper, but also take more creative risks.

7

The Birth of HOLLY[WOOD]

How four penniless Jewish immigrant siblings changed the face of entertainment forever and wrote their own fairy tale

Written by Robin Brown

Jack Warner always wanted to be famous. Actually, make that adored, powerful, rich and famous. Born Jacob Warner in impoverished Canada to Jewish immigrant parents in 1892, he changed his name to something more theatrical: Jack L Warner. As a young man he grew up obsessed with images, hanging around photography studios in the hope of being used for test shots. While his brothers were recognising the potential of early film projectors, investing in a Kinetoscope projector, Jack made money singing in theatres, showing little interest in – or aptitude for – the less glamorous side of show business.

Willed on by his parents and clubbing together with his brothers – Albert, Harry and Sam – Jack toured the Northern states showing old prints of *The Great Train Robbery*, drawing enough cash to buy a series of local theatres and launch their own distribution company, the Duquesne Amusement Company. However, the brothers' ambition didn't stop at a network of provincial theatres. The Warners had their sights set on global domination.

At the turn of the century many others were also heading west to seek a new life. One of these was Harvey Wilcox, who bought 160 acres (64 hectares) of land to the west of Los Angeles in the ironic hope of founding a conservative community. On the train from Kansas, Wilcox and his wife got chatting to a woman who talked of her summer home: Hollywood.

Wilcox's vision of founding a community became a reality and in 1910 Hollywood officially

The birth of Hollywood

JACK WARNER
American, 1892-1978

Brief Bio One of the original group of movie moguls who shaped the nascent Hollywood, Jack L Warner was the cofounder of Warner Bros Studios. With brothers Harry, Sam and Albert he launched Warner Brothers in 1923 and became the dominant force of the four siblings.

Equally feared and admired, Jack was the typical mogul of Hollywood's Golden Age and was known for his ruthlessness in business. Neither actors nor directors were immune from Jack. He even disposed of his own brothers when they outlived their usefulness, discarded his wife and son when he grew tired of them and was known for casual cruelty to staff.
A notorious philanderer, Jack abandoned his wife and son for another woman in 1935. Following the death of his much-loved brother Sam in 1927, Jack's frosty relationship with Harry and Albert came to a head in 1956 when the former sold the studio's rights to films made before 1950 for a paltry sum and later arranged to buy back Warner's stock that had previously been sold, installing himself as president. The brothers never spoke again and Jack refused to attend Harry's funeral in 1958. In 1969, Jack was seen as the last of a dying breed of studio heads and, after seeing his power gradually slip away, retired. Warner Brothers remains one of Hollywood's most powerful studios to this day.

became a part of Los Angeles. At the same time, a group of actors and directors - drawn to the area by the sunny climate, lack of taxes and freedom from patents issued by Thomas Edison's Motion Picture Patents Company - started shooting motion pictures in what is now the film-making capital of the world. In 1911 Hollywood got its first studio, when the Blondeau Tavern on Sunset Boulevard became the Nestor Film Company - firing the starting pistol on a gold rush that would take place over the next two decades.

A few years later, in 1917, Jack Warner had been dispatched to Los Angeles where he bought the rights to *My Four Years In Germany*, a memoir by the US ambassador to Germany who lived in that country during the First World War. In the face of threats from local theatre owners and impressive offers from distributors, the brothers held fast and premiered the movie themselves, making a small fortune in the process. Riding anti-German sentiment following the war, the film was a smash. Warner Brothers now had a place at the top table of American film producers.

In 1918, the siblings formed Warner Brothers West Coast Studios, later incorporated as the more recognisable Warner Brothers in 1923, and moved to Hollywood. Jack shared production duties with brother Sam while Harry and Albert sold distribution rights and they launched enthusiastically into a series of low-budget farces. However, the films were not a success and the company dangled on the edge of a

Making Movies
The main players behind the 1919 picture *Bumping into Broadway*

THE CAMERAMAN
Innovation was key in early film cameras, with devices bulky, hard to move and requiring constant hand cranking. Having to crank a camera while focusing and aiming was difficult, so shooting was often static. Smaller cameras like the Mitchell Standard were introduced in the 1920s but the advent of sound recording posed more problems – namely the issue of sound emanating from the mechanism while recording. Stylistic innovations were slow to appear in early films due to the difficulty of using equipment.

THE DIRECTOR
(HAL ROACH)
Directors were rarely used for the ability to craft sophisticated movies in the silent era – a dynamic that continued into the talkie era. Technical knowledge and the ability to work quickly were more highly prized, with many early directors sourced from producers, actors, writers or entrepreneurs. Hal Roach was an exception, with a career lasting for several decades and well into the

THE STAR
(HAROLD LLOYD)
Stars could earn a lot of money, depending on their levels of fame. Silent film stars such as Charlie Chaplin, Harold Lloyd and Buster Keaton could command film deals worth tens of millions of dollars in today's money. Most had a strong understanding of their appeal and how it should be conveyed – enjoying significant creative freedom. That would all gradually change under the studio system of the late-1920s and throughout the 1930s.

Four brothers with a dream: Harry, Sam, Jack and Albert Warner

A still from 1927's *Tracked By The Police* starring the dog Rin Tin Tin

THE SUPPORTING ARTIST
(SNUB POLLARD)

Supporting artists were kept in steady employment during the churn-'em-out days of silent films. Skills learned in vaudeville and physical theatre translated well in silent films, though many less polished artists found that their unattractive or heavily-accented voices and inability to learn scripts harmed their prospect when talkies took over. Snub Pollard enjoyed some success in the silent era but found mostly bit-part and extra work from the

THE LEADING LADY
(BEBE DANIELS)

Most films had a female protagonist opposite the leading man. The actresses had often learned their craft in theatres, but were mainly cast for their looks. Romances between prominent actors and actresses were not uncommon – studios were known to encourage or even fabricate relationships to generate publicity. Many careers did not survive the transition to talkies – Bebe Daniels

Jack Warner in 1973, shortly after he had been ousted from his own studio

The birth of Hollywood

financial chasm – moving to a down-at-heel neighbourhood that locals referred to as Poverty Row. Salvation was to come in the most unlikely of forms.

A German Shepherd called Rin Tin Tin proved to be the saviour of Warner Brothers. The trained dog – rescued from a battlefield by a US soldier in the First World War – became the star of a series of silent films of derring-do. The canine appeared in over 27 Hollywood films for Warner Bros, becoming famous around the world. Noting Warner Brothers' flirtation with bankruptcy, Jack called Rin Tin Tin "the mortgage lifter."

> "Noting Warner Brothers' flirtation with bankruptcy, Jack called Rin Tin Tin 'the mortgage lifter'"

The German Shepherd was so popular in Hollywood that the Academy of Motion Pictures voted the dog best actor in 1929; sadly the Academy insisted that a human actor take the Oscar. The Rin Tin Tin films were written by Darryl F Zanuck, who later became Jack Warner's executive producer and right-hand man before his dislike of the Warners drove him to what would become 20th Century Fox. Adding names such as director Ernst Lubitsch and star John Barrymore to Warner Brothers' roster boosted sales and also lent the studio some respectability.

On the back of these successes – and fearing being shut out by the established studios – the Warners expanded, purchasing theatre companies, building a laboratory to develop film and investing in new hardware. Warners led the way with a vertical model. Rather than being a cog in a larger mechanism, the studio owned it all, from production to distribution to exhibition. Most moguls came from theatre companies so already had distribution tied up (some had virtual monopolies in certain cities) while adding production allowed for the greatest return on investment. The Warners had to beg, steal and borrow to be able to take on the existing studios.

As well as Warner Brothers, four other big studios were to emerge in the 1920s, which would become Hollywood studios recognised today: Paramount was headed by Adolph Zukor and had a reputation for quality silent films; 20th Century Fox was created from a merger in 1935, headed by Warner's old colleague Darryl F Zanuck; MGM had a huge talent roster and produced many of the era's most famous pictures; RKO concentrated their efforts on films noir.

By the 1920s, most US film production occurred in or near Hollywood. By the end of the decade, there were 20 Hollywood studios averaging about 800 film releases in a year – far in excess of modern Hollywood. Films were being manufactured in modular format, aping the success of Henry Ford's production-line process. Swashbucklers, historical or biblical epics and melodramas were most popular, though Warners would blaze a trail with gangster capers and Universal became known for its horror films. Meanwhile, Charlie Chaplin, Buster Keaton, Harold Lloyd and Laurel & Hardy were popular for their comedic movies.

The studio system that emerged enforced long-term contracts for stars and rigid control of both them and directors. This system ensured strong profits and a de facto monopoly – by 1929, the 'Big Five' studios produced over 90 per cent of the fiction titles in the States. Studios also distributed their films internationally, hogging the profits at every step of film-making and distribution.

The studios didn't just control the logistics of film-making though. They would snap up promising, good-looking young actors and actresses and construct a new

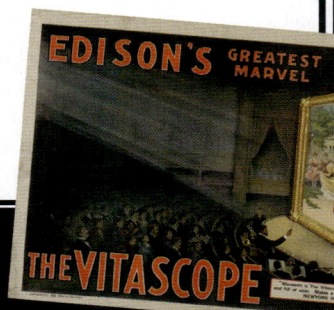

The Birth Of Cinema

By the late-19th century a number of basic methods for showing moving images existed, but none were able to show genuine sequential images filmed by one camera, usually relying on optical illusions or a bank of multiple cameras to replicate moving images. In 1888, Thomas Edison registered a patent for a device that would "do for the eye what the phonograph does for the ear" – record and reproduce objects in motion. Despite his realisation of the Kinetoscope, the invention could only be used by one person at a time. Edison recognised that films projected for large audiences would be a lot more profitable.

The inventor backed another device, the Thomas Armat-designed Vitascope, and publicly demonstrated it on 23 April 1896, at Koster and Bial's Music Hall in New York City. The audience was treated to moving pictures of dancing, a beach, burlesque boxing match and snippets from plays – all were described gushingly as 'wonderfully real and singularly exhilarating.' It was the first public showing of a motion picture on a screen in the States, a feat recognised today in a plaque erected next to Macy's Department Store in New York city.

The event opened up the way for motion pictures to be developed on a mass scale. Ever the businessman, Edison soon dispensed with the Vitascope, patenting his own version, the Projecting Kinetoscope, a few months later.

11

The Warner Brothers' studio lot in its early years

public image for them, often changing their names, putting them through vocal coaching - a necessity for many in the emerging talkie era - and even forcing some to undergo plastic surgery. Studios would choose which films their star made, arrange their romantic lives and force them to adhere to strict moral codes. There was significant irony to this. Jack Warner was used to having his pick of the starlets, enjoying the power that came with the success of the Warner Brothers' talkies.

In 1925, buoyed by financial and moral support from United Artists - an independent founded by Douglas Fairbanks Sr, Mark Pickford and Charlie Chaplin - the Warners embarked on a set of acquisitions, appointments and impulsive purchases. Chief among them was a bunch of old machinery from a radio station, because Sam and Jack had an idea. While silent films had their appeal - they were universal due to their lack of a specific language and sound-synchronisation technology was appallingly basic - the two brothers recognised the fantastic possibilities offered by talking pictures.

Chief among the new technologies they pursued was the new Vitaphone film sound process that allowed for synchronisation of sound and moving images, with sounds played on a gramophone. By the mid-1920s it was clear to Jack, despite his initial personal doubts, that the studio that successfully developed sound would reap immense

"Sam Warner fell into a coma and died at the age of 40, the day before The Jazz Singer's premiere"

rewards. Other studios were investing heavily in the technology so Warners couldn't afford to be left behind. While the resulting Vitaphone technology was basic, Warner Brothers quickly kitted out their theatres with new kit, cementing them as the leaders of the new media but at the cost of $3 million; it was an enormous gamble.

Championed by Sam Warner as a cheaper alternative to paying for live music in theatres, and in the face of resistance from Harry, the new technology paved the way for 1926's *Don Juan*. Although music and sound effects featured, there was no synchronised speech. Still, the reception to the film was overwhelmingly positive - it had changed the face of the industry. But while the studio enjoyed critical success, the bottom line wasn't nearly so healthy and the cost of producing the film and fitting out theatres with the new Vitaphone projectors almost wiped them out.

With the studio mortgaged up to the hilt, the brothers embarked on another ambitious plan: the next project would feature synchronised dialogue. 1927's *The Jazz Singer* was the first to include speech and was a smash hit, earning Warner Brothers millions of dollars, despite a budget that was considered exorbitant at the time, concerns over their star's acting abilities and the quality of the script. Realising Jolson's claim to the audience that "you ain't heard nothin' yet", Warner's stock went stratospheric; at $132 a share it was worth nearly seven times the value prior to *The Jazz Singer*. The gamble had paid off, and handsomely too - the film ensured the studio was now swimming in cash.

The celebrations would be short-lived, though. Jack had noticed that his brother Sam had been struggling with his balance and suffering from nosebleeds - the result of undiagnosed infections caused by abscessed teeth. Following months of ill health, Sam Warner fell into a coma and died at the age of 40, the day before *The Jazz Singer*'s premiere.

While he was devastated by the loss of his closest brother, this was Jack's moment. Without Sam, he became the studio's head of production, inheriting his brother's drive but combining it with a fire and no-nonsense attitude. Unlike Sam, who was generally liked, Jack gained a reputation as an uncaring boss - happy to slash costs and lay off staff for the sake of the bottom line. Under his

The birth of Hollywood

Sam Warner with his wife Lina and daughter Lita in 1925

leadership the studio gambled the astonishing sum of $100 million on the purchase of rival film studio First National. When The Wall Street Crash of 1929 - while not denting the film industry as badly as other industries - occured it meant that, for a while, money was tight.

The studio's response was to ramp up production to a staggering 80 films a year by 1929. With no one to check his behaviour, Jack became notorious as one of the most unpleasant men in Hollywood - in a town filled with unpleasant men no mean achievement. Further acquisitions and expansion would make Warner Bros one of the Big Five studios and Jack Warner one of Hollywood's most powerful players - he was, by this point, a huge success by any reasonable measure. Warner Bros had matched, then bought out and finally beaten rivals into submission, becoming the equal of the four biggest studios, MGM, 20th Century Fox, RKO and Paramount by 1930. It had taken 20 years but the Warner Brothers had done it.

The impact of Warner Bros is hard to overstate. With the release of *The Jazz Singer* the brothers revolutionised the industry - some stars were finished overnight while others saw new opportunities opening up. Silent films were dead within one or two years. Beyond that the structure of Warner Bros - with stars under contract, films made in-house at studios, owned outright and distributed to theatres owned by the studio - combined with pioneering use of new technologies and rampant acquisition of theatre chains and other studios amounted to an economic powerhouse. The four brothers were instrumental in introducing the studio system that Hollywood would become known for - and it was unbeatable.

From poor outsiders, immigrants, they had sweated, gambled, bartered and sacrificed to reach the apex of Hollywood. Jack Warner - who had once sung, badly, for pennies - was a powerful studio boss; the Golden Age of Hollywood arriving. For an ambitious boy who had always yearned for power, respect and adulation, it was a classic rags-to-riches story, worthy of a film script from one of Hollywood's greatest studios.

THE EARLY YEARS OF HOLLYWOOD BY THE NUMBERS

800
The number of movies produced, per year, in Hollywood at the height of its popularity

130,000
Number of residents in Hollywood by 1925 - up from a mere 30,000 in 1919

1923
The erection of the Hollywood sign; it first read 'Hollywoodland' but lost the suffix in 1949

$1.6billion
Inflation-adjusted gross earned by *Gone With The Wind* on release in 1939 - still the highest of any film

400
The number of US movie theatres wired for sound in 1927; by 1930 silent films were almost obsolete

$3.9million
The cost of the silent era's most expensive film, the 1925 version of *Ben-Hur*

2,500
Total number of screen performers in *Gone With The Wind*

Places to Explore

GOLDEN AGE TOURS & SITES
Discover the studios, stars and props that built one of Hollywood's most successful eras

1 PARAMOUNT PICTURES STUDIO TOUR
MELROSE AVENUE, HOLLYWOOD

Having been founded in 1912, Paramount Pictures Studio is the longest operating major studio in Hollywood. It was here that classics such as *King Kong (1933)*, *Sunset Boulevard (1950)* and *Breakfast At Tiffany's (1961)* were filmed, as well as later successes like *The Godfather (1972)* and *Star Trek The Motion Picture (1979)*.

Films and TV series are still being produced on-site, allowing you to get close to the classics while also learning about how the modern production process works. In the foyer you'll find an array of costumes created by Edith Head, one of Hollywood's most famous designers who won eight Academy Awards for her work.

When she became chief designer at Paramount in 1938, she was the first woman ever to lead a design department at a major studio, designing costumes for stars like Grace Kelly and Audrey Hepburn. You can also visit the Prop Warehouse and see famous backlots like the New York Street backlot and the iconic Bronson Gate that appeared in *Sunset Boulevard*.

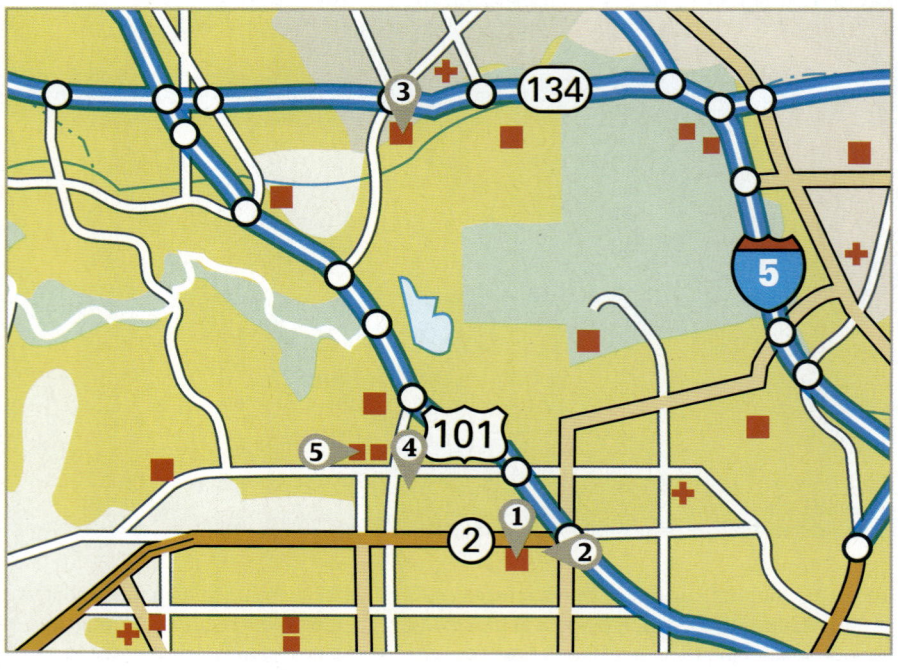

Costumes designed by Edith Head appear alongside uniforms from *Star Trek*

The Bronson Gate at the entrance to the studio appeared in the 1950 film *Sunset Boulevard*

2 HOLLYWOOD FOREVER CEMETERY
SANTA MONICA BOULEVARD, LOS ANGELES

Behind Paramount Pictures Studio lies a tranquil expanse of green overlooked by the famous white Hollywood sign on the hillside above. This is Hollywood Forever Cemetery, where many of the greats have found their final resting place and where many tourists flock each year to pay their respects to their favourite stars. The cemetery was founded in 1899 and is beautifully laid out, with light and airy mausoleums like the Judy Garland Pavilion and a large lake surrounded by monuments and statues.

Hattie McDaniel from *Gone With The Wind* was eventually memorialised with a pink cenotaph beside the lake in 1999

The site is impressively vast, but you can pick up a map from the flower shop by the entrance to help you navigate your way around. Near the centre of the park lies Mel Blanc, the famed *Looney Tunes* voice actor, while Peter Lorre, Mickey Rooney and Rudolph Valentino rest in the Cathedral Mausoleum on the east side.

The marble tomb of Douglas Fairbanks lies just outside this, along with a bronze statue of the dog who played Toto in *The Wizard Of Oz*.

A monument to the Cairn Terrier named Terry who played Toto in *The Wizard Of Oz*

Places to Explore

A cart will take you on a tour around backlots spread across 110 acres

Learn about 100 years of Warner Bros. history in their welcome centre

3 WARNER BROS. STUDIO: CLASSICS TOUR
WARNER BOULEVARD, BURBANK

Warner Brothers Pictures was founded more than 100 years ago in 1923 by four brothers named Harry, Albert, Samuel and Jack. The Hollywood studio that you can visit today was managed by Sam and Jack and was responsible for many classics such as *The Maltese Falcon (1941)*, *Casablanca (1942)*, *Rebel Without A Cause (1955)* and *My Fair Lady (1964)*, along with westerns like *Blazing Saddles (1974)* and TV series *Cheyenne* which debuted in 1955.

Fans of the Golden Age of Hollywood can see many of the places where filming took place by taking their three-hour Classics Tour. The welcome centre introduces you to the 100-year history of Warner Bros. Studio before you board a cart to explore the studio's extensive backlots with the help of a studio guide. You'll see the Midwest Street backlot, which has been featured in nearly 400 movies and shows and is where films such as *The Music Man*, *East Of Eden* and *Rebel Without A Cause* were filmed, and you can also see the last remaining exterior set from *Casablanca* on the French Street backlot.

Some may wish to pay a trip to the fountain featured in the opening credits of the TV show *Friends* and may also be interested to know that the same fountain appeared in earlier comedies by *The Three Stooges*. Stage 48 includes a self-guided exhibition where you can see costumes and memorabilia from *Casablanca* and *My Fair Lady*, along with sets from modern TV shows like *Friends* and *The Big Bang Theory*.

The Art Deco style Max Factor building now contains the Hollywood Museum

4 THE HOLLYWOOD MUSEUM
N. HIGHLAND AVE, HOLLYWOOD

Housed in the historic Max Factor Building, where Hollywood's "make-up king" transformed the looks of stars like Joan Crawford, Bette Davis, Katharine Hepburn and Lucille Ball, is the Hollywood Museum.

Purchased by Max Factor in 1928 and opened in 1935, this building became a revered make-up salon and attracted a host of aspiring film stars looking to create a glamorous on-screen look.

The building has been renovated in its original Art Deco style and you can visit several of Max Factor's restored make-up rooms today, which include some of their original displays and details about the techniques used. It also now contains the largest collection of Hollywood memorabilia in the world, featuring over 10,000 authentic objects displayed across more than 35,000 square feet of exhibition space.

There are hundreds of costumes on display, including Marilyn Monroe's million-dollar dress, costumes worn by Shirley Temple, and Dorothy Gale's ruby slippers. You can also see cars like Cary Grant's Rolls-Royce, along with a range of props, photographs, scripts, and the earliest Technicolor film ever shot.

5 HOLLYWOOD BOULEVARD
HOLLYWOOD BOULEVARD, LA

Head for a walk along Hollywood Boulevard and you can discover two world-famous Hollywood sites in one go: the stars that make up the Walk of Fame and the forecourt of Grauman's Chinese Theatre. Based on an idea initially devised by EM Stuart in 1953, the Walk of Fame has become an iconic symbol of Hollywood, with stars in the colours of coral and gold lining the pavement, each dedicated to a key figure from the entertainment industry.

Beginning with silent film actors like Olive Borden, Ronald Colman and Louise Fazenda, the stars are still being added to with around 24 ceremonies taking place each year and more than 2,700 stars installed so far. In an earlier tradition, the forecourt of Grauman's Chinese Theatre at 6925 Hollywood Boulevard is scattered with signatures and imprints set down in cement by various different stars.

The idea came to theatre owner Sid Grauman when silent film star Norma Talmadge visited in 1927 and accidentally stepped in the new theatre's drying cement. Since then, many of Hollywood's greatest stars have been memorialised here and the ceremonies have been used as an opportunity to promote upcoming films. Most slabs include handprints and footprints with an accompanying name signed in the cement, but some stars have left more unusual imprints, such as Betty Grable's leg, John Barrymore's face, George Burns' cigar, and Marilyn Monroe's earring.

Stars have been continuously added to the Walk of Fame since 1960

Sid Grauman came up with this novel way to celebrate Hollywood stars in 1927

Hall of Fame

HOLLYWOOD INFLUENCERS

Ten of the most impactful men and women in the evolution of Tinseltown

FRANCES MARION
AMERICAN, 1888 – 1973

Having arrived in Hollywood in the silent era when a script could be little more than a handful of scenarios to play out, Marion helped to define the screenwriter role. She started as an actress, but quickly transitioned behind the camera, writing in both the silent and talkie eras for some of the biggest performers of the time. She was a star writer for MGM, credited with some of its great success, eventually making over 300 movies in her career.

Charlie Chaplin
British, 1889 – 1977

One of the most famous names and faces from the silent era of cinema, 'The Little Tramp' helped to transform the comic character archetype of cinema from a sidekick role to the star. In fact, Chaplin was one of the first truly global stars thanks to a string of sympathetic everyman performances that could be enjoyed by everyone. He also changed the business of Hollywood when he co-founded United Artists in 1919 to help produce and distribute his films. They backed independent artists to create their visions until it was bought out by MGM in the 1980s.

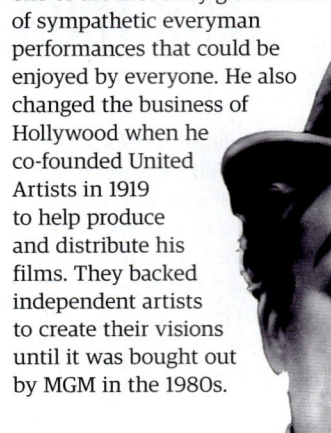

Chaplin's re-entry permit to America was revoked in 1952 over accusations he was a communist sympathiser.

Marilyn Monroe
American, 1926 – 1962

There were plenty of Hollywood 'stars' before Marilyn Monroe, but few who could be argued to have been bigger after her. Making her name in the 1950s, Monroe upended traditional images of femininity at the time, becoming a fashion and style icon as well as a box office smash. The way in which she played with and against her sexualised image, often for comic effect, was also trend-setting. The tragic end of her life put Hollywood's treatment of its stars in the spotlight too.

Singer Ella Fitzgerald credited Monroe for her big break, promising a club owner she would attend if Fitzgerald was booked.

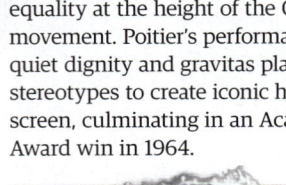

SIDNEY POITIER
AMERICAN, 1927 – 2022

In 2022 *Variety* described Poitier as the actor who "redefined America". It's a bold statement, but one backed up by a string of films through the late 1950s and into the 60s and 70s that challenged conceptions of race and equality at the height of the Civil Rights movement. Poitier's performances of quiet dignity and gravitas played against stereotypes to create iconic heroes on screen, culminating in an Academy Award win in 1964.

MARY PICKFORD
CANADIAN, 1892 – 1979

Pickford started out as a superstar of the silent era, but that was only the beginning of her impact on cinema. She was a co-founder of United Artists in 1919 alongside Chaplin, giving more power to the creative talents behind Hollywood's success. And then she helped to found the Academy of Motion Picture Arts and Sciences in 1927, the body that today is best known for its Oscars ceremony (she also won best actress in its second year).

Hollywood Influencers

LOUIS B MAYER
AMERICAN, 1884 – 1957

The most powerful of the studio moguls in the Golden Age, Mayer helped to shape Hollywood as it became the cultural force we know today. He started out owning movie theatres before opening his own studios in Hollywood, then merging with another to form MGM (Metro-Goldwyn-Mayer), which he led. He spearheaded the glitz and glamour of films targeted at the masses, promising MGM had "more stars than there are in heaven."

Alfred Hitchcock
British, 1899 – 1980

The concept of the 'auteur' director in cinema, a film-maker whose vision is all-powerful and often comes with identifiable elements, is now common in Hollywood. The first man to truly cement such a legacy was Alfred Hitchcock. The British director became known as the 'Master of Suspense' thanks to a run of tense thrillers like *Rear Window* and *Vertigo*, melding artistic flourishes of German expressionism into his popular Hollywood flicks. His impact was so great as to earn the eponymous adjective of 'Hitchcockian' for any film that touches upon the core elements of his style.

Dorothy Arzner
American, 1897 – 1979

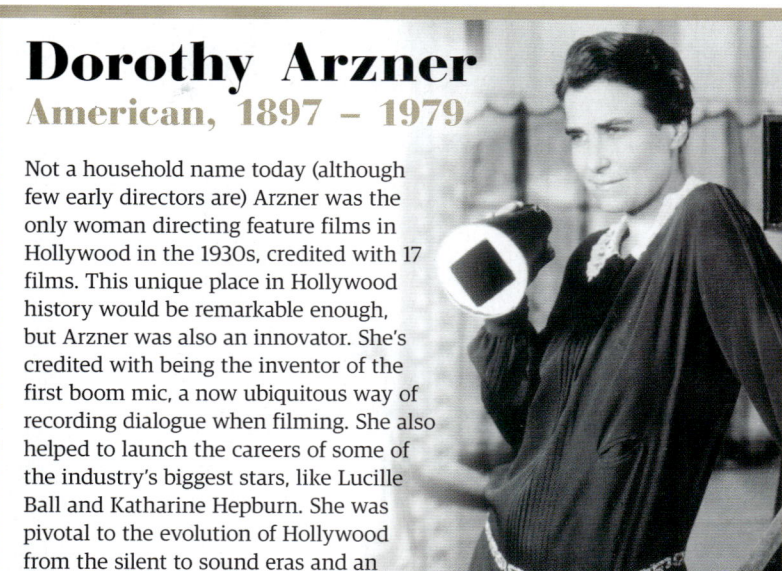

Not a household name today (although few early directors are) Arzner was the only woman directing feature films in Hollywood in the 1930s, credited with 17 films. This unique place in Hollywood history would be remarkable enough, but Arzner was also an innovator. She's credited with being the inventor of the first boom mic, a now ubiquitous way of recording dialogue when filming. She also helped to launch the careers of some of the industry's biggest stars, like Lucille Ball and Katharine Hepburn. She was pivotal to the evolution of Hollywood from the silent to sound eras and an inspiration to many who followed her.

Walt Disney
American, 1901 – 1966

The name Disney today is synonymous with family entertainment and some of the most popular and money-making movies in history, but the man who started it all began as a cartoonist. Achieving some success with a short animation based on *Alice In Wonderland*, Walt started an animation studio in Hollywood with his brother Roy in 1923. From there was born Mickey Mouse and a pantheon of other animal characters as well as the first full-length animated feature film, *Snow White And The Seven Dwarfs* (1937). And that's before we even get into the theme parks.

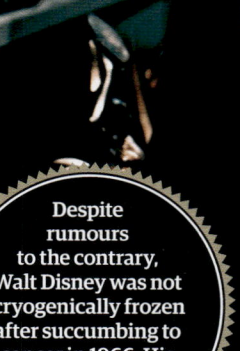

MARLON BRANDO
AMERICAN, 1924 – 2004

When it comes to the evolution of acting in Hollywood, one name stands above all others: Marlon Brando. He was one of a number of actors in his generation to study under Stella Adler to become a 'method' actor. Moving to Hollywood having established himself in New York theatres, his grounded performances in films like *A Streetcar Named Desire* were a revelation. The contrast of Brando's gritty, emotional performances against the affected Golden Age style marked a new era of cinema.

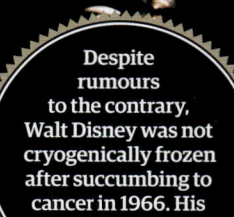

Despite rumours to the contrary, Walt Disney was not cryogenically frozen after succumbing to cancer in 1966. His remains were cremated.

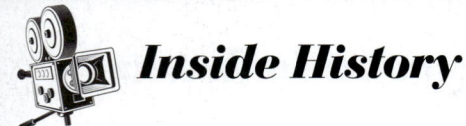 *Inside History*

GOLDEN AGE FILM SET

Hollywood
1930s – 1945

The Golden Age of Hollywood saw some of the most iconic films ever produced, from *Gone With The Wind* (1939) to *Citizen Kane* (1941). Between 1930 and 1945, Tinseltown was dominated by a method of production known as the 'Studio System', which saw even distribution and screening of films under the control of major studios such as 20th Century Fox and Warner Brothers. During this period directors, writers, set designers and even stars were all under contract to specific studios. Each studio owned vast areas of land used for production, from huge backlots to gigantic soundstages.

Sound stages, as their name suggests, developed more readily following the advent of 'talkies' in the 1920s and 1930s. They were designed primarily to allow audio to be recorded at the same time as the film. Early soundstages in the silent era could not be reliant on electrical lighting, as the technology was not yet powerful enough to light the space needed. As such they had glass roofs that allowed the film crews to utilise natural light while shooting. The first examples of sound stages as we know them today appeared in 1928 and were huge warehouse-like structures, allowing for the construction of vast sets.

The making of a film is usually split into three distinct phases. 'Pre-production' describes the early stages including everything from scriptwriting to set design, 'Production' usually refers to principal photography, meaning when the majority of the film will be shot, and 'post production' sees the footage edited with music and other effects added. The 'film crew' is the term used to describe everyone working on the production side of filmmaking, from the director to lighting technicians.

LIGHTING TECHNICIAN
The chief lighting technician and electrician works under the Director of Photography. Their role is to make sure that the lighting plan agreed with the DOP and director is carried out. Sometimes referred to as 'The Gaffer', this term originates in the 16th century and is thought to be a contraction of 'godfather'. By the 19th century the term referred to supervisors in working environments, and it is believed this is where it made the transition to the film industry.

CINEMATOGRAPHER
Also known as the Director of Photography (or DOP for short), the role of the cinematographer is to work alongside the director to design the look of the film and is responsible for both the camera and lighting crews. The profession has a rich history, with the American Society of Cinematographers formed in Hollywood in 1919.

DIRECTOR
The director takes creative responsibility for the entire film, creating a mood and style that best suits the script. During the days of the old Hollywood studio system, directors most likely would have had a contract with a studio. Although there are examples of directors exercising personal freedom during this period, they often had to work with actors or writers who were chosen by the studio.

CAMERA
Today, films can be shot on anything from an iPhone (2015's *Tangerine*) to Zoom (*Host*, 2020). However, in early Hollywood digital cameras did not exist and film stock had to be used. What was more, cameras were large, bulky devices that could be difficult to move. Films shot in special forms (such as three-strip technicolour or 3D during the 1950s) required special cameras.

Golden Age Film Set

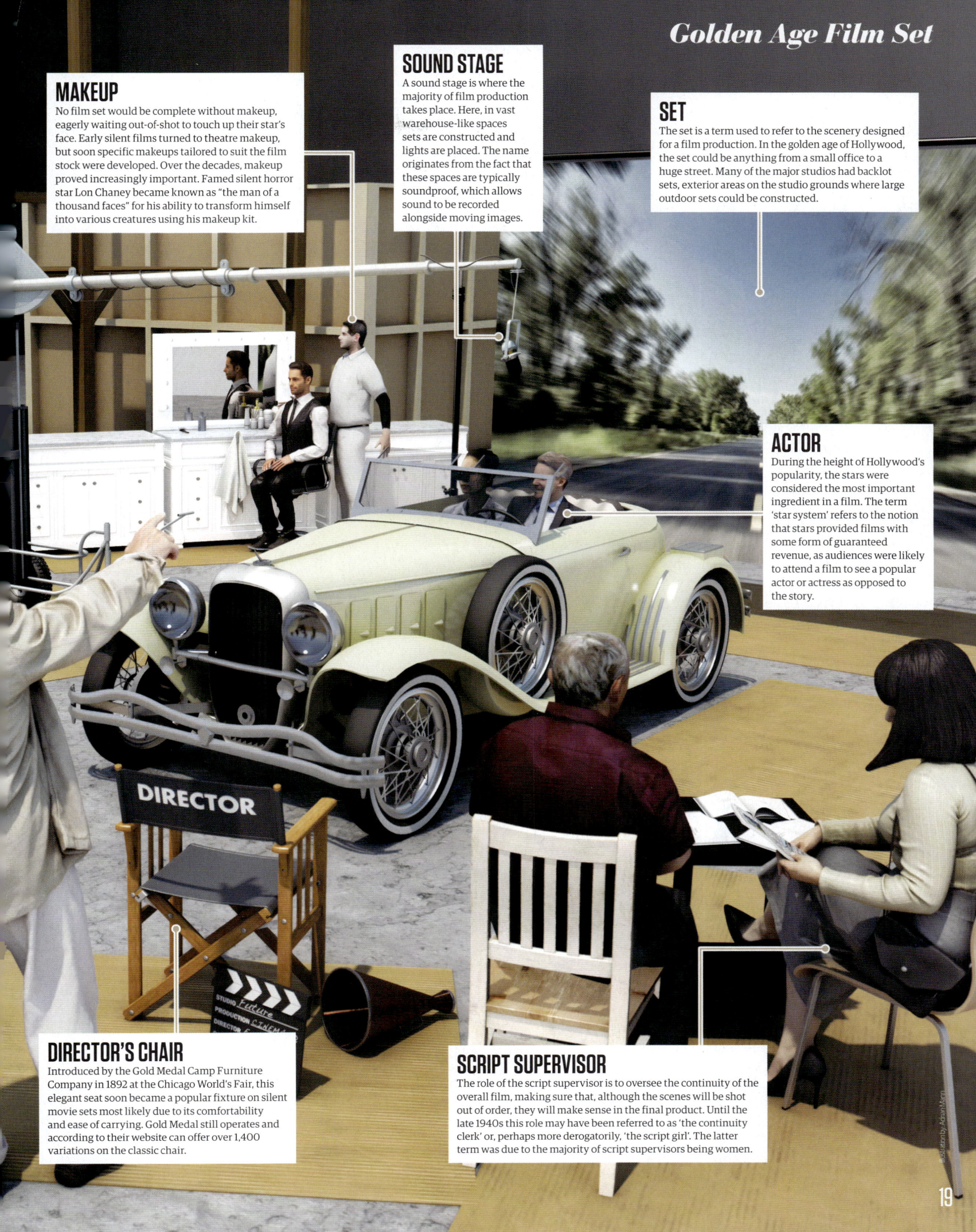

MAKEUP
No film set would be complete without makeup, eagerly waiting out-of-shot to touch up their star's face. Early silent films turned to theatre makeup, but soon specific makeups tailored to suit the film stock were developed. Over the decades, makeup proved increasingly important. Famed silent horror star Lon Chaney became known as "the man of a thousand faces" for his ability to transform himself into various creatures using his makeup kit.

SOUND STAGE
A sound stage is where the majority of film production takes place. Here, in vast warehouse-like spaces sets are constructed and lights are placed. The name originates from the fact that these spaces are typically soundproof, which allows sound to be recorded alongside moving images.

SET
The set is a term used to refer to the scenery designed for a film production. In the golden age of Hollywood, the set could be anything from a small office to a huge street. Many of the major studios had backlot sets, exterior areas on the studio grounds where large outdoor sets could be constructed.

ACTOR
During the height of Hollywood's popularity, the stars were considered the most important ingredient in a film. The term 'star system' refers to the notion that stars provided films with some form of guaranteed revenue, as audiences were likely to attend a film to see a popular actor or actress as opposed to the story.

DIRECTOR'S CHAIR
Introduced by the Gold Medal Camp Furniture Company in 1892 at the Chicago World's Fair, this elegant seat soon became a popular fixture on silent movie sets most likely due to its comfortability and ease of carrying. Gold Medal still operates and according to their website can offer over 1,400 variations on the classic chair.

SCRIPT SUPERVISOR
The role of the script supervisor is to oversee the continuity of the overall film, making sure that, although the scenes will be shot out of order, they will make sense in the final product. Until the late 1940s this role may have been referred to as 'the continuity clerk' or, perhaps more derogatorily, 'the script girl'. The latter term was due to the majority of script supervisors being women.

HOLLYWOOD GOES TO WAR

The movie stars who traded in the glitz and glamour of the silver screen for the sacrifice and service of World War II

Written by Grace Freeman

The Second World War was a time of deep economical, political, and military unrest - and its severe impact was felt not only by civilians, but by well-known faces of film, too. A multitude of known actors, producers, and singers of Hollywood's golden age played their part in the war effort - with those who were eligible to do so signing up for service and others fulfilling duties in a plethora of valuable ways - either abroad or on the home-front, often sacrificing their income and lifestyle to do so.

Some were already known performers and, as such, were able to use their celebrity status to encourage further enlistment and influence produced propaganda; others were yet to achieve stardom, serving only in response to the booming call of duty at the time. The talented leaders of Hollywood's greatest cinematic era all bear legacies that have long outlived them, but many of them have lesser-known stories to tell - stories that carry the most winning of roles and the finest of honours, far more eminent than those earned on the silver screen.

Hollywood Goes To War

JAMES STEWART
American film actor

America's everyman was one of the only soldiers in the military to reach the rank of colonel within four years

James 'Jimmy' Stewart - award-winning star of *A Philadelphia Story* - was the first American film star to don a military uniform in the Second World War. Due to personal interest he already held a commercial flying licence and attempted to enlist in the Army Air Corps in 1940, but was below the weight requirements and subsequently rejected. Following this, he trained to gain further weight and was ultimately inducted into the army in 1941.

Once enlisted Stewart applied again for admission into the Air Corps and received his instructions as second lieutenant at the start of 1942. Shortly after the Army Air Force commissioned him to appear in a short recruitment film, *Winning Your Wings*; this appeared in cinemas nationwide and resulted in over 150,000 new enlisting airmen.

Over the next two years, he was promoted to first lieutenant, then captain, as he trained amateur pilots across states. Following an aviation mission to Germany in 1944, he advanced to major and was awarded the Distinguished Flying Cross, the Air Medal, and the French Croix de Guerre; by 1945, he had reached the rank of colonel - making him one of the only Americans in military history to do so in such a short space of time.

PAUL NEWMAN
American film actor, director, and producer

The nicknamed 'King Cool' only discovered that he was colour blind upon entering training for the Navy

His first big break in Hollywood didn't come until *The Silver Chalice* in 1954, but Paul Newman enlisted in the army over a decade prior to this. He initially enrolled in the V-12 programme, which aimed to induct a large number of qualified officers for both the Navy and the Marines, but he was later dismissed upon discovery of being colour blind during training.

Following this Newman completed training as both a radioman and a rear gunner, before qualifying in torpedo bombers, which were specifically designed for attacks on naval ships. He served in the Pacific Theatre in Hawaii, which was the centre of operations for the United States throughout the Pacific War, fought from 1941 until 1945.

In 1945 he was assigned to the aircraft carrier Bunker Hill, along with the rest of his unit, although the leading pilot of his particular aircraft contracted an ear infection, which kept the plane from boarding the vessel. The ship was attacked by kamikazes only two days later and a large number of its passengers were killed, including other members of Newman's squadron.

21

HEDY LAMARR
Austrian-American film actress and inventor

Heralded as one of the most beautiful women in the world, she was an ingenious inventor

Although she was one of MGM Studios' biggest stars at the time of the outbreak of the Second World War, Hedy Lamarr spent her spare time creating and developing inventions - she often collaborated closely with famous aviator Howard Hughes and made valuable contributions to the evolution of his aircraft designs - and was less than eager to continue to use her celebrity status to sell war bonds.

Upon learning that radio-controlled torpedoes were easily blocked and interfered with by enemy fleets, she designed a device with a signal whose frequency could not be tracked or interrupted, allowing Allied torpedoes to remain undetected across various channels - and, along with friend and fellow inventor George Antheil, the blueprint was created and patented.

Despite the inventiveness and significance of the device, it was deemed too technically hard to implement and was dismissed by the Armed Forces; it was over 20 years before an updated version of their creation was used by the navy during the Cold War and Lamarr's key contribution to military technology was recognised. This wireless development would go on to shape further modern inventions and their security, including Bluetooth, GPS, and Wi-Fi.

Hollywood Goes To War

CLARK GABLE
American film actor

Following the attacks on Pearl Harbour and the loss of his wife within only weeks of one another, the actor enlisted in the army

Often referred to as 'The King of Hollywood', Clark Gable joined the Army Air Force in 1942, following the untimely death of his wife and actress Carole Lombard, who had been killed during a plane crash upon her flight home from a war bond rally in Indiana - she was subsequently declared to be the first American female casualty of the Second World War.

Prior to her death Lombard had encouraged him to enlist in the war effort, but both MGM Studios and President Roosevelt were vocally reluctant for his involvement; he eventually joined in 1942, with the aim of specialising in aerial gunnery and was promoted to second lieutenant upon completing his training. Gable, just like James Stewart, shot war recruitment films to encourage enlistment, and it wasn't until the following year that he was dispatched abroad for service.

In 1943 he flew on five combat missions to Germany, earning both the Air Medal and the Distinguished Flying Cross. During one particular flight his aircraft was attacked and he narrowly avoided being hit by gunfire; when news of this reached MGM, his duty was relieved to being non-combative and, although he was promoted to major in 1944, he received no further orders to serve.

REEL OF HONOUR
During the war Hollywood still produced some of its finest films

Casablanca (1942)
Starring Humphrey Bogart and Ingrid Bergman and famed for its many iconic lines, *Casablanca* was released in 1942, becoming a growing success and winning the Academy Award for Best Picture. Set during the current combat, it followed an American emigrant who is forced to choose between the woman he loves and helping both her and her husband – a fighter in the Czech Resistance – to escape from the city of Casablanca.

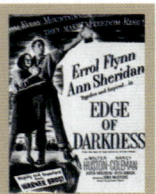

Edge of Darkness (1943)
Also known as *Norway in Revolt*, war drama *Edge of Darkness* is adapted from the novel of the same name. Starring Errol Flynn it follows the occupants of a Norwegian village who, after two years succumbing to German rule, rise up in resistance. It was directed by Lewis Milestone, who had worked on *All Quiet On The Western Front* – adapted, too, from the acclaimed novel written by a German soldier after the Great War.

The Great Dictator (1940)
The Great Dictator was written, directed, and produced by Charlie Chaplin – who also stars as one of its leads, ruthless dictator Adenoid Hynkel. In its most famous scene a barber impersonating Hynkel speaks out against the Nazi regime. Chaplin later confessed that, had he known about the extent of the horrors of the concentration camps of the time, he would not have been able to make the film.

Anchors Aweigh (1945)
Frank Sinatra and Gene Kelly were able to bring some light relief to the silver screen, in *Anchors Aweigh*. The film follows two sailors singing and dancing their way around Hollywood, as they're granted leave from the navy and help an aspiring actress to get an audition. Most-remembered for its scene where Kelly dances with a cartoon Jerry Mouse, the film also offers a glimpse of the studios' headquarters during the war.

CHARLES BRONSON
Lithuanian-American actor
During his years of service the actor participated in over 20 aerial missions across the Pacific Ocean

Before he was a wild vigilante taking up the cause of the defenceless with Steve McQueen in *The Magnificent Seven* and *The Great Escape*, Charles Bronson enlisted in the army in 1943, at the age of 22. He joined the Army Air Forces and first served in the 760th Flexible Gunnery Training Squadron.

In 1945, he trained as an aerial gunner in Guam within the 39th Bombardment Group, assigned to a B-29 bomber plane and participating in dangerous combat missions against Japan. During his service in the unit, Bronson flew in 25 missions, during one of which he sustained significant injuries to his arms. As a result of these wounds, he retired from active duty and was rewarded with the Purple Heart for his three years of service.

Following this, he used his entitlement to the GI Bill, offered to all ex-military servicemen, to study at art school, before taking up acting classes and securing small parts in films for more than a decade - until his big break came in 1960 as one of the cowboying septuplets.

GLENN MILLER
American big-band composer
The composer and band-leader used his much-loved music for morale, entertainment, and propaganda

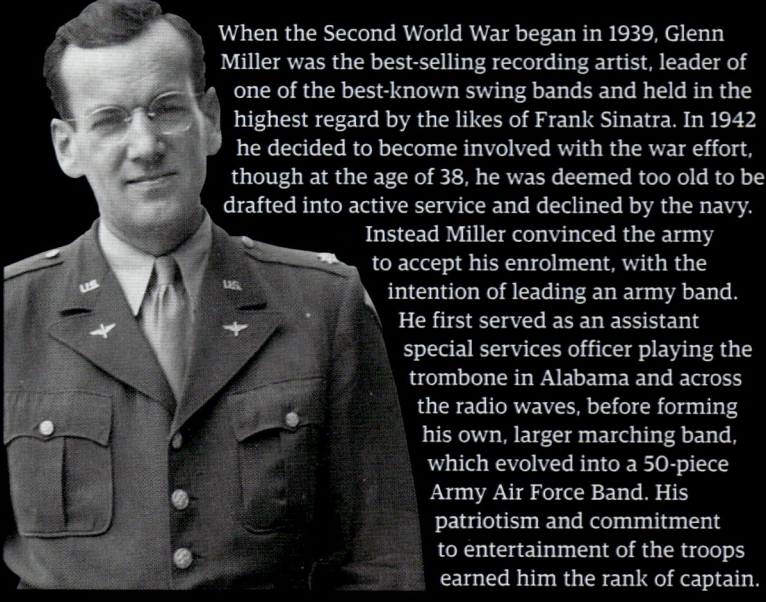

When the Second World War began in 1939, Glenn Miller was the best-selling recording artist, leader of one of the best-known swing bands and held in the highest regard by the likes of Frank Sinatra. In 1942 he decided to become involved with the war effort, though at the age of 38, he was deemed too old to be drafted into active service and declined by the navy. Instead Miller convinced the army to accept his enrolment, with the intention of leading an army band. He first served as an assistant special services officer playing the trombone in Alabama and across the radio waves, before forming his own, larger marching band, which evolved into a 50-piece Army Air Force Band. His patriotism and commitment to entertainment of the troops earned him the rank of captain.

KIRK DOUGLAS
American actor and film-maker
After being rejected from the army, the actor served in the navy for three years before being discharged as a result of his wounds

Born Issur Danielovitch, Kirk Douglas changed his name and enlisted in the Navy at 1941, at the age of 25 and almost immediately after the United States had entered the Second World War. After not passing his psychology test and failing to be accepted into the Army, he enrolled in the Navy - despite his poor eyesight.

Douglas trained at the University of Notre Dame in Indiana, where the navy had installed a training camp, and graduated as a naval infantry officer. Following this he served as a gunnery and communications officer for the anti-submarine patrol aboard the USS PC-1137, which sailed across the Pacific Ocean. He was stationed here for much of 1942 and 1943, patrolling the war-zone for Japanese submarines, and it was during one of these vigils that he was injured, suffering internal wounds when an explosive charge detonated prematurely.

Douglas convalesced for some months in hospital in San Diego, before being permanently discharged from active service in 1944. After this, he returned to working in radio and theatre and had planned to remain a stage actor until he was recommended for his first on-screen role - by friend and starlet Lauren Bacall.

Hollywood Goes To War

ROCK HUDSON
American film actor

When the actor was still known only as Roy Harold Scherer, the then-teenager enrolled as a mechanic in the navy

Rock Hudson - a leading man in Hollywood during the 1950s and 1960s and known for his on-screen romances with actress Doris Day - enlisted into the Navy in 1944, at the age of 19 and almost immediately after he had graduated from high school the previous year.

Known then only as Roy Harold Scherer, he trained in Chicago at Naval Station Great Lakes - the largest naval training station and the navy's only boot camp in the United States - before travelling to the Philippines on the SS Lew Wallace with over 1,000 other servicemen. Under orders to report to Aviation Repair, he worked as an aircraft mechanic until the end of the Second World War.

Following the end of combat, Hudson returned to San Francisco aboard an aircraft carrier and was discharged from service in 1946; it was after this that he moved to Los Angeles and, after securing a talent agent to represent him, made his film debut in 1948 - *Fighter Squadron* was, somewhat aptly, an aviation war film in which he only had one line.

AUDREY HEPBURN
Belgian-born British film actress

At around the age of 13, the iconic actress participated in a series of activities to support the Dutch resistance movement

Audrey Hepburn, one of the greatest stars of the screen of Hollywood's golden age, was only ten years old when the Second World War broke out in 1939. Upon Britain's declaration of war on Germany her mother moved her and the family back to the Netherlands, where they had lived previously, in the hope that it would remain neutral in the combat, as it had during the Great War.

Less than a year later, the country was invaded by Germany - an occupation that was to last for the next five years - and Hepburn adopted the alias Edda van Heemstra, so as to not sound too British during the enemy's rule. When the family moved to a nearby city, she began to take part in silent dance performances, to raise money for the Dutch resistance movement, as well as volunteering at the local hospital and delivering food to Allies hiding close by; the family also hid a paratrooper in their home during 1944's Battle of Arnhem.

A Dutch famine followed the Normandy landings of the same year and Hepburn contracted both anaemia and respiratory problems as a result of malnutrition. After the war ended in 1945, she trained in ballet in Amsterdam, before moving to London to work in the West End and getting her early TV and film roles.

HENRY FONDA
American film and theatre actor

Although keen to enlist at the time - and persistent in his enrolment - the actor was considered by many to be too old to serve

By the time that the Second World War was underway, Henry Fonda had already tread the boards of Broadway, made his critically-acclaimed Hollywood debut, and been nominated for an Academy Award for his performance in the 1940 film *The Grapes Of Wrath* - but he put quick pause to the make-believe, saying that he didn't "want to be in a fake war in a studio".

At the then-old age of 37, Fonda was persistent in his enrolment and enlisted in the navy in the summer of 1942, with an eagerness to contribute more than footage for recruitment films. He trained to become a quartermaster and sailed briefly on the USS Satterlee, then applied to become an officer - though, due to his age at the time, was commissioned instead as a lieutenant.

He assisted in the planning and enforcement of aerial missions in the Pacific Theatre, and was awarded the Bronze Star Medal for his efforts. After three years of service, Fonda left active duty towards the end of 1945 and at the cessation of the war, though he continued to rank in reserve until his official resignation in 1948.

Ancient

ANCIENT

The Fall of the Roman Empire (1964)	28
Cleopatra (1963)	30
300 (2006)	34
Ben-Hur (1959)	36
Gladiator (2000)	38
Spartacus (1960)	42
Troy (2004)	44
Pompeii (2014)	46
Alexander (2004)	48

 Ancient

THE FALL OF THE ROMAN EMPIRE

Director: Anthony Mann **Starring:** Sophia Loren, Stephen Boyd, Alec Guinness, Christopher Plummer **Country:** Italy **Year:** 1964

Did golden-age Hollywood stick to the facts of this calamitous period?

This film shares many plot points with the 2000 movie Gladiator

A common trope of Hollywood history is that tinseltown loves a trend. If a movie concept does well, you can bet there will be a handful of scripts suddenly greenlit that seem oddly similar. For the late 1950s and early 1960s, that was historical epics. Off the back of films like Ben-Hur (1956), Spartacus (1959) and El Cid (1961), it seemed that audiences couldn't get enough of swords, sandals and romantic melodrama.

That was until Cleopatra (1963) and The Fall of the Roman Empire both flopped at the boxoffice. This film seemed to have things in its favour. It had El Cid's Anthony Mann at the helm and a stellar cast. The warning bells should have rung though when many stars wanted to steer clear. Both Charlton Heston and Kirk Douglas apparently turned down the opportunity to play the lead role.

In the end this $19 million movie brought in only $4.8 million in the United States. The producer of the film, Samuel Broston, filed for Chapter 11 bankruptcy following its release and the historical epic in Hollywood took a sharp decline in frequency.

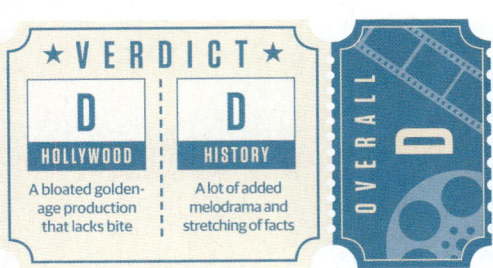

VERDICT
- **D HOLLYWOOD** — A bloated golden-age production that lacks bite
- **D HISTORY** — A lot of added melodrama and stretching of facts
- **OVERALL D**

01 Marcus Aurelius (Guinness) campaigns against the German tribes and gathers regional leaders of the empire to him. He promises them the rights of Roman citizens. He made no such offer and in fact crushed the Quadi (Germanic) tribes in the north during his reign.

02 Aurelius is poisoned by the supporters of his son, Commodus, after he tells general Livius (Stephen Boyd) that he will be his successor. In fact Commodus was already co-emperor, Livius is a fictional character and Aurelius died from natural causes aged 58.

03 Commodus appears to become mad with power once his father has died, taxing the provinces, proclaiming himself a god and even renaming Rome after himself. Some of this is true, as Rome was renamed Commodiana under his leadership.

04 Aurelius laments that he can't make his daughter Lucilla his heir, but instead she is married off to the king of Armenia. She is later nearly burned at the stake with German rebels. In fact she was married to a Syrian general and was executed by Commodus.

05 While the film claims to show the beginning of the end of the Roman Empire, the events of this film are about 300 years before the Western Empire fell. This happened when Odoacer, the Germanic king, took Rome and the seal of the Empire was sent east.

The Fall of the Roman Empire

Italian movie icon Sophia Loren pictured on set as Lucilla in the 1964 epic

The real Empress Lucilla was hugely influential, but was killed under the orders of her son, Commodus

Real Power of Rome

With an impressive array of connections to the Imperial throne, this noblewoman had a vast amount of influence and control in empire

Lucilla was the daughter of one emperor (Marcus Aurelius), the wife of another (Lucius Verus), and the sister of a third (Commodus). Few women had the opportunity to experience such a close connection to the heart of power in Rome, and Lucilla evidently relished the opportunities for influence which they afforded her.

Lucilla was born and raised in Rome in the mid- C2nd AD, at a time of relative and fairly unusual stability within the Imperial regime, under the so-called 'Good Emperors' of Rome. As the second daughter, and third child, of Marcus Aurelius and his wife Faustina, it was clear from early on that Lucilla would serve a useful role as part of a political marriage to strengthen the Imperial regime. She was duty promised to, and then married to, Marcus Aurelius' co-Emperor Lucius Verus, before she was 17 years old (and perhaps as young as 14). Following her marriage, Lucilla remained in Rome, ruling on behalf of her often-absent husband, who spent much of his time in conflict on the edges of the Empire. Verus' untimely death in AD 169, just five years after their marriage, left Lucilla a young widow, who would soon be married against her will to Tiberius Claudius Pompeianus Quintianus, one of her father's best generals. Unfortunately for Lucilla, her new husband was unable to match the political prospects of her former; he was relatively unambitious, declining the opportunity to be named Aurelius' heir. Lucilla was relegated to the fringes of political influence, a position she seems to have found frustrating - certainly, she would later attempt to recover her position of power at the top of the Imperial regime.

Lucilla must have hoped that her husband would reconsider his position after the death of her father in AD 180, but saw her prospects quashed when her brother Commodus instead became the new emperor.

Within a few years, Lucilla despaired of Commodus' rule and instigated a plot to assassinate him and place herself and Pompeianus Quintianus on the throne - although she evidently demurred from involving her husband in the plot. The attempt failed, and Lucilla was exiled to Capri, where she was later executed, while Pompeianus Quintianus, innocent of involvement in the plot, was allowed to live, and actually outlasted Commodus.

Lucilla was raised from childhood to Imperial influence, and must have expected that the power she wielded as the wife of Lucius Verus would have been long-lasting, an ambition which would ultimately be cut short by his early death. She was not content to be relegated to the sidelines, and hoped to regain her former glory through her new husband, but found herself thwarted by his lack of ambition. Lucilla ultimately gambled on a coup to replace her brother on the Imperial throne with her husband; she failed, and paid with her life.

 Ancient

CLEOPATRA

Director: Joseph L Mankiewicz, Rouben Mamoulian, Darryl F Zanuck **Starring:** Elizabeth Taylor, Richard Burton **Country:** UK, USA **Year:** 1963

Was this classic film as liberal with historical fact as it was with its budget?

Elizabeth Taylor wore 65 different costumes for the role

One of history's most iconic figures, and one half of the most tragic romances ever, the story of Cleopatra has captivated readers and audiences for centuries. After being ousted from the throne of Egypt by her younger brother Ptolemy (Richard O'Sullivan), Cleopatra (Elizabeth Taylor) solicits the support of Julius Caesar (Rex Harrison) to restore her rule.

Their alliance – and love affair – is cut short when Caesar is assassinated and Rome is plunged into civil war and division. Years later, Caesar's close friend Mark Anthony (Richard Burton) is stunned by Cleopatra's beauty, and the pair begin a romance, as well as a military alliance. However, the murky world of Roman politics is never far away, and when Anthony's rival Octavian (Roddy McDowall) declares war on Egypt, Cleopatra's throne as well as her life hangs in the balance.

With grand-scale set pieces, unbelievable costumes and a cast of Hollywood royalty – not to mention the allure of Burton and Taylor's real off-screen affair – this Sixties epic may have a list of anachronisms longer than the Nile, but its place in movie history is undeniable.

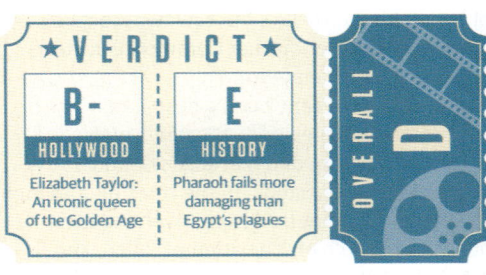

VERDICT
- **Hollywood: B−** Elizabeth Taylor: An iconic queen of the Golden Age
- **History: E** Pharaoh fails more damaging than Egypt's plagues
- **Overall: D**

01 Cleopatra dies by suicide by clasping a snake to her breast until it bites her. But beside the fact that the snake used in the film was a harmless garden snake (not an Egyptian cobra), historians believe she was bitten on her arm or that she simply poisoned herself.

02 Cicero is shown to be active in Roman politics and plays a major part in plotting Caesar's death. Actually Cicero didn't enter the senate when Caesar was ruler and played no part in his assassination, although he did write in support of Brutus's cause.

03 Despite the film being set in the last century BCE, the décor used is from a mixture of different reigns from many Egyptian kings and queens. This includes Queen Hetepheres, who lived around 2,600 years before Cleopatra ruled this illustrious ancient civilisation.

04 The film largely ignores the militaria of Caesar's period in favour of the armour and shields that were used a century later. Not a single soldier in the Oscar-winning movie has a crest indicating their rank, and there were in fact many centurions in Caesar's army.

05 Although the Arch of Constantine shown in the opening sequence was authentically and painstakingly replicated by the filmmakers, the real Arch isn't located near the Forum at all, and it wasn't even built until a full 350 years after Cleopatra entered Rome.

Cleopatra

The affair between Taylor and Burton made headlines, but didn't draw enough viewers to cinemas to make back the money spent on the film

The film that nearly toppled Hollywood

Patrick Humphries explains how Cleopatra's scandal-hit production marked the decline of the old studio system

Patrick Humphries is a civil servant turned journalist, writing for *NME*, *Melody Maker*, *Evening Standard*, *Guardian*, *The Times* and many more. His previous books include *A Little Bit Funny: The Elton John Story*, *Rolling Stones 69* and *With The Beatles*.

Does *Cleopatra* act as a pivot between old and new Hollywood?
I think it does. I mean, it's a terrible film, but the backstory is fantastic, which is what really appealed to me. I think Paramount did a drama series about the making of *The Godfather*, and I think they could do one about the making of *Cleopatra* because just the scale of it, even now, it's unbelievable.

Did it really do so much damage that it brought the Hollywood epics to an end?
It's not the one film that sank the studios, but it's certainly one of the first nails in the coffin.

Cinema was fighting a rearguard action in the 1950s with television. Why pay to go out when you can stay at home and see movies? So, the way Hollywood fought back is by producing big, spectacular epics in colour, stereo sound. They would be roadshow presentations to try and make it as much of an event as possible. So, there would be two performances a day and you'd get a souvenir programme like going to the theatre. These were big, big productions, which you couldn't possibly expect to see on TV. The biggest of them all was *Cleopatra*.

What was the landscape *Cleopatra* was developed against?
Hollywood had a good run in the 1950s. They found the *Bible* delivered good box office numbers. There was a series of very successful films during the '50s, *The Robe* (1953), *Demetrius And The Gladiators* (1954), *Quo Vadis* (1951), etc. They were big-budget films that really filled the screen. The biggest of them all, of course, was *Ben-Hur* (1959), which came in at $15 million, which was an awful lot at the time. Now 20th Century Fox, like all of the

31

Ancient

[Caption: Cleopatra's famous entrance into Rome in the film involved 20,000 extras in full costume]

CLEOPATRA AND THE UNDOING OF HOLLYWOOD IS OUT NOW FROM THE HISTORY PRESS

[Caption: With an ever-escalating budget, Cleopatra led 20th Century Fox to the verge of bankruptcy]

studios, was struggling. For some inexplicable reason they thought they could do a version of *Cleopatra* based on an earlier version that the studio had done. They needed something big and Elizabeth Taylor was a huge star at the time, and they got in touch with her. Originally it was going to be a $2 million, 60-day shoot with contract player Joan Collins as Cleopatra to be filmed in Hollywood, around Los Angeles, in the deserts around California to replicate Ancient Egypt. That never happened.

So, they wanted a big star; Taylor had just won an Oscar, so they told her we want you to play Cleopatra. Apparently she's in the shower and she told her then husband, "tell them I will do it for a million dollars" expecting them to say "no way". Nobody's ever been paid a million dollars for any one film. And they agreed. So, that's when it all started going horribly wrong.

How impactful was the Taylor/Burton relationship to the film's reception?
The original cast was Stephen Boyd, who was coming in hot off of *Ben-Hur*, and Peter Finch to play Caesar. They had other commitments,

so they had to shut it down. The crunch came when the studio had to decide, do they bite the bullet and wipe off what by then would have been about six or seven million dollars, or shut it down and relocate to Rome, because what else could possibly go wrong?

Well, they made the decision to go to Rome and that's when the trouble really started because, of course, Richard Burton came on set. He was married to his long-suffering Welsh wife, Sybil, who put up with all manner of indiscretions and betrayals. And Elizabeth Taylor was married to her fourth husband, Eddie Fisher. When they got together on set in Rome the chemistry was palpable, and that's when the affair started.

Then, of course, the scandal broke and it really was front-page news. It knocked the Cuban Missile Crisis and the Berlin Wall off the front page. As I say in the book, there's one journalist who went to the White House to see President Kennedy, as the Cuban Missile Crisis was building up a head of steam, and he was taken to one side by Jacqueline Kennedy who said, "Do you think Richard Burton and Elizabeth Taylor will stay together?" The world was spellbound by them.

The film's budget ultimately ballooned to a staggering $44 million, so how did things end up for the filmmakers?
In fairness to Mankiewicz, he wrote the script screenplay and his vision was always two films. It was going to be Cleopatra and Caesar as one film and then Cleopatra and Mark Antony as the second film. They would then need to show them consecutive nights or release them the next year, or whatever. But the studio was just hemorrhaging money and they needed to get something, anything out to cash in on the Burton/Taylor scandal.

And when it finally opened, the reviews were pretty damning. There's one positive review which was later recanted. It did eventually go into profit, but as one of the 20th Century Fox directors said, "yes, it did go into profit, but it took the studio with it".

How close was *Cleopatra* to being truly disastrous for the future of the big studios in Hollywood?
Very close indeed. Take $44 million compared to the cost of other films at the time; *A Hard Day's Night*, for example, cost £190,000, and yes, it was in black and white, but the scale of the *Cleopatra* disaster is apparent.

At the end of the book, with regards to *Cleopatra*, I quote Churchill on El Alamein that "it's not the beginning of the end, but it is the end of the beginning". I think of it as the line in the sand. Before that, Hollywood was pretty much unsurpassable and after that, I think it took a very, very bad knocking.

WHAT DID CLEOPATRA REALLY LOOK LIKE?

The burning question historians keep trying to answer

For a historical figure as well-known as Cleopatra, it's odd that we really have no sense of what she looked like. The muse for so many artists, poets and writers over the centuries, the true visage of the last pharaoh of Egypt is muddied by both time and inaccurate repetition.

Thanks to being on the wrong side of the Roman civil war, it's believed that many examples of contemporary portraits of her were destroyed by Octavian, Julius Caesar's heir. What we're left with is around ten coins (approved for distribution by Cleopatra, so questionable in accuracy), a handful of statues (most in very stylised forms) and some contemporary accounts of her appearance (mostly contradictory).

But historians continue to pick away to find the truth. What we can be confident in saying is that she was not Egyptian, having been born to the Macedonian Ptolemaic line, but it's also unlikely that she looked like a contemporary Greek. Her family line had lived in Egypt for 250 years, after all.

For our own re-creation, we turned to the research of Dr Sally-Ann Ashton, an Egyptologist who worked on a more recent rendering of Cleopatra. Her work, which contributed to BBC documentary *Cleopatra: Portrait Of A Killer*, drew from statues and an understanding that she would very likely have had mixed Greek and African heritage.

But is this all a distraction? While her racial background and depiction is of contemporary interest and relevance, the obsession with Cleopatra's looks, whether she was the most attractive woman in the world or ugly, were not that relevant to her ability as a ruler. Much of the debate around her appearance in her own time was to push the clonversation away from her keen political acumen; to diminish her legitimacy to rule. It was easier to think of her as a seductress than as a shrewd political operator.

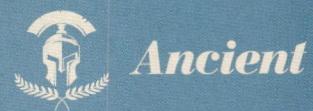 Ancient

300

Name of movie: 300 **Director:** Zack Snyder **Starring:** Gerard Butler, Lena Heady, Dominic West **Country:** US **Year:** 2006

Prophecies, treachery, an indomitable warrior culture, a giant god-king, biceps, enhanced six-packs… This. Is. Sparta. Kinda.

King Leonidas (Gerard Butler) is ruler of ancient Sparta at a time when a mighty Persian army is on the warpath. When an envoy from the Persian god-king Xerxes arrives in Sparta and asks Leonidas to submit to Persia, Leonidas instead kicks him into a bottomless pit. He then pays a visit to the ephors, five prophets with political power who tell Leonidas not to wage war during the Carneia festival. Leonidas defies them however, by taking 300 of his warriors north to Thermopylae, joined by other Greek armies along the way.

Leonidas encounters a severely deformed Spartan, Ephialtes, who asks to join his army. Leonidas refuses and Ephialtes slinks away to betray Sparta to Xerxes, in return for wealth, women and status. The Spartans and their allies manage to repel several waves of Persians, including a battle with the mighty Immortals, before Ephialtes shows Xerxes a goat path that allows his armies to outflank the Spartans, sealing their fate. A critical flop yet a huge commercial success, *300* is based on the Frank Miller comic novel series and is shot with a heavy overlay for a dark comicbook effect.

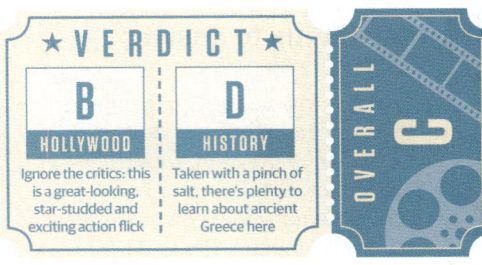

VERDICT
Hollywood: B — Ignore the critics: this is a great-looking, star-studded and exciting action flick
History: D — Taken with a pinch of salt, there's plenty to learn about ancient Greece here
Overall: C

Miller's comic novel was inspired by a movie called The 300 Spartans

01 Xerxes' envoy demands "earth and water" of Leonidas as a token of Sparta's submission to Persia. This is mentioned in several books by the ancient historian Herodotus, who writes that King Darius of Persia sent his envoys to the Athenians.

02 King Xerxes I was a real ruler of the Achaemenid (Persian) empire from 522-486 BCE. He was not the god-like giant portrayed in *300*, although the real Xerxes was almost more terrifying: on one occasion he murdered his brother's entire family.

03 The agoge really was a Spartan warrior's training program that saw sons taken from their mothers at a young age and thrown into a violent rite of passage. However, Leonidas himself would have been exempt from it as the royal firstborn and a future king.

04 Arguably the most obvious historical inaccuracy in *300* is the Spartan soldiers' garb. Snyder has them fighting bare-chested in hot pants, leather strapping and fancy red capes - a ludicrous premise in an era when almost everyone worth fighting wore armour.

05 Leonidas did lead an army against the Persians, but there were closer to 7,000 under his command from across the whole of Greece, not just Sparta. Also, the ephors didn't object to the war,h because the Persians had been seen as a serious threat for years.

The enduring myth of Spartan prowess on the battlefield is just that - a myth

Debunking the Spartans

"The lies told about ancient Sparta are nearly as old as the city itself," says historian and author Myke Cole. Here he peels back five of the biggest myths and legends surrounding the ancient city state

Myth 1: The suicide mission

Nearly everything we think we know about the Battle of Thermopylae (480 BCE) is wrong. There were probably around 1,000 Spartans (the famous 300 were just the noble elite part of the Spartan force) and that's not counting their slaves, who also fought. Each Spartan noble would have had at least one slave, but at the Battle of Plataea in 479 BCE, each had seven.

If this were the case at Thermopylae, then the Spartans would have had an additional 2,100 slave troops. This Spartan force was part of a larger army of around 7,000 allied Greeks. Far from being a suicide mission, Herodotus tells us they expected to be reinforced. And far from a glorious defeat, it was an utter disaster, a speed bump for the Persians, who went on to capture and burn Athens after a paltry delay of just three days. The defeat was so disastrous that the Spartan myth was likely coined at this time as an effort to shore up Greek morale and keep the rest of the Greeks from surrendering.

Leonidas' celebrated taunt "Come and take them" to Xerxes' demand that the Spartans surrender their arms conveniently ignores the fact that Xerxes did come and take them, after killing Leonidas and all of his men, cutting off the king's head and sticking it on a pole.

Myth 2: They never ran away

The Spartans withdrew, retreated, backed down and fled the field of battle far too many times to document here. Their fear of Athenian naval supremacy was well known. After their victory at the Battle of Corcyra in 427 BCE, the Spartan fleet hoisted their sails and ran the moment Athenian reinforcements arrived. They famously backed down again in 411 BCE, despite the fact that their navy was much improved, buoyed by gold from the very Persians they fought at Thermopylae.

But the Spartans didn't just flee on the water. Their most famous defeat at the hands of the rival city state of Thebes - the Battle of Leuctra in 371 BCE - snapped Sparta's spine and ended their relevance as a military power in Ancient Greece. The defeat was so total that a second Spartan army, though certainly positioned to engage the Thebans, backed off rather than face them in the field.

Myth 3: 'No Surrender'

The best known example of a Spartan surrender is perhaps the most instructive. During Sparta's long and wasteful war with Athens, the Peloponnesian War (really, multiple wars spanning more than 50 years), the Athenians established an epiteichisma (a forward operating base) in Spartan territory. In the course of trying to drive the Athenians out, 120 of the elite Spartan citizens found themselves cut off on the island of Sphacteria in 425 BCE.

By all accounts, they fought bravely, living up to their legend. But when the Athenians surrounded them by scaling a cliff the Spartans believed to be unclimbable, they surrendered. What happened to those surrendering Spartans debunks another lie.

Myth 4: Punishing survivors

According to myth, the 120 captives from Sphacteria should have been termed tresantes - 'tremblers' who would live as outcasts should they ever return to Sparta - unable to hold public office, excluded from gymnastics, games and communal dining or from conducting business, forced to dress in rags and subjected to beatings by their own countrymen.

However, none of this happened when these 120 men were returned to the city state. Some lip service was paid, but in the end they were not really punished. These were elite men from powerful families and, as is so common with the rich and powerful, the rules did not apply to them.

Myth 5: They hated wealth

The idea that Spartans hated wealth and even refused to use gold and silver coins was promulgated by the Greek philosopher Plutarch in his famous *Life of Lycurgus* - a biography of Sparta's almost certainly mythic founder. Plutarch claimed that the Spartans redistributed all wealth so that each man would only have what he needed to serve in the army and no more..

Most historians agree that Spartan wealth inequality was so exaggerated that it caused the oliganthropia - Sparta's military manpower crisis that saw its elite citizen warriors dwindle until it finally resorted to arming its slaves. Service in the military elite was dependent on a Spartan's ability to pay his communal mess dues, and as wealth in the city state accrued in fewer and fewer hands over the years, fewer and fewer could afford to cover the bill and found themselves cast out of the elite.

There are numerous accounts of Spartan kings and notable leaders accused of taking bribes. Perhaps most famous is the Spartan king Leotychidas, who after Thermopylae campaigned against the Thessalians - northern Greeks who had bent the knee to the Persians. His campaign was so ineffective that it came as no surprise when a glove packed with silver was found in his tent.

THE BRONZE LIE
MYKE'S NEW BOOK DEBUNKING THE BIGGEST MYTHS OF ANCIENT SPARTA IS OUT NOW IN ALL GOOD STORES

Ancient

BEN-HUR

Director: William Wyler **Starring:** Charlton Heston, Jack Hawkins, Haya Harareet, Stephen Boyd **Country:** USA **Year:** 1959

This Hollywood epic won a record 11 Academy Awards — but does it make the cut for historical accuracy?

Considered by many to be the quintessential 'Golden Age' Hollywood movie, director William Wyler's classic follows the tradition of the religious epic, following the path of such monumental works as *The Robe* (1953) and *The Ten Commandments* (1956). Set in the first century A.D - during the time of Jesus - the narrative follows a story of comradeship, betrayal, revenge and spiritual awakening.

Based on the 19th century novel of the same name, Wyler's film was the first to bring the tale to the big screen in full colour and sound, thrilling audiences with its grand staging, effects and stunts - the spectacular chariot race in the final act was in particular singled out for praise.

At the 1960 Academy Awards the movie received an unprecedented 12 nominations, winning all but one of these, making it jointly the most successful production in the history of the Oscars. During production, heated disagreements surrounding the screenplay, which was penned by several different writers, remains the cause of some controversy, with claims that scenes were altered, inserted and cut.

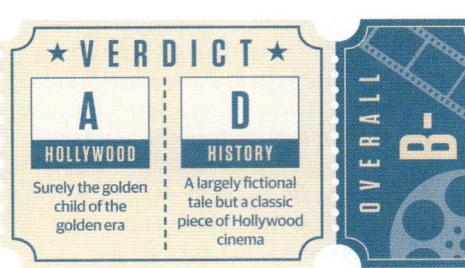

VERDICT
A HOLLYWOOD — Surely the golden child of the golden era
D HISTORY — A largely fictional tale but a classic piece of Hollywood cinema
OVERALL B-

15,000 extras were used in the climactic chariot scene

01 The film is based on the 19th-century historical fiction novel *Ben-Hur: A Tale of Christ* by Lew Wallace. The main character, Judah Ben-Hur, is a fictional Jewish prince but his life runs parallel to Jesus Christ, who he encounters.

02 Towards the beginning, the Roman tribune, Messala, asks Ben-Hur, at this point his friend, to provide him with information on anti-Roman Jews. Ben-Hur refuses to betray his own people and the film correctly portrays the tensions between the Romans and the Jews.

03 In the movie, Ben-Hur is depicted as one of the galley slaves, the enslaved men who powered the Roman ships. However, this is inaccurate because slaves were not used in this capacity at this time — the ships were actually powered by free men.

04 Alongside the inaccuracy regarding galley slaves, the battle against the Macedonian pirates is also completely false. The film is set during the lifetime of Jesus, between 4 BCE to roughly 30 CE, at which point there were no pirates with large warships.

05 The iconic chariot race towards the end of the movie portrays just how dangerous the sport was, if a bit toned down. As well as this, it correctly shows how successful chariot racers could gain a life of fame, glory and wealth through the sport.

The Golden Gate, also known as the Gate of Mercy, is believed by Christians and Muslims to be the gate through which Jesus entered Jerusalem

Why is Jerusalem so Important?

Simon Sebag Montefiore explains the ancient origins and enduring significance of this historic city

Was there anything that made Jerusalem special before it became the centre of three of the world's major religions?
The development of Jerusalem as the universal holy city is one of the strangest phenomena of geopolitics and religious development. The fact is that there was nothing special about it, except the fact that it was a fortress/hill and there was a spring next to it. It was a natural place for people to build a settlement of sorts. Secondly it was a natural place to build a holy place, which were often associated in pagan religions with a high place like a mountain. Of course, the spring made it ideal for settlement too.

It wasn't on any major trade routes. It was far from the sea. It was a mountain in the blistering Judean desert. In those days we think there was much more fauna and forestry than there is now, but that's another thing. It was very unlikely to become the holy city of the Western world.

In telling the story of early Jerusalem, how challenging is it to find sources that can be relied upon?
There are very few sources and you can't just use the Bible. What's interesting is the obsession with King David. That's a big question that

As a historian and author, Simon Sebag Montefiore has written several books on a wide range of topics, such as Stalin, the Romanovs and the speeches that changed the world. His bestseller, *Jerusalem*, was published in 2011 and covers the full history of the city.

everyone is obsessed with: did King David exist and is there proof of his existence? And therefore it is regarded as very political because if we can't find evidence of his existence and of the First Temple, then it has political implications today. But in fact this is a huge red herring because first of all, there is evidence in a stele that was found, the Tel Dan Stele, which mentions the House of David. So there is evidence that David was the founder of this kingdom and it seems highly likely that he was.

You start your story with the Roman siege of Jerusalem in 70 CE. Could you explain a little why that siege is so important to what

Ben-Hur

Jerusalem has come to mean today?
It's very important. It's a disaster and a drama on the scale of the Battle of Berlin in 1945 or Stalingrad or the Siege of Leningrad. It's one of the astonishing set pieces of human tragedy that is fascinating. Also, it has huge religious and political implications. It marks the end of Jewish independence in the Holy Land, and with a short interlude there wasn't really another Jewish realm until 1948. Secondly, in terms of the Roman Empire, it meant that from then on Jews were banned from Jerusalem itself and it was really seen as the withdrawal of the divine favour or blessing from the Jewish people.

That has huge implications because first, it lead to the change in the Jewish religion itself. Before that the Jewish religion was completely based around the Temple in Jerusalem and about the sacrifices of animals outside the Holy of Holies. That was Temple Judaism and after this Judaism changed forever and the Old Testament, but especially the five books of Moses [Torah], became a portable Jerusalem for Jewish people.

That's the way it has remained to this day. Secondly, the Christian religion up until then still worshipped as a Jewish faction within the Temple. When they saw that the Temple had fallen, they separated from the mother religion forever and modern Christianity comes from that moment too. Thirdly, 600 years later it was this event and then the development of Christianity after it that made Muhammad convinced that he was the third and final revelation of God. The first was the Jews, but that ended in 70 CE when the Temple was destroyed. The second was Christianity and he regarded Jesus as a prophet. And the third was Muhammad himself and the final revelation that became Islam. 70 CE is when all modern religion began in the Western world.

How much of ancient Jerusalem still exists?
There's a lot to see there and that's the exciting thing about Jerusalem. The ancientness of a holy place adds to its holiness. That's why so much of Jerusalem has been preserved in different ways. There are amazing things to see. My favourite place is the Golden Gate on the Eastern Wall, which is very ancient and may have been built by Heraclius or the Umayyad Caliph, we're not really sure. It's the most beautiful place and it's the place where all three religions believe Armageddon, Judgement Day, will start. There's tonnes to see there and one of the great joys of Jerusalem is that you can actually touch these stones.

JERUSALEM: THE BIOGRAPHY IS OUT NOW PUBLISHED BY WEIDENFELD & NICOLSON

Ancient

GLADIATOR

Director: Ridley Scott **Starring:** Russell Crowe, Joaquin Phoenix, Oliver Reed, Derek Jacobi, Connie Nielsen **Country:** USA **Year:** 2000

Father to a murdered son, husband to a murdered wife – and little adherence to historical accuracy…

This five-time Academy Award-winning historical epic had box office smash hit written in its stars: directed by Ridley Scott and with several generations of major acting talent in its cast, including Oliver Reed, Connie Nielsen and Joaquin Phoenix. *Gladiator* is the tale of the Roman general Maximus Decimus Aurelius (Russell Crowe). As a fearless and gifted soldier, a respected general who has led the Roman army to many victories, and a true servant of Rome, Maximus had earned the unwavering trust of the aging Emperor Marcus Aurelius (Richard Harris).

But Maximus has a dramatic turn in fortunes following the death of the Emperor. Commodus (Phoenix), the emperor's son, seizes the throne for himself despite Marcus Aurelius's final decree to hand Rome back to the senate. With Aurelius' favourite general a serious threat to his ambitions, Commodus orders the execution of Maximus and his family. General Maximus escapes, only to become a slave. A slave who becomes a gladiator. A gladiator who defies an emperor…

Gladiators were rarely killed, they were too valuable

VERDICT
- **HOLLYWOOD: A** — An instant classic worthy of *Ben Hur* or *Spartacus*
- **HISTORY: D** — Not quite A-level Roman history revision material
- **OVERALL: C+**

01 The opening scene shows the Romans fighting Germanic tribes in a forest made up of a single type of tree. Managed forests of this kind were not introduced until the 1500s. Catapults and ballistae wouldn't have been used in a wooded environment.

02 Most Roman buildings would not have been white and wouldn't have looked as ancient and weather-beaten as they do in the movie. Many would have been new and freshly painted in a variety of colours, as would the statues and carvings that appear in the streets.

03 Rome wasn't founded as a republic. In fact, the Eternal City started life as a monarchical state ruled by the Alban kings, before becoming a republic in 509 BCE and an empire in 27 BCE. Marcus Aurelius never intended to return it to a republican state.

04 Even under the most tyrannical of imperial machinations Maximus couldn't have disappeared to be enslaved. More likely he would have been legally banished, so wouldn't have been able to return to Rome to compete in the Colosseum.

05 There is no evidence that Emperor Marcus Aurelius was murdered by his son Commodus. He actually died in Vindobona (modern-day Vienna). He also did not ban gladiatorial combat, though he did regulate the games to make them less deadly.

A gladiator seeks a judgement from the crowd in this painting by Jean Léon Gérôme

Gladiator

This 3rd century CE gladiator tombstone from modern-day Turkey displays the typical equipment of a Thracian gladiator, including his distinctive curved sword

Real History of the Gladiators

Brutal reality of Rome's most famous bloodsport uncovered

One of the most well-known legacies of Ancient Rome is the spectator events of the arena, in particular gladiatorial contests. Some may be familiar with Roman institutions such as the Plebeian Council or the Centuriate Assembly, but almost everyone has heard of the gladiators and the Colosseum. This is due in no small part to Hollywood blockbusters like *Spartacus* and *Gladiator*. The historical accuracy of most of these cinematic depictions, however, often leaves something to be desired.

One topic of debate among historians has been the origin of gladiatorial contests. Such combat existed in Italy prior to its emergence in Rome, but a consensus beyond this has been difficult to achieve. Some researchers argue that gladiators originated in the Etruscan society of north-central Italy, a belief based largely upon ancient testimony that the term 'lanista', the standard Roman word for a gladiatorial trainer, was Etruscan in origin. However, the available evidence supports the idea that gladiatorial combat originated among the Campanians of south-central Italy. A series of late 4th century BCE tomb-paintings from Campania, for example, depict duels between armed men. The Roman historian Livy records that Rome's Campanian allies during the same period were in the practice of dressing up gladiators in the armour of their enemy, the Samnites, and forcing them to fight duels to entertain guests at banquets.

The earliest recorded gladiatorial duels in Rome were staged in a funerary context, a far cry from the later massive spectacles of the Colosseum. In 264 BCE, for example, the sons of Decimus Junius Brutus staged a combat involving three pairs of gladiators in the Forum Boarium ('Cattle Market') for their deceased father. In these early funerary events the fighting skill of the participants, as well as the blood they spilled, was meant to honour the deceased, an obligation that those staging such events were happy to fulfil. This idea of family obligation towards dead relatives, or the obligation of later Roman magistrates to stage combat events for thousands of spectators, was central to such contests. In fact, one of the most common terms used for the spectacles of the arena, 'munus' ('munera' in the plural), means 'duty'.

Gladiatorial events gradually became larger and more popular in Rome over the succeeding decades. A truly decisive point in terms of their scale appears to have been reached with the disastrous defeat that the Carthaginian general Hannibal inflicted upon the Romans at Cannae in 216 BCE during the Second Punic War. The deep insecurity that the Romans felt in the aftermath of Cannae evidently led them to desire seeing more and more gladiators, who could be thought of as symbolising their opponents on the battlefield, killed for their entertainment. Certainly, the size of gladiatorial events grew dramatically in the period after Cannae: in the same year as the battle three days of funerary games staged for a certain Marcus Aemilius Lepidus in the Roman forum featured 44 gladiators, while in 183 BCE an event of similar duration dedicated to Publius Licinius involved 120.

As might be expected, the earliest gladiators reflected the groups and ethnicities against which Rome was currently fighting or had recently fought: the 'Samnite' type, followed by

Ancient

the 'Thracians' and 'Gauls', broadly reflected the course of Roman territorial expansion in the Republic. The weapons and armour borne by these types of gladiators, of course, reflected to a degree the equipment used by their namesakes. The characteristic weapon of the 'Thracian' gladiator, for example, was a type of curved sword that was native to the lower Danube region.

Gladiatorial combat, however, was not the only form of violent spectacle that enjoyed popularity during this period. The venationes, or beast-hunts, also became a staple of Roman arena events beginning in the early 2nd century BCE. Like the gladiatorial contests, these spectacles were not entirely a Roman invention, but evolved from precedents found elsewhere. One such forerunner was the widespread cross-cultural custom of rulers displaying and/or hunting various exotic animals as a demonstration of their alleged mastery over nature.

The Romans staged a procession of exotic animals in 275 BCE and another 25 years later, both of which featured spoils of war: namely, the war elephants that the Romans had recently captured from Pyrrhus and the Carthaginians. Over the succeeding decades such processions, staged in venues like the Circus Maximus (the great chariot-racing stadium of Rome), were ever more frequently organised in peacetime as well. By the end of the 3rd century BCE, displays of African animals like ostriches had become quite common.

The fate of the animals involved in these early processions is not certain. The first explicitly attested venatio in Rome, in which animals were not merely displayed but also killed for the public's amusement, occurred in 186 BCE when Marcus Fulvius Nobilior staged such an event to celebrate his recent military victories. The factors behind Nobilior's decision to introduce a violent element into his animal spectacle are not certain. It may be that contemporary Romans, increasingly enamoured of bloody entertainment, found non-violent animal processions somewhat boring in comparison.

The dramatic expansion of Rome in the last two centuries of the Republic provided ample scope for the further growth of such events. The tens of thousands of military prisoners captured by the Romans during this period were a ready source of forced recruits for the arena. Similarly, the annexation of territory in such regions as Asia Minor, Syria and north Africa provided ready access to a large number of exotic animals such as lions, thereby allowing spectacle organisers (editores) to increase the variety and popularity of their events.

As the arena spectacles grew in both scope and popularity, the various aspects of their production gradually became more organised. By the late Republic, for example, Roman magistrates staged munera on a regular basis, often as a means of securing popular support for upcoming elections in the city. By the late Republic several ludi, or training-schools for the arena, were owned by wealthy Romans, along with various familiae, groups of gladiators and their requisite support and training personnel. It was these groups that supplied the massive late-Republican spectacles of prominent Romans like Pompey and Julius Caesar. The most famous of these Republican ludi was located at Capua in southern Italy, from which Spartacus and his followers escaped and began their insurrection against the Roman state in 73 BCE.

At the same time as the organisation and infrastructure of arena spectacles became more sophisticated, the structures in which they were staged gradually became more elaborate as well. The earliest gladiatorial and animal events in Rome were staged in venues originally built for other purposes, which offered ample space and/or seating. Venationes and other animal events were staged on the level track of the Circus Maximus that ran around the arena for chariot racing, while gladiatorial contests often took place in the open space of the Roman forum. In the last two centuries BCE, alterations and additions were made at both of these locations to facilitate such events. Iron animal cages, for example, were added to the Circus Maximus, while wooden balconies known

The remains of the Colosseum in Rome. The galleries of the basement (hypogeum) in the centre once held almost 200 animal cages

A section of the Borghese mosaic, which depicts a range of gladiators

> "Gladiatorial combat was not the only form of violent spectacle that enjoyed popularity during this period"

Gladiator

EMPERORS IN THE ARENA

The glamour of victory might have enticed even the most powerful men in Rome

CALIGULA
Reign: 37-41 CE

The reign of Caligula is an infamous chapter of Roman history, although contemporary records are rather biased against the emperor, making it hard to decipher fact from malicious fiction. One story about Caligula claims that when those accused of treason were sentenced to public execution he sometimes fought them as gladiators.

HADRIAN
Reign: 117-138 CE

Like many emperors, Hadrian was a big fan of gladiatorial games and put on a particularly extravagant display to mark his 43rd birthday in which hundreds of animals were slaughtered and gifts were thrown into the crowd. Hadrian also took part in some staged fights in which there was no risk of death to himself or his opponent.

COMMODUS
Reign: 177-192 CE

Most famously portrayed in the film *Gladiator*, Commodus did indeed venture into the arena to show off his prowess with a blade. Rather than taking on prominent gladiators, however, he preferred to face off against beasts or fighters who would immediately submit to him after receiving a wound.

---

as maeniana were added to a number of buildings surrounding the open space of the Roman forum for the convenience of spectators.

The building most associated with the Roman munera, of course, is the amphitheatre. The earliest stone amphitheatre in Italy, dating to approximately 70 BCE, is found not in Rome, however, but in Pompeii. One of the main reasons why no amphitheatres predating the Colosseum exist in Rome today is that, because of a longstanding senatorial ban on the building of such permanent spectator venues during the Republic, many of the structures that were erected for various munera during that period were temporary.

The growth of the munera over the last few centuries of the Republic culminated in the spectacles of Caesar. As part of his quadruple triumph in 46 BCE, Caesar staged a combat between cavalry, 40 elephants and approximately 500 infantry in the Circus Maximus, as well as both venationes and gladiatorial munera in the Roman forum. For the latter events, he not only erected a temporary 'hunting-theatre', but even had a number of subterranean galleries built beneath it. These held the animals and equipment that were to be used in the spectacle above. Caesar also put on a massive naumachia, or staged naval combat, involving thousands of prisoners of war.

This detail from a Roman mosaic depicts a secutor (left) in combat with a retiarius. Behind them stands the referee with his stick, ready to punish any rule infractions

41

Ancient

SPARTACUS

Director: Stanley Kubrick **Starring:** Kirk Douglas, Laurence Olivier, Tony Curtis **Country:** USA **Year:** 1960

Does this tale of rebel gladiators hold up in the arena of historical records?

Released in 1960 and loosely based on historical accounts from ancient historians, this Roman epic is set in the first century BCE and stars Kirk Douglas as the eponymous slave. Unbroken by his servitude in a mining pit, Spartacus is chosen by a wealthy Roman entrepreneur, Batiatus (Peter Ustinov), who sees potential in the indomitable Thracian and wants him to train as a gladiator at his school.

When the Roman senator Crassus (Laurence Olivier) visits the school and pays Batiatus to watch slaves duel to the death, Spartacus is defeated in combat. However, instead of killing Spartacus, his opponent defies the senator and is instead killed by a soldier. The following day, Batiatus sends the slave girl that Spartacus had formed a relationship with to Crassus in Rome. Brimming with righteous indignation, Spartacus kills his trainer, which leads to a riot. The slaves overwhelm the guards and escape to the Roman countryside, where Spartacus is elected their leader. They organise, and with the help of Cilician pirates, their numbers grow enough to threaten the Roman Senate.

The real Spartacus led a rebellion against Rome in 73 BCE

VERDICT
- **A HOLLYWOOD** — A jaw-dropping movie in an era that predates CGI
- **C HISTORY** — A retelling certainly not constrained by accuracy
- **OVERALL B**

01 Spartacus claims to be the descendant of a long line of slaves, going back to his grandfather. This is not based on any historical record. In fact, while he was from Thrace, it's thought that he was a Roman soldier and then imprisoned and enslaved.

02 Although trained as a gladiator at Capua, which was a well-known school, Spartacus never actually fights in an arena, which is accurate. The uprising of the slaves beginning in the school's kitchen also tracks with the historical record of events in 73 BCE.

03 Spartacus did lead his men to a stunning victory over Clodius, the Roman praetor. The film shows this as a surprise night attack against a poorly prepared camp. In reality, it was even more daring, as they abseiled down Mount Vesuvius to flank the Romans.

04 Spartacus and his army make it their aim to free every slave in every town in the film, but such a motive is not established in the historical records. They are estimated to have freed around 90,000 enslaved people as they travelled Italy, however.

05 The most famous scene of the film, as Spartacus's men stand in turn to claim "I'm Spartacus!" is unfortunately fictitious. Spartacus died in battle thanks to a spear to the thigh. It is true, however, that some surviving rebels were crucified.

SPARTACUS'S REBELLION

The slave uprising rocked the Roman world and was almost victorious

Plotting and escape
73 BCE
01 While based at the Capuan gladiatorial training school owned by Gnaeus Cornelius Lentulus Batiatus, Spartacus hatched a plan to break free of the camp. Despite their attempts at secrecy the plot is betrayed, but Spartacus still manages to muster between 70 and 80 willing slaves – many of whom were former soldiers – to join his escape.

The military arrives
73 BCE
02 After breaking free, the group elects three individuals to lead them; two Gallic slaves, Crixus and Oenomaus and Spartacus. The group ransacks military equipment from the camp and takes on a small force sent to quash them. Spartacus's group easily defeats the soldiers, plunders the surrounding region and adds more slaves to its number before retiring to a defensive position on Mount Vesuvius.

Praetorian might
73 BCE
03 With news spreading of the revolt, Rome dispatches a militia of 3,000 men to stop the uprising. Praetor Gaius Claudius Glaber leads the reactionary force, blocking the revolt from escaping its base on Vesuvius. Spartacus's men use vines to rappel down the side of the mountain at night, sneaking up on the force and annihilating them.

Breaking the revolt
73-72 BCE
04 The uprising spreads across the nearby regions, freeing slaves and swelling its ranks to over 70,000 fighters. Alarmed at the size of the revolt, the Senate dispatches a consular army to engage the slaves. It's initially successful, with Crixus and around 30,000 slaves being defeated by General Lucius Gellius Publicola.

War under Crassus
71 BCE
05 Despite the loss of Craxis and his forces, Spartacus has led the larger force into the south of Italy, which continued to sweep Roman forces. The Senate grants praetorship to Marcus Licinius Crassus and an army of around almost 50,000 infantrymen. Crassus and Spartacus's first clash ends in defeat for the slave, with a loss of 6,000 men. After being betrayed by pirates, Spartacus's force retreats to Rhegium.

The Battle of the Siler River
71 BCE
06 The legions of Pompey are returning home after the conquest of Hispania, so the Senate orders them to march directly to Crassus's position. With news of the reinforcements reaching Spartacus he attempts to negotiate a truce, but Crassus refuses and kills 12,300 fleeing rebels. Despite the insurmountable odds, Spartacus and his men charge into Crassus's forces. Spartacus dies on the battlefield with his rebel cohorts.

THREE SLAVE REBELLIONS

Spartacus's uprising wasn't the only rebellion to rock the slave trade and 'civilised' society

ZANJ REBELLION
869-883

At its height, the Abbasid Caliphate (one of three powerful Islamic states that controlled much of the Middle East and Asia between 750 and 1517) had one of the biggest slave populations in the world. The Zanj Rebellion, which comprised a number of smaller uprisings that eventually solidified into a single national conflict, saw 500,000 captives rise up against their masters in a violent confrontation that eventually led to the formation of an independent state within Egypt. However, the Abbasid armies eventually regrouped and crushed what was left of the uprising soon after.

HAITIAN REBELLION
21 April 1791 - 1 January 1804

Toward the end of the 1780s, Saint-Domingue was the most profitable possession controlled by France. It produced a staggering 60 per cent of the world's coffee and around 40 per cent of all sugar reserves, but it did so by working its slaves into a mortality rate that far exceeded the island's birth rate. Inspired by the shock waves of the French Revolution, an uprising was concocted by freeman and military genius François-Dominique Toussaint Louverture. After almost 13 bloody years the French were driven off the island and the republic of Haiti was established.

SECOND ROMAN SERVILE WAR
104-100 BCE

Taking place over 30 years after the very first major servile conflict, the uprising led by slave leader Tryphon grew to such a size that it took considerable military might on the part of the Roman Republic to bring it to heel. The revolt broke out when most of the slave population on the island of Sicily walked out on their masters en masse. Refusing to return to servitude, the slaves formed into a force of around 2,000 cavalry and 20,000 infantry. Despite its considerable presence, the consul general Manius Aquillius eventually put the rebellion down.

Ancient

TROY

Director: Wolfgang Petersen **Starring:** Brad Pitt, Eric Bana, Orlando Bloom, Diane Kruger **Country:** USA **Year:** 2004

Does this all-star ancient epic live up to the real legend?

The face that launched a thousand ships; the anatomical weak spot of even the greatest warrior; hiding an army inside a giant wooden horse: the story of Troy is embedded in Western culture more than many may appreciate. So when director Wolfgang Petersen and writer David Benioff (future *Game of Thrones* co-creator) were tasked with bringing Homer's tale to 21st-century audiences, it was just as well they had a legendary cast to match the Greek mythology.

Brad Pitt is at the peak of his powers as the demi-god Achilles, while Eric Bana does a credible job in the role of the Trojan prince Hector. Although the pair's duel is undoubtedly a highlight for those seeking some sword-and-sandal sparring, heavy lifting is done by supporting performances from Sean Bean as Odysseus, Brian Cox as Agamemnon, Diane Kruger as Helen, and bonafide legend Peter O'Toole as King Priam.

An epic worldwide taking just shy of half a billion dollars gross took *Troy* into the top-ten earners of 2004, even while many of its stars would later go on to bemoan its lack of depth.

Brad Pitt injured his Achilles tendon during filming

VERDICT
- **B HOLLYWOOD** — A legendary cast with memorable set pieces
- **D HISTORY** — Only a few flaws short of a Greek tragedy
- **OVERALL C**

01 While in the film the siege of Troy begins and ends within a couple of weeks, in Homer's *Iliad* the war actually lasts over ten years. This means a lot of the events and even whole characters in the original text are entirely cut from the movie.

02 During fighting in front of Troy's walls, Hector kills the towering Greek hero Ajax with a broken spear. In Homer's *Iliad*, Ajax does indeed fight Hector, but he is not killed on the battlefield. Instead, Ajax falls on his own sword after the end of the war.

03 In a bid to end the war, Paris and Menelaus fight a duel to the death. However, when Menelaus wins, Hector fatally stabs Menelaus before he can perform the coup de grâce. In Homer's text, Menelaus still wins the duel, but survives the war.

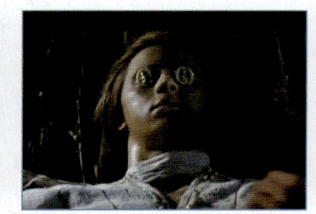

04 At Patroclus' funeral we see Achilles place two coins on his eyes, a tradition that dates back to ancient Greece. However, the earliest known use of coins is dated to around the 6th or 5th century BCE - centuries after the events of the Trojan War.

05 While Patroclus and Achilles are depicted as cousins, Homer describes them as close friends and elsewhere they are portrayed as lovers. A relationship between the two better accounts for Achilles' passionate rage after Patroclus' death.

Troy

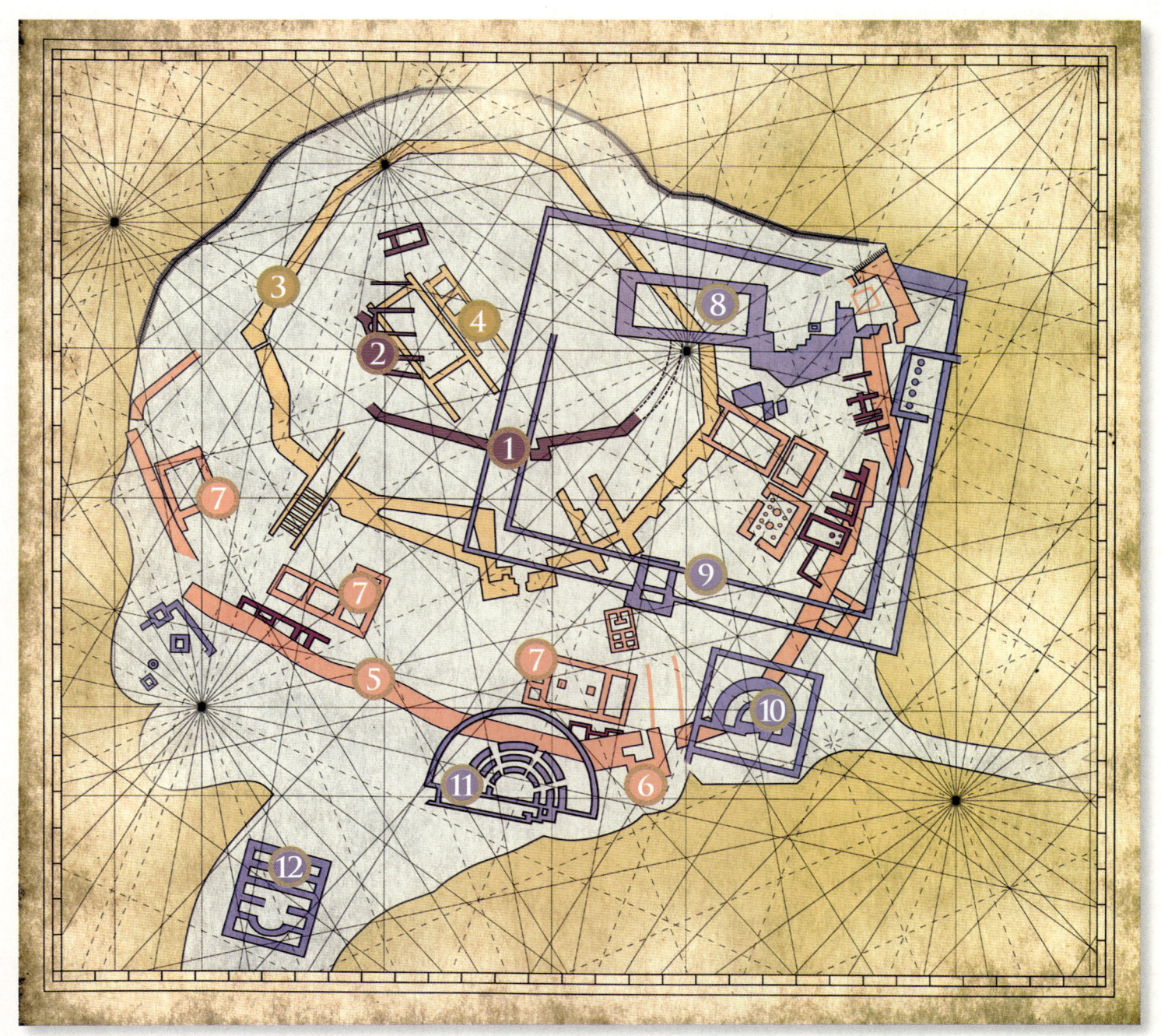

The nine cities of troy

Several layers of the city have been unearthed, revealing its long history

🟣 TROY I
c. 3500 – 2550 BCE

The earliest examples of settlement were found 32 metres above the plain under a mound made from debris from centuries of settlement. Some key features were found including the outer gate and wall of the city (1) and the Megaron or great hall (2).

🟡 TROY II
c. 2450 – 2200 BCE

About 110 metres up are the remains of a much wider complex, about twice the size of the original site. The outer walls around the city (3) were more complete and apparently sloped, which would protect them better against earthquakes. The great hall appears to be built on top of the previous one (4).

🟠 TROY VI
c. 1700 – 1250 BCE

The remains of this level of the city include even greater walls (5) and defensive towers next to them (6). Showing the growing prestige and wealth of Troy by the Middle Bronze Age, the city now boasts a wider array of housing and storage buildings (7) to better supply the population. Evidence of Minoan pottery points to the growing trade in the region too.

🟣 TROY VII
c. 1250 – 1080 BCE

This era of the city saw much of the previous incarnation rebuilt and built upon following an earthquake. Housing appears to have gotten closer together and done more cheaply, which might indicate that the population was growing significantly at this stage. This could well have been the city as described by Homer.

🟣 TROY VIII – XI
c. 1000 – 500 CE

Now a Greek colonial settlement, the site is dominated by a Temple of Athena (8) surrounded by a wider temple complex including courtyards (9). Alexander the Great is said to have attended the temple on his way to the Battle of the Granicus in 334 BCE. To the south are signs of the Roman occupation of the city with a bouleuterion or assembly house (10), odeon for entertainment (11) and a bath house (12).

45

Ancient

POMPEII

Director: Paul WS Anderson **Starring:** Kit Harrington, Keifer Sutherland, Emily Browning, Carrie-Anne Moss **Country:** USA **Year:** 2014

Can love overcome an erupting volcano and a pyroclastic flow? No, probably not…

The tragedy of Pompeii is one of history's most shocking and captivating stories. Buried under burning-hot ash in 79 CE, the city was preserved in incredible detail, the bodies of the victims of Mount Vesuvius' eruption captured in their moment of death. The ruined remains of the city are some of our most incredible archaeological sites for evidence of daily life in ancient Roman Italy.

Enter //Resident Evil// and //Alien Vs Predator// director Paul WS Anderson to bring this tragic event to the big screen. He's not considered a heavyweight director, but his box office success can't be denied. What's more, this seems to have been a real passion project for him having read extensively on the topic. He brought his action directing skills to bear in making the eruption as accurate as possible.

With a budget estimated to be around $100 million and a box office return of $117 million, the film was a mild success, but took a bit of a kicking from critics. Star Kit Harrington later joked on SNL that the film was "more of a disaster than the event it was based on."

Our record of the eruption comes from Pliny the Younger who witnessed the event from across the bay of Naples

VERDICT
- **E HOLLYWOOD** — Isn't this just *Gladiator* smashed together with *Titanic*?
- **C HISTORY** — While the story is fictional, the key event sticks largely to the science
- **OVERALL D**

01 Before the eruption in 79 CE, we see that the city of Pompeii is shaken by earthquakes, with only mild alarm by its citizens. This is accurate to how such eruptions were experienced and would have seemed normal to the people of Pompeii.

02 After Vesuvius explodes, a pyroclastic flow speeds down the volcano and into the city, burning everything it touches. This is accurate to this kind of eruption and what happened to Pompeii. The flow is thought to have reached temperatures of 300° C.

03 The burning cloud that hits Pompeii is joined by fireballs and a giant tsunami that sends ships flying into the city. Neither of these things happened. There was a tsunami, but nowhere near this size and while large chunks of rock fell, they were not on fire or molten.

04 All the main characters are fictional, although Milo and Cassia are inspired by 'The Two Maidens'. These remains were found embracing at Pompeii and were thought to be two women, but more recent DNA analysis suggests they were actually both men.

05 The city itself is impressively re-created with even the location of key buildings being based on the remains (such as the amphitheatre). Items on sale in the market were based on discoveries made by researchers and lidar was used to get the topography correct.

Pompeii

Preserving Pompeii

Looking after a city that's over 2,000 years old is far from an easy task

01 REGIO V

The current excavations are taking place here, uncovering a part of the city that hasn't seen the light of day since the eruption in 79 CE.

New technologies like lasers and drones are being used to uncover the half-hectare area in what's been called one of the biggest postwar digs in the world.

02 VILLA OF THE MYSTERIES

From 1924 to 1961, a considerable amount of excavating took place. One of the buildings to be uncovered in this period was the Villa of the Mysteries, a well-preserved villa on the outskirts of Pompeii. Archaeologists also dug up most of Regio I and II.

03 VIA DELL'ABBONDANZA

While today this street makes up the majority of the 'Pompeii for all' walking route, it was heavily bombed during World War II, hampering excavation efforts. It was around this time that Vesuvius erupted again and parts of the area were evacuated.

04 HOUSE OF THE GLADIATORS

In 2010, tragedy struck. The House of the Gladiators, which had been struck during the bombing raid in the 1940s, suddenly collapsed after a bout of heavy rainfall in the Bay of Naples. Thought to be a relatively sturdy building, its collapse shocked many.

05 ADVERSE CONDITIONS

Because the city of Pompeii isn't covered by anything, it's open to the elements – and that creates problems for us today. A lot of what has been uncovered by archaeologists over the years has suffered from wind, rain, light damage and even tourists and archaeologists themselves.

06 STILL UNDERGROUND

Just under one-third of Pompeii still lies unexcavated underground. Arguably, this is the safest place for the buildings as here they can't be damaged by the elements or the people constantly traipsing through. It's uncertain if digs will take place here in the future.

Ancient

ALEXANDER

Director: Oliver Stone Starring: Colin Farrell, Angelina Jolie, Val Kilmer, Anthony Hopkins Country: USA Year: 2004

A bombastic big-screen retelling of one of history's legendary figures, but does it lose focus on facts for action and spectacle?

Building on the massive success of Ridley Scott's *Gladiator* in 2000, Oliver Stone looked to bring his own homage to the Hollywood epic to screens with *Alexander*. Its star-studded cast included screen legends like Anthony Hopkins and Christopher Plummer, established stars Angelina Jolie and Val Kilmer, and relative newcomers Colin Farrell, Jared Leto and Rosario Dawson.

This wasn't Stone's first foray into historical drama, of course, having made his name with *Platoon*, *Born on the Fourth of July*, *The Doors*, *JFK* and *Nixon*. This scale of sword-and-sandal adventure was a little different, but with a budget of $155 million it was able to do a lot with its settings, costumes and scale of action.

However a who's who of acting talent, Oscar-winning director and large budget didn't save *Alexander* from box office struggles. It's estimated that the movie took about $167 million globally, which is a few million more than the budget, but begins to dwindle when advertising is taken into account. Controversy also swirled around Alexander's depiction as bisexual, while critics found it to be ambitious, but overstuffed and dull.

VERDICT

- **HOLLYWOOD: C** — The stars were out and chewing up the scenery
- **HISTORY: D** — Trades a lot of history for glitz and glamour
- **OVERALL: D+**

Angelina Jolie is less than one year older than her 'son' Farrell in the movie

01 Philip II (Kilmer) is depicted as having a scar over his right eye, possibly taken from a reconstruction in 1984 of what were believed to his remains. Those remains were later proven to not be the king's, which would have been known when the film was made.

02 Alexander (Farrell) is shown wearing an elaborate lion head helmet into battle. There is no record of him wearing any such headgear. Plutarch records his helmet being simple iron. The other equipment of the Macedonian military is considered accurate.

03 The Battle of Gaugemela has been widely praised by experts for faithfully portraying the battle formations and tactics used. However, a number of other battles are ignored and the later battle in India should have been on a river bank, not in a jungle.

04 The film depicts Alexander being involved sexually with both men and women. This appears to track with the historical evidence. We know he had multiple wives, at least one child, as well as relationships with Bagoas and Hephaestion (Jared Leto).

05 The film is narrated by Alexander's successor in Egypt, Ptolemy (Anthony Hopkins) in Alexandria. At one point we see the lighthouse, Pharos, in the background. This lighthouse was commissioned by Ptolemy, but was not finished in his lifetime.

The Myth Maker

Here are six legends and stories that surrounded Alexander, some of which he happily fostered

GORDIAN KNOT
On his march through Anatolia, Alexander reached Gordium. There he was shown a cart lashed to a pole with an intricate knot that only the future king of Asia could untie. Alexander wrestled with the knot for several moments before proclaiming: "It makes no difference how they are loosed", drew his sword and sliced the knot in two.

SON OF ZEUS
Alexander may have truly believed that he was the son of Zeus. His mother Olympias claimed a bolt of lightning shot into her womb and his father had a dream in which he pressed a seal against her womb with a figure of a lion on it. Supposedly in later years Alexander visited the Oracle of Zeus-Ammon to seek confirmation.

THE TAMING OF BUCEPHALUS
Phillip II had been offered the horse Bucephalus, but was uninterested in it due to its wild nature. Alexander bet his father he could tame the horse, where others had failed. Realising its shadow was the cause of its distress, he turned it towards the sun. A prophecy claimed the rider of the horse would rule the world.

BURNING OF THE TEMPLE OF ARTEMIS
On the night of Alexander's birth the Temple of Artemis was torched by a man named Herostratus, seeking notoriety. Any mention of Herostratus's name was forbidden under pain of death. It was believed Artemis was present at the boy's birth and so neglected her temple.

ORACLE AT DELPHI
In 336 BCE Alexander marched his men to the oracle, Pythia, at Delphi, wishing to hear confirmation he'd conquer the entire ancient world. Upon arrival, he was told she was unable to see him. Enraged, Alexander dragged Pythia by the hair until she screamed: "You are invincible!" He replied, "I have my answer."

PAINTINGS OF APELLES
A renowned painter in ancient Greece, Apelles painted Alexander several times, with one renowned version showing him holding a lightning bolt. One story tells that when painting Alexander's concubine Campaspe, Apelles fell in love and as a reward for the skill of the painter, Alexander gave her to him.

ALEXANDER THE (NOT SO) GREAT

Despite his title, Alexander was known for his wanton cruelty and savagery against his enemies

BURNING OF PERSEPOLIS
The Persian capital Persepolis housed numerous works of art and treasures. During the Persian invasion of Greece in 480 BCE, many Greek villages, cities and temples had been raised by the army of Xerxes I. It's often thought that the memory of these crimes led Alexander and his men to torch the city, though several accounts state he was drunk.

CONSPIRACY OF THE PAGES
Alexander was served by many pages, one of whom, Hermolaus, killed a boar that was marked for Alexander. Publicly flogged, Hermolaus was humiliated. He, along with his lover and several others, conspired to kill the king while he slept. But Alexander spent the night drinking and failed to return. The plan revealed, the boys were stoned to death by the Macedonian court.

CLEITUS KILLED
During the Battle of Granicus, Alexander was attacked by Persian satraps and was saved by Cleitus. Alexander gave Cleitus the satrapy of Bactria and organised a banquet to celebrate. When both men were heavily intoxicated, an argument began in which Cleitus claimed Alexander's achievements were due to his father. Furious, Alexander grabbed a spear and murdered Cleitus.

BATIS BRUTALISED
Batis was the commander of the city of Gaza during a fierce battle and following defeat was brought before Alexander. Ordered to submit, Batis remained silent. Enraged, Alexander dragged him through the city attached to his chariot. Alexander boasted that he'd replicated the acts of his ancestor Achilles against his enemy Hector – except Hector had already been dead.

49

Drama

50

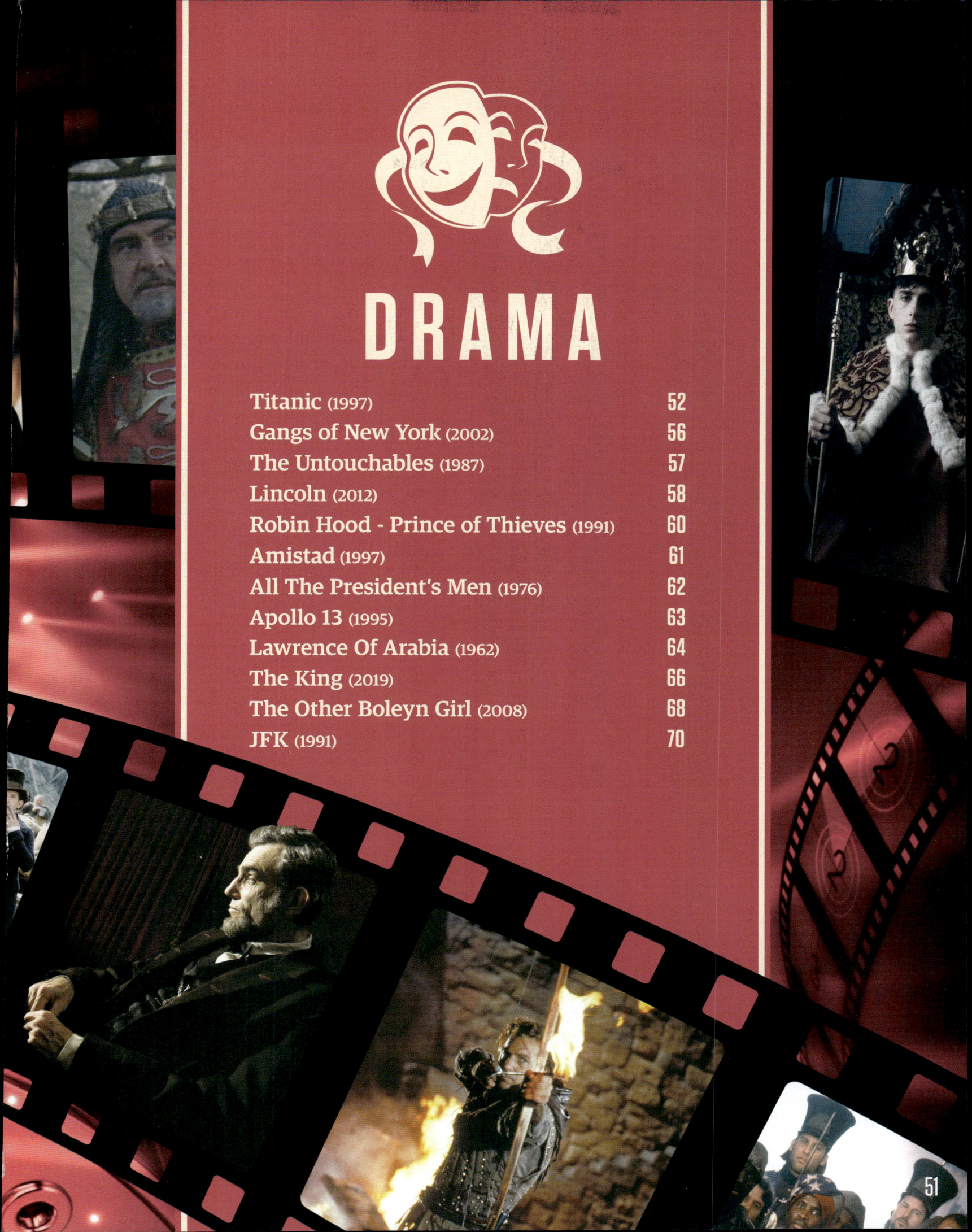

DRAMA

Titanic (1997)	52
Gangs of New York (2002)	56
The Untouchables (1987)	57
Lincoln (2012)	58
Robin Hood - Prince of Thieves (1991)	60
Amistad (1997)	61
All The President's Men (1976)	62
Apollo 13 (1995)	63
Lawrence Of Arabia (1962)	64
The King (2019)	66
The Other Boleyn Girl (2008)	68
JFK (1991)	70

Drama

TITANIC

Director: James Cameron **Starring:** Leonardo DiCaprio, Kate Winslet **Country:** USA **Year:** 1997

When you start scrutinising the details of this epic blockbuster, you can't avoid that sinking feeling…

When dashing artist Jack (Leonardo DiCaprio) saves the life of a beautiful young aristocrat named Rose (Kate Winslet), the pair have an instant connection. Though Jack is a penniless drifter and Rose is from a rich upper-class family, the pair soon fall for eachother. There are just two problems.

First, Rose is unhappily engaged to sneering, arrogant industrialist Cal (Billy Zane), who attempts to split the young couple apart when he uncovers their relationship. The other problem? They are on board the RMS Titanic, on course to hit an iceberg and sink. Part romance, part disaster drama, director James Cameron's faithful retelling of Titanic's fateful first and final voyage is one of Hollywood's highest ever grossing movies.

Awash with all the cutting-edge CGI effects the Nineties had to offer, including a painstakingly accurate rendering of the vessel, we follow Rose and Jack's romance turn into a struggle for survival. The film's final act, as the doomed ship begins to sink and break apart, is a terrifying depiction of how the real catastrophe unfolded more than a century ago.

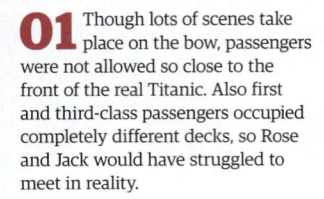

James Cameron dove to the real Titanic wreck 12 times during his research

★ VERDICT ★

A	B-
HOLLYWOOD	HISTORY
A star-studded $2 billion blockbuster	Jack could have definitely fit on that door…

OVERALL B+

01 Though lots of scenes take place on the bow, passengers were not allowed so close to the front of the real Titanic. Also first and third-class passengers occupied completely different decks, so Rose and Jack would have struggled to meet in reality.

02 A virtual model of RMS Titanic was created for the film. Only the starboard (right) side was built and mirrored for use as the port (left) side. This means the side of the ship we see docked is not as Titanic would have appeared, as it wasn't exactly symmetrical.

03 Once the lifeboats return to find survivors, we see the crewmen searching for people in the water. Though in the film they are using large torches that emit a strong white beam, flashlights of this strength and quality weren't in mass production at the time.

04 Towards the film's climax, crowds flock around the lifeboats. Lt. William Murdoch, the first officer, is shown threatening the passengers and shooting one dead before killing himself. There are conflicting accounts of Murdoch's exact actions during the sinking.

05 As Rose gazes up to the sky while floating on a broken door, the star field she sees is actually wrong for the ship's position. Astrophysicist Neil deGrasse Tyson informed James Cameron of the inaccuracy, who amended it in a re-release in 2012.

Titanic

Five Real Survivors of Titanic

The tales of real men and women who miraculously beat the odds or sacrificed it all on a cold April night in 1912

Despite the common misconception, RMS Titanic was never called 'unsinkable' in the run up to its maiden voyage. In fact, it wasn't until after the sinking that it became known as such. It was 'practically unsinkable', but so was every other luxury liner of the period. These ships just didn't sink – that was the end of it – and there was nothing special about Titanic in this regard. It was because of this general attitude of superiority over the sea that Titanic carried only enough lifeboats for half of the passengers on board, and none of the crew members were trained in how to conduct an evacuation. The officers, later criticised for releasing lifeboats half full, simply had no idea how many people could safely board the boats.

Nobody had the slightest notion that the ship would, or even could, sink.

With no procedures in place to protect them and a ship completely unprepared for evacuation, when Titanic hit an iceberg on 12 April 1912, those on board had to fend for themselves. For some, death was inevitable, but for others it was a noble choice – such as the devoted wife who refused to leave her husband, and the band that played until the final moment. In less than three hours, hundreds of lives were changed, and more were ended. From penniless immigrants to multi-millionaires, every man, woman and child on board had a life, a story and a destiny. Their tales of heroism, sacrifice and survival have intrigued people for more than 100 years; these are just five of them.

Joseph's daughter, Louise, became one of the oldest survivors of the Titanic disaster, dying in 1998 aged 87

JOSEPH LAROCHE
Second-class passenger, 1886-1912
Titanic's forgotten black hero

— 1 —

Although Laroche was an educated man with an engineering degree, he struggled to find work because of rampant racism in France. So to pay for his daughter's medical bills, Laroche made the decision to return to his native Haiti with his family of two daughters, and another child on the way. The family first planned to travel on SS France, but changed their tickets to Titanic when they discovered they would not be able to dine with their children.

When Titanic struck the iceberg, Laroche quickly became aware that something was wrong. He woke his wife, Juliette, then put as many of their valuables as he could carry in his pockets. With their young daughters still sleeping, Laroche and Juliette carried the girls up to the deck. Joseph led his pregnant wife and daughters to a lifeboat, possibly lifeboat 8, safely, however, he could not follow them. Sadly, no more of Joseph's story is known. He died in the sinking and his body was never recovered. However, his wife and children survived, and Juliette went on to have a baby boy that she named Joseph in her late husband's honour.

53

Drama

MARGARET BROWN

First-class passenger, 1867-1932

The unsinkable fireball that fought for survivors

Also known as the 'Unsinkable Molly Brown', Margaret Brown was born the poor daughter of Irish immigrants. Although she dreamed of marrying a rich man, she fell in love with James Joseph Brown, a miner, and married him, later saying: "I decided that I'd be better off with a poor man whom I loved than with a wealthy one whose money had attracted me." The couple had two children and struggled with money. However, James eventually became superintendent of the mine and, thanks to his own enterprising ideas, became a hugely successful and wealthy businessman.

Margaret had boarded Titanic to visit her grandchild who was ill in New York. It was a last-minute decision, and many of her family members were unaware she was actually on board. When the ship hit the iceberg, the energetic woman leapt into action, helping several women and children into the lifeboats. After much persuasion, she eventually climbed aboard lifeboat 6 and encouraged the other women to row it with her, working hard to keep their spirits up. Quartermaster Robert Hichens was in charge of the lifeboat and Margaret reportedly clashed over the issue of going back for survivors. Margaret was determined to return for the people in the water as they still had room in the lifeboat, but Hichens feared that the people would swarm the boat and drag them down. It is unknown whether Margaret did manage to persuade him to go back or not.

However, it was her actions after the tragedy that drew the most attention. Upon boarding Carpathia, she assisted survivors, handing out food and blankets. By the time the ship arrived in New York, she had established a survivors' committee and been elected the chair of it, as well as raising $10,000 for passengers who had lost everything. She refused to leave the ship until all survivors had been reunited with friends and family or received medical assistance. With her sense of humour still intact, she wrote to her daughter: "After being brined, salted, and pickled in mid ocean I am now high and dry... I have had flowers, letters, telegrams from people until I am befuddled. They are petitioning Congress to give me a medal... If I must call a specialist to examine my head it is due to the title of Heroine of the Titanic."

Margaret went on to become a fierce activist of women's rights and was one of the first women to run for Congress before females even had the right to vote. During World War I she established a relief station for soldiers and was bestowed with medals and honours. After her death, she became known as the 'Unsinkable Molly Brown'.

A 1960 Broadway musical was produced based on Brown's life

Construction of Titanic began in 1909 and took about 26 months to complete

WALLACE HARTLEY & THE TITANIC BAND

Musicians

The final performance of eight brave men

The legend of the musicians on Titanic is one of the most well-known stories of heroism, and for good reason. The Titanic band featured eight men ranging from the age of 20 to 33, who all travelled in second class. Bandleader Wallace Hartley led them during their performances at tea time, Sunday services and an array of different occasions on board the ship, while a separate trio played outside the A La Carte restaurant and the Café Parisien. Therefore, when Hartley united the band on the night of the sinking, it was likely the first time they had all played together.

Shortly after midnight, when the lifeboats were beginning to be loaded, Hartley assembled the band in the first-class lounge and began to play. His aim was to calm the passengers. When the majority of people moved onto the boat deck, and the severity of the situation became clear, Hartley moved his band to the deck. As the ship filled with water and the decks began to slant, the band continued to play until their final moments. None of the band members survived, but the remarkable heroism and sacrifice shown by each of the men entered into legend.

Titanic

As the ship descended into the water, Joughin was positioned at the topmost part

CHARLES JOUGHIN
Head baker, 1878-1956

The baker saved by cunning, luck and a dose of alcohol

— 4 —

Joughin was no stranger to the sea, having embarked on his first voyage aged 11. He was a skilled cook and became chief baker for many White Star Line steamships, a role he was serving in on Titanic's ill-fated maiden voyage. When the ship struck the iceberg, Joughin was asleep in his bunk. The shock woke him and he soon learned that lifeboats were preparing to launch. Understanding that passengers would need provisions, he instructed the 13 men working under him to carry four loaves each and load them into the boats.

Understandably shaken, Joughin returned to his cabin and had a quick drink of whisky to calm his nerves. Then, at about 12.30am, he approached the boat he had been assigned, number 10. Joughin helped the women and children onto the lifeboat, but when it was half full, many were hesitant to climb in, believing they were safer on Titanic than in the perilous waters of the Atlantic. With the terrified crowd unable to listen to reason, Joughin marched down to the promenade deck, dragged them up the stairs and threw them into the lifeboat. Eventually the boat was close enough to full, but Joughin declined to climb on board, believing the sailors already there would be proficient.

Once the lifeboat had departed, Joughin returned to his quarters and had another drop of liquor. When he re-emerged, all the lifeboats were gone. So Joughin went down to B-Deck and threw deck chairs over the side for flotation devices. After throwing about 50 overboard, he went to the pantry for a drink of water, but heard a loud crash. Joughin dashed outside and saw crowds of people clambering to get to the poop deck. The ship lurched and threw them into a heap, but Joughin kept his footing. He grabbed the safety rail and positioned himself outside the ship as it went down. As the vessel sunk, Joughin rode it down, clutching the rail. His unique position made him the last survivor to leave Titanic.

As the ship hit the water, Joughin wasn't pulled down. In fact, he managed to almost step off, barely getting his hair wet. Joughin trod water for two hours until he glimpsed the upturned collapsible boat covered with men. One held his hand as he clung to the side, his legs submerged in the freezing water. He stayed afloat until they were rescued. The only injury he sustained was swollen feet, which many attributed to the alcohol he consumed, believing just the right amount can slow down heat loss.

Joughin briefly features as a character in the 1997 Titanic film, and is seen clinging onto the rail

THOMAS BYLES
Second-class passenger, 1870-1912

The priest providing comfort amid the panic

— 5 —

Father Thomas Byles was a Catholic priest travelling on board Titanic to officiate the wedding of his younger brother. On the day of the sinking, he preached a sermon to second and third-class passengers about their new life in the USA and a need for a spiritual lifeboat to avoid temptation. Byles was frequently seen walking on deck praying, and it was there that he was stood when the ship hit the iceberg. When the ship began to sink, he helped third-class passengers reach the deck and escape on lifeboats. As the situation gradually worsened, he moved through the panicked crowds alone, giving absolution and reciting the rosary to the trapped passengers. Twice he was invited on board a lifeboat, and both times he refused. As the passengers' deaths became imminent, Byles remained by their side, comforting them with words of god and granting absolution to those who sought it. When the ship went down, Byles was upon it, preaching the word of the lord until the very end and bringing light to the darkest of times.

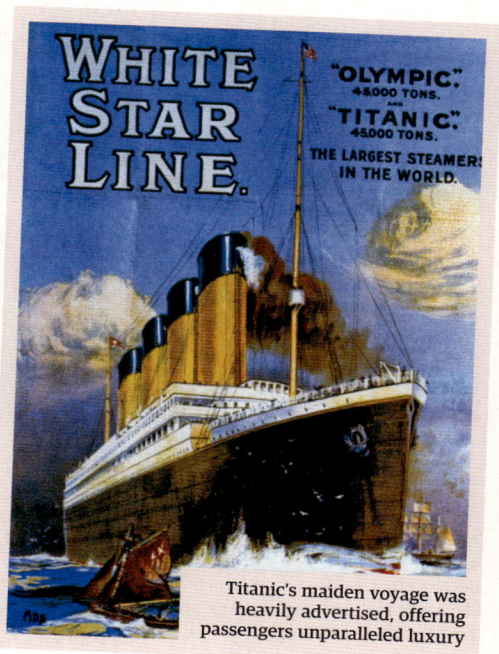

Titanic's maiden voyage was heavily advertised, offering passengers unparalleled luxury

Drama

GANGS OF NEW YORK

Director: Martin Scorsese **Starring:** Leonardo DiCaprio, Cameron Diaz, Daniel Day-Lewis **Country:** USA **Year:** 2002

Does this film butcher the realities of life in the notorious New York slum?

Set in the impoverished and crime-stricken slums of mid-19th century New York, this revenge epic sees Daniel Day-Lewis play gang leader William "Bill the Butcher" Cutting. After killing "priest" Vallon, the leader of the immigrant Dead Rabbits gang, Cutting takes control of New York's Five Points territories and absorbs the Dead Rabbits members into his own gang.

Vallon's young son witnesses his father's murder and swears revenge. Sixteen years later, he emerges from the orphanage and returns to New York, calling himself "Amsterdam". Amsterdam (Leonardo Di Caprio) is recruited into Cutting's gang and begins to plot his murder using the knife that cut his own father down. When Amsterdam's plot is unveiled to Cutting, the Butcher beats, burns and banishes Amsterdam from the city. But Amsterdam is dead set on revenge and, after rallying former members of the Dead Rabbits, a pitched battle in Paradise Square is dispersed by Union Army soldiers. Cutting is wounded by gunfire and Amsterdam shows no mercy, plunging the knife into his chest.

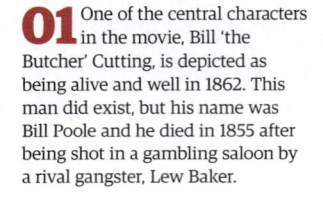

To train for this role, method actor Day-Lewis picked fights with strangers

VERDICT
- **Hollywood: B** — Day-Lewis is terrifyingly convincing as Bill the Butcher
- **History: C** — Scorsese didn't stray too far from his source material
- **Overall: C+**

01 One of the central characters in the movie, Bill 'the Butcher' Cutting, is depicted as being alive and well in 1862. This man did exist, but his name was Bill Poole and he died in 1855 after being shot in a gambling saloon by a rival gangster, Lew Baker.

02 One member of Amsterdam's gang is a young black man, but it is extremely unlikely they would have allowed black people to join them. During the draft riots Irish immigrants attacked blacks, killing at least 119 and also targeting numerous black orphanages.

03 Throughout the movie various characters are shown drinking out of pewter mugs, and the bars are full of them. However, people stopped drinking from pewter cups in the 18th century, so glass tumblers would have been far more accurate.

04 Throughout the film Amsterdam (DiCaprio) and his father repeatedly recite a section of the Prayer to St Michael. The first time Priest Vallon speaks the prayer before the street battle is in 1846, but the prayer wasn't written until 1886 by Pope Leo XIII.

05 The film's final confrontation between the Irish and the 'natives' occurs during the Draft Riots, but in reality the showdown happened on 4-5 July 1857, not 1863. Still, it was between the Bowery Boys (Natives) and the Dead Rabbits (Irish) as depicted.

THE UNTOUCHABLES

Director: Brian De Palma **Starring:** Kevin Costner, Sean Connery, Robert De Niro **Country:** USA **Year:** 1987

Set during the 1920s Prohibition era, is it time to call last orders on this classic depiction of infamous mob boss Al Capone?

The story of America's most notorious gangster, Al Capone, and his eventual downfall, has been told numerous times in the century since the height of the Prohibition era. A certified king of the crime drama after *Scarface* (1983), Brian de Palma focuses instead on the men who eventually caught Capone.

Federal agent Elliot Ness (Kevin Costner) leads the eponymous unit to crack open Capone's illegal liquor empire, all the while gathering evidence to nail the kingpin for his crimes. Ness finds a mentor in local beat cop Jim Malone (Sean Connery) who challenges the agent to take the fight to Capone in the 'Chicago way'.

Though he is only on-screen for a small amount of time, Robert De Niro's performance as Capone is one of his most memorable. He reportedly was compelled to wear padding in order to properly portray the gangster's larger body size. Connery meanwhile received the film's only Academy Award, for his supporting role as Malone - it was the first and only time he would be nominated for an Oscar in his long career.

VERDICT

A- HOLLYWOOD Some of the biggest names in the business at their best

C HISTORY Just a few minor federal crimes against history

OVERALL B

The scene at the train station is a homage to Battleship Potemkin (1925)

01 The film's courtroom climax pits Al Capone against federal agent Eliot Ness, resulting in an adrenaline-pumping rooftop chase, but this is entirely fantastical. In reality, no such showdown occurred and the two men never came face to face.

02 Costner's portrayal of Ness is that of a hard-working family man with high morals, enforcing Prohibition among his force. The real Eliot Ness had a chequered career, a host of failed marriages and is rumoured to have struggled with alcoholism.

03 Frank Nitti meets his grisly fate after Ness throws him off the roof of a building, but this is inaccurate. The real Nitti managed Capone's empire while he was in prison and was charged with extortion, but he ended his own life before the trial.

04 The 'Untouchables' of the film comprises of Eliot Ness, Oscar Wallace, Jim Malone and George Stone, but in his biography Ness reports that there were actually ten men on the team, none of whom share names with the characters depicted in the film.

05 Despite his client's protests, Capone's lawyer pleads guilty at the trial, but this is simply wrong. A defence lawyer is not allowed to plead guilty without his client's consent and the real Capone actually pled not guilty and the trial went to verdict.

Drama

LINCOLN

Director: Steven Spielberg **Starring:** Daniel Day-Lewis, Sally Field, David Strathairn **Country:** USA **Year:** 2012

Do we stand divided on the accuracy of this ambitious film?

In one of his standout roles, among a litany of critically acclaimed performances, Daniel Day Lewis became the 16th US President, brilliantly adopting his mannerisms, posture and even growing the iconic beard. Steven Spielberg's narrative begins in the final year of the American Civil War, with victory over the Confederacy in sight, but the 13th Amendment – abolishing slavery – still hanging in the balance.

With the Confederates willing to negotiate an end to the war, Lincoln is faced with the dilemma of bringing peace to a unified nation blighted by slavery, or continuing the fight until the amendment can be successfully passed.

Day-Lewis' utter commitment to his performance as the 16th US President, right down to emulating his voice without any existing audio recording as reference, earned him his third Academy Award. Sally Field also received a nomination for her supporting role as First Lady Mary Todd Lincoln, as did Tommy Lee Jones for his portrayal of abolitionist politician Thaddeus Stevens.

Liam Neeson was originally cast to play Lincoln

VERDICT
- **A HOLLYWOOD** – One of the all-time greatest directors and actors together
- **B HISTORY** – Only a few historical blunders to be found
- **OVERALL: B+**

01 In the film, two congressmen from Connecticut vote against the Thirteenth Amendment, however, all four of Connecticut's congressmen voted in its favour in 1865. The screenwriter said this was altered to convey just how narrow the margin was.

02 Lincoln's dialogue is littered with curse words throughout the film. Although he may have used the occasional swear word while telling a story, he very rarely swore. Contemporary accounts reveal that Lincoln objected when people swore in his presence.

03 In real life, Lincoln's relationship with his oldest son was as strained as it is in the film, however, it is unlikely that he ever slapped him. There's no evidence that this occurred, and accounts of Lincoln often focus on how he loathed personal violence.

04 When Lincoln is in his deathbed in the film, he is dressed in a nightgown and laid on his side. In reality, Lincoln was so tall that he had to be laid diagonally across the bed. The president was also naked, as doctors stripped him to search for other wounds.

05 The secretary of state did use lobbyists to recruit votes for the amendment. The wavering democrats were offered a variety of inducements to obtain their votes. While we can't be sure what was offered to the democrats, every part of this plot is completely true.

Lincoln's Vices and Virtues

VIRTUES

Arch politician
Aided by stunning speech-making, Lincoln was as skilled a political operator as there has ever been. His genius lay in courting different opinions, often at odds with his own, then setting a course, and bringing those of differing views along with him.

Forbearance
President Lincoln set off along a difficult, painful path with an iron resolve. He faced criticism and scorn from many quarters but he did not waver, believing the cause of protecting the Union was a duty he had to accomplish.

A hands-on leader
From strategic planning to appointing or dismissing generals, Lincoln was an active, interventionist commander-in-chief during the civil war. Furthermore, he was also equally busy in attending units of active soldiers to raise moral, or visiting the wounded in hospitals.

Honesty
Acquiring the moniker 'Honest Abe' from his days as a young storekeeper, it stuck with Lincoln through his career as a lawyer and later in the White House. His integrity informed both friend and foe alike exactly where they stood with him.

Humour
There was a lighter side to Lincoln. He told stories, yarns, jokes and anecdotes throughout his life to win over audiences, to illustrate certain points, and sometimes just to lighten the mood in cabinet before facing up to important decisions.

VICES

"The vision thing"
George Bush Senior's remark was about his inability to articulate ideas to shape the nation. Lincoln, by his own words, was similarly inhibited when he wrote: "I claim not to have controlled events, but confess plainly that events have controlled me."

Race and colonisation
For far too long, Lincoln clung stubbornly to his political hero Henry Clay's views on racial separation via colonisation. Perhaps the lack of vision contributed, but for such a practical politician, it was an extraordinarily impractical solution to support.

Civil rights
Lincoln exercised unprecedented executive power at the onset of the war, including suspending habeas corpus and shutting down opposition newspapers. His measures drew criticism not only from opponents and but also some supporters, who feared he had exceeded his authority.

Foolhardiness with his own safety
Warned of assassination plots against him, Lincoln shunned the use of bodyguards. He frequently rode alone at night, and was shot in August 1864. He escaped injury, though his stovepipe hat was later found holed by a musket ball.

Remoteness
For a man capable of working with politicians of many different views, Lincoln made few close friends. He allowed people to get only so close, being variously described as "not a social man by any means" and even "secretive."

Drama

ROBIN HOOD: PRINCE OF THIEVES

Director: Kevin Reynolds **Starring:** Kevin Costner, Morgan Freeman, Alan Rickman, Mary Elizabeth Mastrantonio **Country:** USA **Year:** 1991

The existence of folk hero Robin Hood has always been debated, but was the research for the rest of this film on target?

This 1991 take on the popular English folk tale sees Robin Hood (Kevin Costner) break out of a dungeon in Jerusalem having been captured during King Richard the Lionheart's third crusade. As he makes his escape with his wounded brother-in-arms Peter Dubois, Robin frees Azeem (Morgan Freeman), a Moorish prisoner who then swears his own life to Robin. Peter later dies but not before making Robin promise to protect his sister, Marian.

After months at sea, Robin and Azeem reach English shores, only to find that the Sheriff of Nottingham has ambitions to take the throne in King Richard's absence and has murdered Robin's father, Lord Locksley. Despite his noble birth, Robin wins over a motley group of outlaws in Sherwood Forest and with the help of Marian, begins to wage a guerrilla war against Nottingham and his cronies.

Director Kevin Reynold's *Robin Hood: Prince of Thieves* was released in the same year as John Irvin's more traditional *Robin Hood* – though critics gave Prince of Thieves middling reviews, it was a huge box office success.

Alan Rickman improvised many of the Sheriff's most memorable lines

★ VERDICT ★
C HOLLYWOOD — Worth watching for Alan Rickman's Sheriff of Nottingham alone
E- HISTORY — Far-fetched fantasy, even for an adaptation of a folk tale
OVERALL D

01 On their way to Locksley Castle, Robin and Azeem encounter the Sheriff's soldiers and Robin warns that they are on his land. They are actually walking across Hadrian's Wall in Northumberland, which is 320 kilometres (200 miles) north.

02 At several points in the film we see Azeem using a makeshift refracting telescope. However, these instruments were not invented until several hundred years later, at the start of the 17th century. This design was famously refined by Galileo Galilei in 1609.

03 The film's religious ceremonies are conducted more or less entirely in English, but in 1194 England was still Catholic. This means that all Church ceremonies, including weddings, mass and so on would have been conducted in Latin.

04 When Robin returns to England with Azeem, he claims they will 'celebrate with my father' by nightfall. However, Dover, on the south coast of England where they land, is some 320 kilometres (200 miles) away from Nottingham so the journey would take days.

05 The film ends with King Richard I arriving in what appears to be fall. Although he did return in the year 1194, he landed in March and was gone again by May. Needless to say, he also would not have spoken with Sean Connery's distinctive Scottish accent.

AMISTAD

Director: Steven Spielberg **Starring:** Djimon Hounsou, Matthew McConaughey, Morgan Freeman **Country:** USA **Year:** 1997

A Hollywood courtroom epic that twists the facts a little hard for drama's sake

The case of the mutiny on La Amistad in 1839 came at a pivotal moment in US history. On 2 July that year, 53 West Africans were being transported by Spanish slavers off the coast of Cuba. When one of the captives, Joseph Cinqué (Djimon Hounsou), was able to free himself and his fellow Africans, together they took over the ship, killing most of its crew. However, when La Amistad arrived in American waters, the Africans' freedom was far from guaranteed.

A high-profile court case was begun to determine whether the Africans were indeed free, or returned to slavery. The case had political implications in the US, where the balance of power between Free States in the North and Slave States in the South was increasingly fractious. For the movie Steven Spielberg had some of Hollywood's big names under his direction, including Anthony Hopkins as former president John Quincy Adams, and Morgan Freeman as Theodore Joadson. Meanwhile, future star of *12 Years A Slave* Chiwetel Ejiofor made his movie debut as British sailor James Covey, who returns the freed Africans to Sierra Leone.

VERDICT

B HOLLYWOOD — A suspenseful courtroom drama with a message

C- HISTORY — Gets the broad facts right, with some artistic licence

OVERALL: C+

The real survivng captives from La Amistad returned home in 1842

01 The film opens with the revolt on the La Amistad as captured Africans seize the ship, only to be taken to the shores of New York and arrested. The details of the uprising are all consistent with what we know of travelling the 'middle passage'.

02 At several points in the film we see Azeem using a makeshift refracting telescope. However, these instruments were not invented until several hundred years later, at the start of the 17th century. This design was famously refined by Galileo Galilei in 1609.

03 President Martin Van Buren (Nigel Hawthorne) interferes in the district court case by switching judges. In fact the judge remained the same throughout and had been pro-slavery, but still found in favour of the defence.

04 The spectre of civil war breaking out if the case goes in favour of the Africans is mentioned by several characters, including pro-South Democrat John C Calhoun (Jeremy Northam). In reality the idea of secession, not war, was foremost in people's minds.

05 Former president John Quincy Adams makes the final argument before the Supreme Court having previously refused to help. In reality he'd advised the defence throughout. His actual speech was eight hours and scathing of the Van Buren administration.

Drama

ALL THE PRESIDENT'S MEN

Director: Alan J Pakula **Starring:** Robert Redford, Dustin Hoffman, Jason Robards, Hal Holbrook **Country:** USA **Year:** 1976

This thriller brings the breaking of the Watergate scandal to the big screen, but does it get the facts right?

The 1970s saw a wave of what has been called the Paranoid Thrillers with movies like *The Day of the Jackal*, *3 Days of the Condor* and *The Conversation* all examining different shadowy events. One of the last was also a film about the event that capped off a period of growing distrust in the federal government in America. Alan J Pakula's *All the President's Men* is about the Watergate scandal or more specifically about how it was exposed, primarily by the journalism of Carl Bernstein and Bob Woodward of the Washington Post.

Pakula was coming off the back of two other thrillers in Klute and The Parallax View, but this is his most celebrated story. Made only two years after the events, it's based on the accounts of Woodward and Bernstein themselves (they even helped in the casting) and shows how they pulled on the threads of a mysterious break-in of the Democratic National Committee headquarters to discover it was being covered up by the White House under Richard Nixon.

Made on a budget of $8.5 million dollars it managed to make an impressive $70 million at the box office and earned four Oscars.

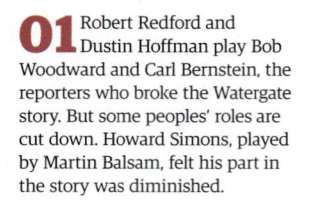

The phrase "follow the money" comes from this movie

VERDICT
A- HOLLYWOOD A gripping thriller about uncovering a government conspiracy
B- HISTORY Manages the balance of fact and entertainment relatively well
OVERALL B

01 Robert Redford and Dustin Hoffman play Bob Woodward and Carl Bernstein, the reporters who broke the Watergate story. But some peoples' roles are cut down. Howard Simons, played by Martin Balsam, felt his part in the story was diminished.

02 Most of the film takes place in the newsroom of *The Washington Post*. Denied access to shoot at the real offices, designers took accurate measurements, ordered identical desks, and even had a brick from the *Post* supplied so they could make fibreglass replicas.

03 In the 2013 documentary *All The President's Men Revisited*, Redford says they struggled with how to portray Nixon. As such, news footage of him is used. But the film only covers the first seven months of the investigation, avoiding involving Nixon to any great degree.

04 Hal Holbrook plays the informant Deep Throat. W Mark Felt, then associate director of the FBI, later revealed he was Deep Throat, but at the time of filming this was not known, so the character is portrayed in a shadowy, semi-mythical fashion.

05 Jason Robards won an Oscar for his portrayal of executive editor Ben Bradlee. One scene shows him encouraging the reporters to continue with the story despite the danger, but Woodward claimed Bradlee's response in real life was "What the hell do we do now?"

APOLLO 13

Director: Ron Howard **Starring:** Tom Hanks, Bill Paxton, Kevin Bacon **Country:** USA **Year:** 1995

Is this depiction of the famous rescue mission grounded in reality?

One of the most well-known movies about the Apollo programme is a dramatic retelling of its most infamous disaster. The ill-fated spaceflight of Jim Lovell (Tom Hanks), Fred Haise (Bill Paxton) and Jack Swigert (Kevin Bacon) as part of the Apollo 13 mission was intended to be NASA's third landing on the Moon. Instead, a malfunction with their craft leaves the astronauts in peril, and unable to make their landing on the lunar surface. While the team at Houston frantically improvise solutions to return the crew safely, the astronauts guide their stricken spacecraft around the Moon and carry out difficult manoeuvres to set them back on course for Earth.

The production went to great lengths in order to bring the Apollo mission to life, including having the real Jim Lovell on set to advise the cast, and even filming in zero gravity conditions. The result was a huge box office success, grossing over $355 million, as well as earning nine Academy Award nominations, with two wins.

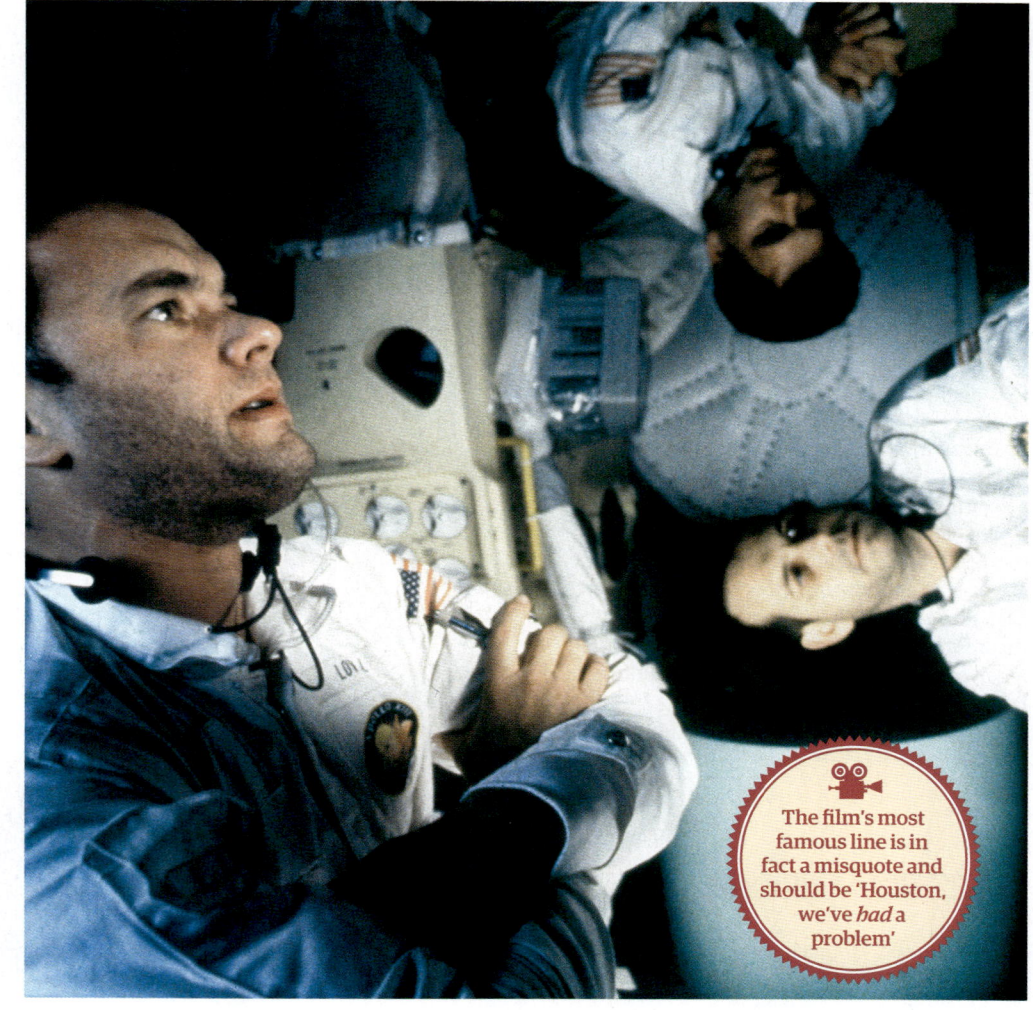

VERDICT
- **A HOLLYWOOD** — An all-time classic and a masterclass in suspense
- **B HISTORY** — Attention to detail that shoots for the stars
- **OVERALL: B+**

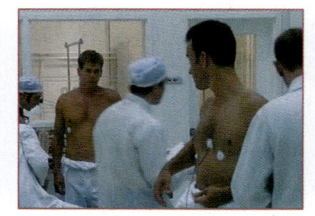

The film's most famous line is in fact a misquote and should be 'Houston, we've had a problem'

01 The phrase "Houston, we have a problem" was never actually uttered. The actual exchange started with Jack Swigert saying "I believe we have a problem here" and when he was asked to repeat his words, he said "Houston, we've *had* a problem."

02 The astronauts' families are shown wishing goodbye to their loved ones on the other side of a road. This was used to prevent the transmission of disease, but not until the Space Shuttle programme some ten years after the events that are shown in the film.

03 In the film, mission controllers try to work out how to make the resources in the spacecraft last. Although partly true, the movie depicts the men inventing the methods on the spot, when in reality NASA had a procedure in place for events such as this.

04 The famous NASA 'worm' letter logo is clearly shown on a window when the astronauts are getting into their spacesuits. This is inaccurate as that particular logo was not used by the agency until 1975, while the events of the film take place in 1970.

05 The film has been praised for its exact replicas of the modules and control rooms, and real zero-gravity scenes were filmed in the same aeroplane used by NASA. Nearly all the dialogue between the astronauts and ground control was taken direct from transcripts.

Drama

LAWRENCE OF ARABIA

Director: David Lean **Starring:** Peter O'Toole, Alec Guinness, Anthony Quinn **Country:** UK **Year:** 1962

It may have swept the board at the 1963 Oscars, but how many awards will it win for historical accuracy?

One of the most enigmatic figures of the First World War, T. E. Lawrence's role in the Arab revolt between 1916 and 1918 was immortalised by Peter O'Toole in this breakout performance. Sent by the British to liaise with the Arab leader Prince Faisal (Alec Guinness), Lawrence finds the revolt un-unified and un-coordinated, lacking the strategy needed to overthrow Ottoman rule. Lawrence becomes frustrated when his seemingly unconventional approach to warfare is challenged by his British superiors, but his innovative and daring guerrilla tactics eventually succeed in destroying the Ottoman Hejaz railway, key to the enemy's control of the region.

Considered one of the all-time great pieces of cinema, director David Lean's work was also assigned special status in the US, where it was added to a list of films 'deemed worthy of preservation' according to the *LA Times*. Beyond an astonishing box office performance that saw worldwide earnings almost five-times its production budget, *Lawrence of Arabia* also received seven Academy Awards, including for Best Director and Best Picture.

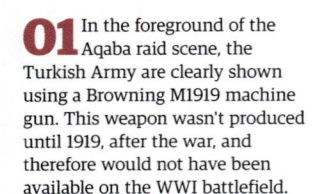

The film was banned in several countries for its depiction of Arab culture

VERDICT
- **HOLLYWOOD: A** — A true masterpiece of 20th century cinema
- **HISTORY: C** — Some oases of facts among the huge desert of fiction
- **OVERALL: B**

01 In the foreground of the Aqaba raid scene, the Turkish Army are clearly shown using a Browning M1919 machine gun. This weapon wasn't produced until 1919, after the war, and therefore would not have been available on the WWI battlefield.

02 When we first see General Allenby, he wears Overseas Service Chevrons on his lower right sleeve. These features were only introduced for officers in very late 1917, several months after the attack on the Hejaz Railway, which took place in early 1917.

03 In the movie, Farraj (Michel Ray) is mortally wounded when a detonator going off in his clothing. However, in his post-war memoir *The Seven Pillars of Wisdom*, T.E. Lawrence describes that Farraj was in fact wounded by a gunshot.

04 The idea that Lawrence's Arab army almost entirely deserted him as he moved further north, as shown over the second half of the film, is inaccurate. According to records, only one or two Arabs actually deserted during the audacious manoeuvre.

05 It is implied in the early scenes of the film with Colonel Brighton (Anthony Quayle) and Prince Faisal (Guinness) that the major sea port Yanbu is 50 miles (80km) south of Wadi Safra, when in reality it is approximately five miles (8km) west.

Lawrence of Arabia

Lawrence at Aqaba, 6 July 1917. He wrote of his role during the Arab Revolt: "I drew these tides of men into my hands and wrote my will across the sky in stars"

Lawrence's Battle for Arabia

Dr Rob Johnson of Pembroke College, University of Oxford, discusses how the famous victory at Aqaba may not have played out quite as dramatically as on screen

The Battle of Aqaba, when Arab troops captured the port by surprising Ottoman forces from in-land, is arguably the most famous event of Lawrence's military career. It had taken months to plan, but Dr Rob Johnson, author of *Lawrence of Arabia on War: The Campaign in the Desert 1916-18*, believes that Lawrence's precise role remains controversial: "There are at least three claimants for who suggested going to Aqaba. One was Colonel Édouard Brémond, a French commander who thought there was a possibility of taking Aqaba because the Allies had taken other ports. However, he was effectively talked out of it by Lawrence because Brémond wanted to make a large Allied landing. Lawrence responded by saying, 'If you do it, you'll be hemmed in like at Gallipoli.'

"The consensus among Lawrence specialists is that [Howeitat leader] Auda Abu Tayi probably came up with the final idea. Auda was to some extent driven by money, prestige and honour. He was also an opportunist and probably took the view that if you captured a port like Rabigh or Yanbu you could help yourself to whatever was in there. It was his audacity that gave the Arabs military success towards Aqaba."

This boldness required the Arab fighters and Lawrence to undertake a journey of hundreds of kilometres through inhospitable terrain. "It was appallingly difficult," says Johnson. "The first stage was crossing the 'al-Houl' ('The Terror'), which was a huge, waterless desert region. We sometimes underestimate how big the desert is, and if you go there at the height of summer (which Lawrence did) it is so hot that your lungs are emptied of air and you have to regulate your breathing.

"Dehydration was a real threat and Lawrence wrote that several men were killed on the journey by snake bites. One fell off his camel and was famously rescued by Lawrence, who went back for him. This quite impressed the Arabs but there were other challenges, including hostility from other tribes and potential betrayal to the Ottomans. Tribal fights could have broken out at any point and there was lots of distrust between groups even when they were together. If the Ottomans had known they were coming they could have easily destroyed them."

These hazards meant that Lawrence's survival was important: "If Lawrence had been killed that would have ended that operation because the other Arabs wanted to raid further up the Hejaz Railway. We know that's important because a British captain called Shakespear (who was attached to Ibn Saud, the future king of Saudi Arabia) was killed in 1915 on a very similar mission. That ended close liaison between the British and Ibn Saud for a year."

Once the Arabs finally reached Aqaba its fall was swift. "They actually took Aqaba by negotiation rather than fighting," says Johnson. "There were sensible Ottomans who realised they were completely cut off and couldn't be resupplied. Perhaps one-third of the Ottoman Army during WWI was probably Arabic rather than Turkish. An Arab conscript was more likely to survive if Aqaba was taken by negotiation. Also, the cavalry charge in David Lean's 1962 film [*Lawrence of Arabia*] was nothing like the reality. There was a sandstorm and the Arabs only rode quickly to get shelter. The dramatic legend of the Arabs entering Aqaba is based on one photograph taken by Lawrence of them riding at speed."

Johnson argues that Aqaba's strategic importance to the Allies has also been overplayed: "We're told that it was strategically significant because it provided a potential naval base for operations into the interior. The problem is the strategic reality. What difference did it make to the campaign when the Arabs took it in July 1917? It didn't. No large-scale Allied force was brought in at that point except Arab regulars who had been trained in Egypt. It wasn't a vital strategic hub for the first six months and was more important to the Arabs than the Allies."

Dr Rob Johnson is a Senior Research Fellow at Pembroke College, Oxford, and author of Lawrence of Arabia on War: The Campaign in the Desert 1916-18

Drama

THE KING

Director: David Michôd **Starring:** Timotheé Chalamet, Robert Pattinson, Joel Edgerton **Country:** UK **Year:** 2019

Shakespeare's Henriad given an abridged and gritty modern retelling, but still lacking in accuracy

The Battle of Agincourt is one of the most famous (if you're English) or infamous (if you're French) battles in history. The ultimate story of a backs-against-the-wall, against-all-odds victory for the plucky underdog has been retold since Shakespeare, and it is from the Bard that this 2019 epic retelling takes its lead. Following Prince Henry's (Timotheé Chalamet) reluctant ascent to the throne of England, he gathers an army to invade France, laying siege to the port town of Harfleur before facing the French on the battlefield. Not afraid to fight dirty, Henry uses the muddy terrain and thick forest on his flanks, to outsmart the French, whom he counts on underestimating the English.

The King's gritty, realistic combat scenes came in for particular praise from critics, with armoured knights hammering one another to the ground, and the muddy conditions of the climactic battle are true to the historic record. Being based on Shakespeare's plays, however, there are more than a few artistic tweaks to the characters as well as the events in this retelling.

★ VERDICT ★

B HOLLYWOOD — Plenty of clattering action and court intrigue to grip audiences

D HISTORY — An interesting character study with occasional brushes of fact

OVERALL C

Timotheé Chalamet's middle name is Hal

01 Since this movie is based on the Shakespeare plays of *Richard II*, *Henry IV Part 1* and *Part 2* and *Henry V*, its depiction of young Prince Hal is closer to those productions. He's reluctant to reign and would much rather drink and party. It's unclear how true that was.

02 Sir John Falstaff is one of Shakespeare's most loved characters and he unsurprisingly appears in this film as Hal's only confidante. He remains, however, a fictional character inspired by a combination of real historical figures, including Sir John Oldcastle.

03 The film paints Henry as a reluctant warrior. Historically, however, Henry seems to have been keen to wage his war as he believed his claim to France's throne was legitimate. He had campaigned since he was 12 and fought his first battle at 16.

04 The details of Agincourt are not that accurate militarily. The French actually had to charge up a muddy hill rather than down and the English lines were defended by spikes, making it even harder. It was these factors that helped the outnumbered English win.

05 Robert Pattinson's Dauphin is a scene-stealing firework when he's on screen, but his death scene at Agincourt couldn't be further from reality. In fact Louis, Duke of Guyenne was nearly 100 miles away from the battle and died from dysentery a few months later.

The King

The paternal relationship between Falstaff and Prince Hal is largely comic but ends in Henry IV, Part II as a tragic betrayal of friendship

The Truth About Falstaff and Prince Hal

William Shakespeare immortalised Henry's youth by depicting a fictional friendship with a disreputable knight

Sir John Falstaff is one of the most famous comic characters in English literature. A fat, vain, cowardly knight who is contemptuous of honourable virtues, Falstaff dominates the two Henry IV plays. He also acts as a "father ruffian" figure to the future Henry V, who is known in the plays as Prince Hal. Falstaff introduces Hal to a hedonistic lifestyle amongst the commoners of Eastcheap, London. Shakespeare's depiction popularised the notion that Henry had a riotous youth before he adopted the serious mantle of kingship. It is a dramatically rich tale – but the reality is quite different.

Falstaff was a fictional creation of Shakespeare's, although he was loosely drawn from two of Henry's contemporaries: Sir John Oldcastle and Sir John Fastolf. Oldcastle was a trusted supporter of Henry who was eventually executed for leading a revolt of heretical proto-Protestants known as Lollards. Meanwhile, Fastolf served as a soldier in Henry V's campaigns in Normandy but was later accused of cowardice after being defeated by Joan of Arc's forces. In truth, little links the two men to Falstaff beyond names and tenuous historical influences. The same is true for the interpretation of Hal.

Henry's military role in Wales did become limited after 1408 and he spent more time in London. Relations with his father Henry IV were bad and historical sources imply that he possibly lived beyond his means. Nevertheless, evidence for his wild behaviour is based on speculation. Published comments that fuelled the rumours only appeared after his death but they were drawn by people who knew him. One contemporary chronicler called Thomas Elmham probably had links with men who knew Henry and may have been one of his royal chaplains.

In his book Pseudo-Elmham, Elmham spoke of his memory of Prince Henry as "an assiduous pursuer of fun, devoted to organ instruments (a medieval double-entendre) which relaxed the rein on his modesty; although under the military service of Mars, he seethed youthfully with the flames of Venus too, and tended to be open to other novelties as befitted the age of his untamed youth".

This description does not fit with other contemporary works that adulated Henry but Elmham's possible connections to the king adds some credence and may reveal an intriguing kernel of truth that might lie behind the legendary tale.

THE SHREWSBURY SCAR

Prince Henry underwent a horrific but successful surgery after defeating Hotspur, which most likely left him facially disfigured

Henry IV may have won the Battle of Shrewsbury but Prince Henry's grave facial wound put his life in danger. He had been hit by an arrow that had penetrated just below the eye and to the side of the nose. The shaft was extracted but the arrowhead remained lodged "in the furthermost part of the bone of the skull to the depth of six inches".

Such a wound required delicate surgery and Henry was taken to Kenilworth Castle in Warwickshire for treatment. Various doctors unsuccessfully tried to remove the arrowhead by "potions and other cures". In the end, a London surgeon called John Bradmore performed the operation. Bradmore had been a convicted criminal, but he was also an innovative medic.

To extract the arrowhead, Bradmore devised a small pair of hollow tongs that had a screw mechanism running through the middle. Henry's wound had to be enlarged before the tongs were inserted. The tool was infused with rose honey before it was placed into the socket of the arrowhead. In his treatise Philomena, Bradmore describes how "by moving it to and fro, little by little (with the help of God) I extracted the arrowhead".

67

Drama

THE OTHER BOLEYN GIRL

Director: Justin Chadwick **Starring:** Natalie Portman, Scarlett Johansson, Eric Bana, Eddie Redmayne, Benedict Cumberbatch **Country:** USA, UK **Year:** 2008

A loosely based adaptation of one of the most dramatic eras of Tudor history

Tudor England was all the rage in the Noughties, fuelled by Philippa Gregory's acclaimed novels, and culminating in the Showtime series *The Tudors*. Based on Gregory's novel, the eponymous 'other Boleyn girl' is Mary Boleyn (Scarlett Johanssen), sister to Anne (Natalie Portman).

The plot follows Mary's overlooked story as the one-time mistress of Henry VIII (Eric Bana), before Anne's rise to the throne of England. When the sisters' uncle the Duke of Norfolk (David Morrissey) and their father Sir Thomas (Mark Rylance) conspire to make Mary the king's new mistress, a battle for the royal bedchamber ensues. Soon the sisters are caught up in scandal and subterfuge, as the maniacal king seeks to secure his throne with a male heir. Anne's marriage to Henry is the the foreboding peak of the Boleyns' trajectory, as Mary witnesses her tragic downfall from the sidelines.

Hollywood's dalliance with the Tudor court may not have yielded the success of Gregory's books – with only modest box office returns – however, the world's fascination with the story of Boleyns remains strong.

VERDICT

C- HOLLYWOOD — Big-name stars, but not enough to save this costume drama

D HISTORY — A mostly fictional interpretation of a Tudor tragedy

OVERALL: D+

There is debate among historians as to which Boleyn sister was the eldest

01 In the film, Anne is instantly presented to the audience as being the eldest of her three siblings, although historians largely agree that Mary was the eldest, having been born in 1500, followed by Anne in 1501, and then their brother George in 1503.

02 According to The Other Boleyn Girl, after Anne's first unsuccessful encounter with the king she is 'exiled' to France to serve the queen, returning to England after a "couple of months," however, evidence shows that Anne was sent to France aged 12 for nine years.

03 Played by Scarlet Johansson, Mary is an innocent and inexperienced virgin prior to her marriage to William Carey, but the King of France once referred to Mary as "a great whore more infamous than the rest," alluding to her reputation at his court.

04 Mary's affair with King Henry VIII is a central focus point in both history and Chadwick's adaptation, however, Mary did not bear a son first but a daughter by the king, and it was widely observed that Henry did not acknowledge this child as his own.

05 In the film, only Anne and George were arrested, charged, convicted and executed for high treason adultery and incest, but Mark Smeaton, Sir Henry Norris, Sir William Brereton and Sir Francis Weston were arrested in connection with Anne's alleged crimes.

The Other Boleyn Girl

How Three Lives Led to a Love Triangle

Anne Boleyn
Anne Boleyn was one of the first Englishwomen to be queen

1501 – Probable birth
Although her birth date was nowhere recorded, Anne is probably born in this year. She spends most of her childhood at Hever Castle, which was the primary seat of the Boleyns.

1513 – Serves Margaret of Austria
Anne travels to serve Margaret of Austria, regent of the Netherlands in Brussels. She reluctantly leaves the following year to transfer to the household of Queen Mary Tudor in France.

1522 – Returns to England
Anne returns to England when it is proposed that she marries her Irish cousin, James Butler, to settle an inheritance dispute concerning the earldom of Ormond. The marriages comes to nothing.

1527 – Agrees to marry Henry VIII
Henry VIII offers to marry Anne, after a long pursuit. She accepts and returns to court. The king opens an ecclesiastical case to try the validity of his marriage.

1529 – The Blackfriars trial
Cardinals Wolsey and Campeggio convene a legatine trial at Blackfriars to investigate Henry's marriage. When Campeggio revokes the case to Rome, Anne and Henry turn on Wolsey, bringing about his ruin.

1532 – Visit to France
Henry VIII and the Boleyn sisters return to France. Their meeting with Francis is a success and he assures them of his support. Soon afterwards, Anne and Henry consummate their relationship.

1533 – Henry VIII marries Anne Boleyn
Henry VIII secretly marries a pregnant Anne Boleyn in January. He then breaks with Rome before annulling his marriage to Katherine. Anne is crowned and gives birth to Princess Elizabeth.

1536 – Miscarriage and execution
The sisters are reconciled before Anne miscarries a son in January. Determined to end his marriage, Henry has Anne arrested on trumped-up charges of adultery. She is executed on 19 May.

Henry VIII
England's most infamous monarch, who ushered in the Reformation

1491 – Henry VIII's birth
Henry VIII is born on 28 June at Greenwich. As the second son of Henry VII, he becomes Prince of Wales following the death of his elder brother in 1502.

1509 – Becomes king
Henry VIII becomes king at the age of 17. He immediately marries Katherine of Aragon, to whom he has been betrothed since childhood. She is the widow of his elder brother.

1519 – The birth of Henry Fitzroy
Elizabeth Blount gives birth to Henry Fitzroy, proving that Henry can father a healthy son. Fitzroy is ennobled in 1525 while Katherine's daughter, Mary, goes to Ludlow as de facto princess of Wales.

1531 – Supreme head of the Church
As a precursor to the Break with Rome, Henry forces the English clergy to accept him as supreme head of the Church of England and begins a series of anti-papal measures.

1547 – Henry VIII dies
Henry VIII dies on 28 January 1547 and is succeeded by his nine-year-old son, Edward VI.

1543 – The third Act of Succession
Anne's daughter, Elizabeth, is restored to the succession along with her elder half-sister, Mary. She eventually succeeds to the throne in 1558 and reigns for more than 44 years.

1536 – The second Act of Succession
Henry passes the second Act of Succession, declaring both his daughters illegitimate. Henry is given the power to name his own successor, with Henry Fitzroy a likely candidate. Fitzroy dies soon afterwards.

1536 – Henry marries Jane Seymour
Henry becomes betrothed to Jane Seymour the day after Anne's execution and marries her shortly afterwards. He marries a further three times after Jane's death in childbirth in 1537.

Mary Boleyn
The less well-known Boleyn sister, who was mistress to two kings

1499 – Probable birth
Mary Boleyn was probably born in 1499 at Blickling Hall in Norfolk. She is the eldest surviving child and raised with her younger sister, Anne, and brother, George.

1514 – Arrival in France
Mary arrives in France to serve the new French queen. She was soon joined by her sister, Anne. Mary and Anne remain behind when their widowed mistress returns to England in 1515.

1520 – Marries William Carey
Some time after returning to England, Mary marries the courtier, William Carey, on 4 February 1520, before taking up a court position in the household of Queen Katherine of Aragon.

1522 – Becomes a royal mistress
Mary became Henry VIII's mistress in around 1522, bearing two children who may have been fathered by the king. Thanks to her prominence, the sisters danced at a court masque that March.

1525 – One relationship ends, another begins
Mary's relationship with Henry ends around this time, with the king instead looking to Anne Boleyn to become his new mistress. She refuses him and returned to Hever.

1528 – William Carey dies
Mary's husband, William Carey, dies suddenly of the sweating sickness, leaving her a widow in her late twenties with two children to raise.

1534 – Secret marriage
Mary secretly marries her servant, William Stafford. She appears at court visibly pregnant and is banished by her furious sister, who lost her own baby soon afterwards.

1543 – Death of Mary Boleyn
Mary dies in obscurity seven years after her sister. She was wealthy, having inherited much of the Boleyn fortune from her parents. She leaves behind a husband and two children.

69

Drama

JFK

Director: Oliver Stone **Starring:** Kevin Costner, Kevin Bacon, Tommy Lee Jones, Donald Sutherland **Country:** USA **Year:** 1991

A film pickled by flawed theories and fantasy, that succeeded in fuelling a generation of conspiracies

Oliver Stone has never been afraid of controversy and that reputation was firmly cemented thanks to the release of JFK. This fiery, righteous biopic of New Orleans district attorney Jim Garrison's attempt to prove a conspiracy in the assassination of President John F Kennedy was a massive hit.

While its budget was a meaty, but relatively modest $40 million, it still managed to pack in some of the biggest names in acting of the early 1990s. Kevin Costner was arriving off the back of The Untouchables, Field of Dreams, Dances With Wolves and Robin Hood: Prince of Thieves, so his star could not have been higher. He was joined by Kevin Bacon, Tommy Lee Jones, Gary Oldman, Sissy Spacek, Joe Pesci, Donald Sutherland and so many more past and future legends.

The movie was controversial as it implicated the highest echelons of the federal government in a conspiracy to murder a sitting president. Was any of it true? Not really, but it caused enough public interest for the Assassination Records Review Board to credit the film with the passage of the 1992 JFK Records Act to release official documents on the assassination.

VERDICT
- **B+ HOLLYWOOD** — A cultural phenomenon that actually forced files to be declassified
- **F HISTORY** — Possibly one of the least accurate films ever made
- **OVERALL: E-**

The real Jim Garrison cameos as author of the Warren Report, Judge Earl Warren

01 David Ferrie (Joe Pesci) confesses to being involved in a plot to assassinate Kennedy. He is subsequently murdered by his co-conspirators. In reality Ferrie maintained his innocence, and died of natural causes, according to the coroner's report.

02 Willie O'Keefe (Bacon) is a convict who was involved in the conspiracy and confesses to Garrison (Costner). This is a composite character, partially based on Perry Russo. He did confess under the use of hypnosis, making his testimony highly questionable.

03 Garrison is given insight of an even deeper plot through an insider called X. He implicates the military industrial complex in the assassination. X is inspired by colonel L Fletcher Prouty who assisted the production, but whose credibility has been challenged.

04 Garrison concludes with explaining the 'magic bullet theory' so impossible that a second gunman must have been involved. This explanation is based on flawed analysis of bullet trajectories, used to make the 1963 Warren Report of the assassination seem ludicrous.

05 The story is based on the trial of Clay Shaw (Jones), accused of conspiring with Lee Harvey Oswald and the CIA to kill Kennedy. He was acquitted by the jury after less than an hour and DA Garrison was accused of charging Shaw for attention.

Eye Witness

The assassination of John F Kennedy
Dallas, USA 22 November 1963

HUGH AYNESWORTH

He was dubbed 'the man who saw too much', having witnessed the assassination of JFK and the shooting of Lee Harvey Oswald by Jack Ruby. Aynesworth was an acclaimed investigative journalist, nominated for the Pulitzer Prize for Reporting six times.

Hugh Aynesworth was standing across the street from the sniper nest, on the day the United States' President John F Kennedy was shot. It wasn't seen as the prime spot for watching the President's parade through Dallas, but it turned out to be the most eventful stretch of the entire motorcade as the limousine made the sharp left turn onto Elm Street and mere moments later, the fatal shots were fired.

32-year-old Aynesworth was there by chance. "I went to the motorcade because almost everyone else in The Dallas Morning News newsroom did the same," he recalls. "Most of them had assignments but I had freedom until 3pm so I thought I'd walk over the four blocks. You don't see a President every day!" Aynesworth's usual beat was space exploration and he was Aviation and Aerospace Editor during the Space Race between the US and the Soviet Union. But there was no escaping the buzz around the President's impending visit, especially after speaking with a group of "arch Conservatives" the day before. "The people that hated Kennedy were going to show up with picket signs and dress in Uncle Sam suits and just show him that they didn't like him and they didn't like his policies," he says. "They wanted publicity and, the day before, the editor sent me to interview a couple of them and they told me they were going to embarrass him in some way at the Trade Mart. Although we expected some picketing and angry shouting perhaps, nobody expected any real trouble."

There was a good turnout along Main Street so in a bid to bag a better view, Aynesworth went to the corner of Elm Street in front of the County Records Building. "The mood of the crowd was jubilant, happy, pleased and impressed with the young President and his beautiful lady," he says. "Everyone was relieved because we'd had that horrible hate JFK ad in the Dallas News and people were expecting there to be an embarrassment

Drama

of sorts. So by the time Kennedy arrived in mid-town, there were cheers of relief." Aynesworth saw the presidential limo take the left at the corner where he stood and remembers the smiling faces of John F Kennedy, his wife Jacqueline, and the Governor of Texas John Connally as they waved to the crowd. "They were very happy, they would have known the reputation of some of these trouble makers," he says. "It was just a happy, happy occasion. Within seconds, it changed."

A shot fired and the President seized his throat, another two shots and his head exploded. "Seconds after the Kennedy car passed, I heard what I thought was a motorcycle backfire," he says. "Seconds later I heard the second shot and immediately I realised it was a rifle shot. Then a third ensued rapidly." In the minutes that followed, panic rippled through the crowd. "People close to me reacted with alarm: some shielded their children, a couple screamed, a couple more threw up their lunch. With the unusual layout of Dealey Plaza, nobody immediately knew what had happened or from where the shots came. Or, for that matter, how many people were shooting and if there were more shots to come. One of the first remarks was from a man who said he had seen Vice President Johnson hit. A motorcycle cop told two women in front of me that the president had been hit. I didn't know what to do, I thought about just running like hell but that layout is so unusual, a couple of buildings on a couple of sides and open space and we didn't know where the shots were coming from." Instead, his journalistic nature prevailed and he began to interview bystanders, writing on envelopes in his pocket.

Even in the heat of the moment stories were contradictory, down to the number of shots fired. "The acoustics were so weird that no one knew what direction the shots were coming from," he reports. "There were all kinds of statements about seeing people in trees or on the grassy knoll. There were people that swore they'd heard 11 or 12 shots and one woman only heard one. I can guarantee you there were three shots. But most people were willing to talk apart from the people who had children and wanted to get the hell out of there." The only real witness according to Aynesworth was a man called Howard Brennan. "He was pointing up to the School Book Depository window, which was the building in front of me, and shouting 'He's up there, I saw him, I saw him.' So I ran over and tried to get him to talk to me but he got two policemen to push me away. Later he told me he was scared for his family because we didn't know if there was more than one person shooting."

Brennan's description of the suspected sniper, later named as Lee Harvey Oswald, was broadcast to law enforcements immediately. It was probably this account that prompted Dallas Police Officer JD Tippit to stop Oswald in the street at 1.15pm, 45 minutes after Kennedy was shot. "After being rebuffed by Brennan, I eased over to a police radio on a cycle," he says, recalling his efforts to learn about what had happened. "Then I heard the report of Officer Tippit being shot and I thought as it was only a few blocks away, it's bound to be connected somehow. I grabbed a television car with two reporters in it, told them what I heard and we sped like mad to the scene. We arrived before most of the cops got there and interviewed everyone we could find. I spoke to six people who had seen Oswald shoot him, or seen him run from the scene, or seen him plant or throw away shells. There were many eyewitnesses to the Tippit killing." Incidentally, this murder was the reason for Oswald's initial arrest, not Kennedy's.

A man-hunt ensued and a false alarm at a decrepit furniture store led to an officer falling through the ground with a bang. As the cops drew their pistols, Aynesworth became aware that he was the only man unarmed. "I thought, 'Boy, I gotta get out of here,'" he laughs. "Then we heard on the radio there was a suspect in the Texas Theatre," he tells us, "so I ran like hell for eight blocks." After speaking to the ticket seller Julia Postal, who couldn't recall whether the murderer

A frame from the Zapruder film, which captured the Kennedy assassination

Hugh (right) interviewing a cab driver who unknowingly picked up Lee Harvey Oswald after the shooting.

After he is sworn into office Lyndon B Johnson, together with Lady Bird and Judge Sarah T Hughes, comforts Jackie Kennedy

Aynesworth worked on the Dallas Morning News at the time of the assassination

JFK

Hugh Aynesworth with Marina Oswald and her daughter, June

> **"I heard what I thought was a motorcycle backfire. Then I heard the second shot and immediately I realised it was a rifle"**

had bought a ticket or not, he inched closer to the front of the theatre. "I peeked through the curtain and saw two men – one in uniform and the other in civilian clothing – coming up the aisles and talking to people who were there," he says, as he watched from a few feet away. "There were only 12 or 13 people in that lower part of the theatre and I saw who I later realised was Oswald shifting one seat over to the right and Officer McDonald told him to stand up. Oswald pulled a pistol out of his pocket and tried to shoot him, but somebody got their hand on the weapon, jammed the firing mechanism and saved him." The police captured him as he yelled, 'I protest this police brutality!'

It was at the theatre that Aynesworth discovered the President had died over a transistor radio. By that point, everyone was listening to the rolling news bulletins and this one stunned its audience. "I was shocked and hurt," he recalls. "It was an unbelievable day." Outside the theatre, a throng had gathered and were calling for the murderer's head. "They were an unruly, mad crowd of about two or three hundred people. They were yelling 'Kill that son of a bitch' and 'Get that communist!' There were people that would have tried to take him, and the police moved pretty fast and got him into a car outside the front door and held the crowd back." It quickly became public knowledge that the prime suspect, a former US Marine, had defected to the Soviet Union four years previously and returned with a Russian wife.

It was during the Cold War and tense relations between the US and the Soviet Union shaped the lives of Kennedy and Oswald, as well as the public's reaction to the assassination, fuelling speculation and conspiracy stories. For Aynesworth, there's no doubt who the killer was. "My thoughts on the Warren Commission? Essentially they got it right, but the investigation was too hurried and left many holes that they could have filled. There was considerable evidence against Oswald and absolutely no evidence of anyone assisting him. As a 65-year veteran of many murder trials, there was more evidence against Oswald than 90 per cent of those convicted in the trials I covered."

After the Kennedy shooting, Aynesworth worked solely on the assassination, which led him to break several stories. The first was how the killer fled the scene and arrived at his rooming house before travelling to his next murder, Officer Tippit, to the theatre where he was caught.

Through investigative journalism, Aynesworth and reporter Larry Grove from The Morning News pieced together the route in the face of witnesses told to keep quiet by the FBI. Once they figured Oswald took a taxi after getting off the bus at Elm Street, they began catching taxis themselves. On every journey they'd replay the same conversation about 'what's-his-name, the guy who gave a ride to the man who shot the President', until the line finally snagged and one driver chirped up, 'You mean Louie?' A chat with Louie and the escape route was mapped out.

Aynesworth later bagged the first print interview with Marina Oswald and with it the scoop that she had persuaded her late husband not to assassinate Richard Nixon, a threat the widow hadn't even shared with the Warren Commission. But the biggest revelation was uncovering Oswald's Russian diary, which The Dallas Morning News ran with the splash 'Secret Diary – Oswald's Thoughts Bared.' And though Aynesworth can credit the breaking of these stories to his journalism, he knows it was just chance that placed him there that day of Kennedy's assassination. "It was just pure dumb luck," he resigns. "I wasn't assigned to any of it. I just made a good judgement when I thought someone shot the cop and I thought they were connected."

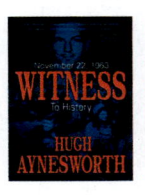

Hugh Aynesworth's thrilling and detailed account of the JFK assassination can be found in his book *November 22, 1963 Witness To History*, published by Brown Books Publishing Group.

War

WAR

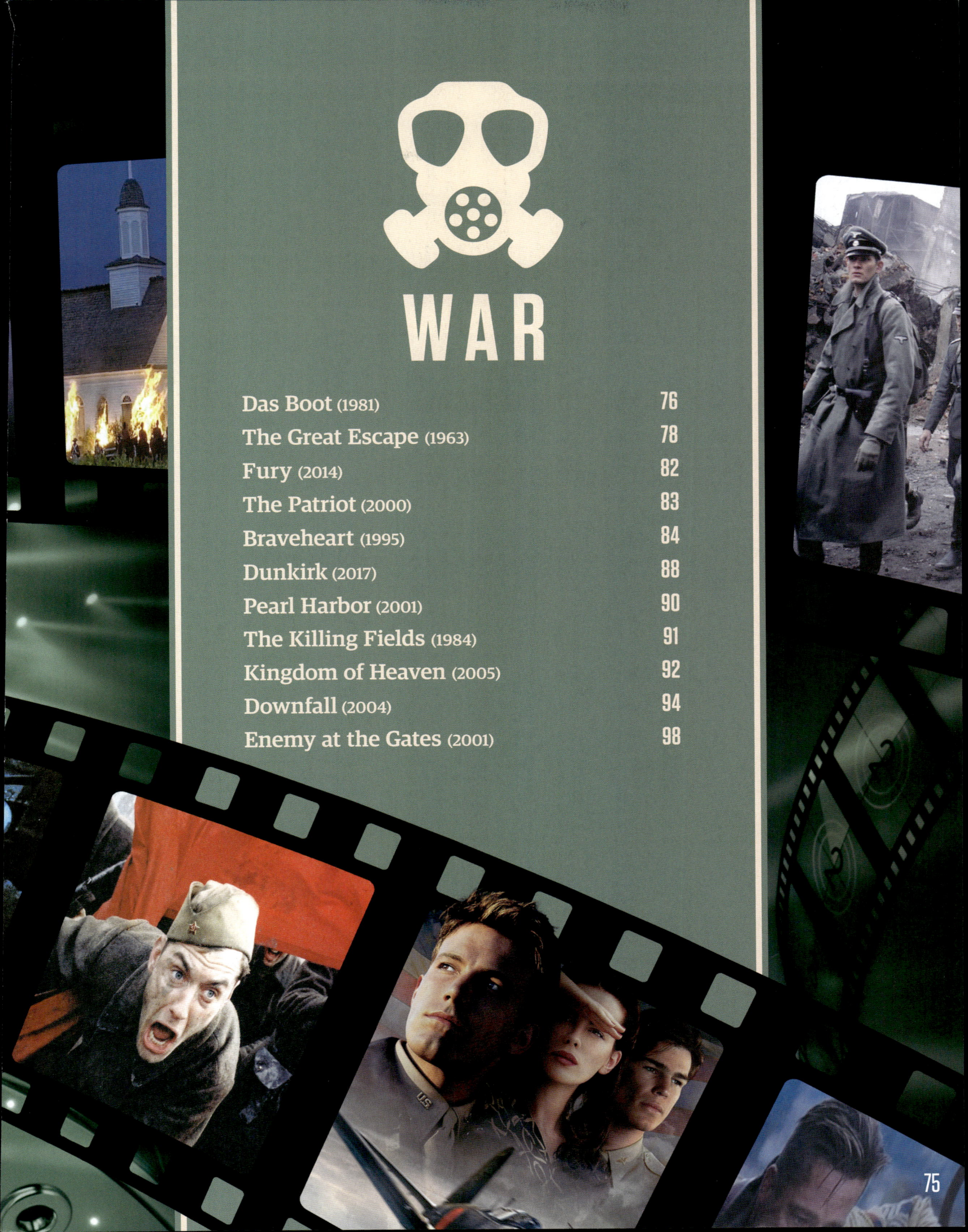

Das Boot (1981)	76
The Great Escape (1963)	78
Fury (2014)	82
The Patriot (2000)	83
Braveheart (1995)	84
Dunkirk (2017)	88
Pearl Harbor (2001)	90
The Killing Fields (1984)	91
Kingdom of Heaven (2005)	92
Downfall (2004)	94
Enemy at the Gates (2001)	98

War

DAS BOOT

Director: Wolfgang Petersen **Starring:** Jürgen Prochnow, Herbert Grönemeyer, Klaus Wennemann **Country:** West Germany **Year:** 1981

Does this claustrophobic war thriller faithfully re-create life inside a Kriegsmarine U-boat?

Before going on to make fantasy epic *The NeverEnding Story* and blockbuster action thriller *Air Force One* Wolfgang Petersen's breakout project was a much darker, subtle war drama set almost entirely in the confines of a submarine. Based on a novel by Lothar-Günther Buchheim, who served on German U-Boats during the Second World War, the film follows the crew of U-96 during the Battle of the Atlantic. After successfully attacking a British convoy, the boat is hunted down by enemy destroyers, and the crew are forced to dive deeper and deeper to escape.

Two full-scale replica models were built for the film, in order to faithfully re-create the claustrophobic conditions experienced by the real wartime submariners. Some crew members begin to crack under the pressure, as they endure isolation, daily mundanity and intense struggles for survival. Despite having a modest budget of only $15 million, Petersen's epic received six Academy Award nominations, and has since become one of the most critically acclaimed war movies of all time.

★ VERDICT ★

A HOLLYWOOD — One of the all-time iconic war movies

B+ HISTORY — A classic that is as gripping as it is accurate

OVERALL A-

The Director's Cut version of the film is an epic 3 hours and 30 minutes long

01 As scary as it must have been being pummelled by Royal Navy depth charges, it is likely that the German submariners would not have panicked as much as they do in the film. The submarine would have been a place of quiet discipline, no matter the peril.

02 The drunken party scene is one of the most controversial moments of the film. Many historians feel as if a party of this magnitude would not have happened on board and there is no chance that the officers on the submarine would have got involved.

03 The U-96 docks in the port of La Rochelle in France at both the start and the end of the film. This is not historically accurate as the events in *Das Boot* take place in November 1941, and at this time, the submarine base at La Rochelle was not functional.

04 When the British bombers attack La Rochelle, they cause devastation. At this point in the war, fighter-bombers would not have had the range or capability to attack the port from British airfields. They could have been carrier-based, but this is doubtful.

05 Until the latter stages of the war, the U-boats were one of the least Nazified areas of the Third Reich. In *Das Boot* the crew are indifferent or outwardly sceptical and the one Nazi member on board is referred to as Hitlerjugendführer (Our Hitler Youth Leader).

U-48 TYPE VII-B

Commissioned: 22 april 1939 **Origin:** Nazi Germany
Length: 66.5m (218.2ft) **Crew:** 44
Range: 6,500 nm surfaced; 90 nm submerged
Displacement: 753 tons surfaced
Engine: 2 X Krupp Germaniawerft diesel engines surfaced; 2 X Allegmeine Elektricitats-Gesellschaft AG (AEG) electric motors submerged
Primary Weapons: 4 X 53.3cm (21in) and 1 X 53.3cm stern torpedo tubes; 14 torpedoes
Secondary Weapons: 88mm SK C/35 naval gun; 20mm C/30 anti-aircraft gun

Das Boot

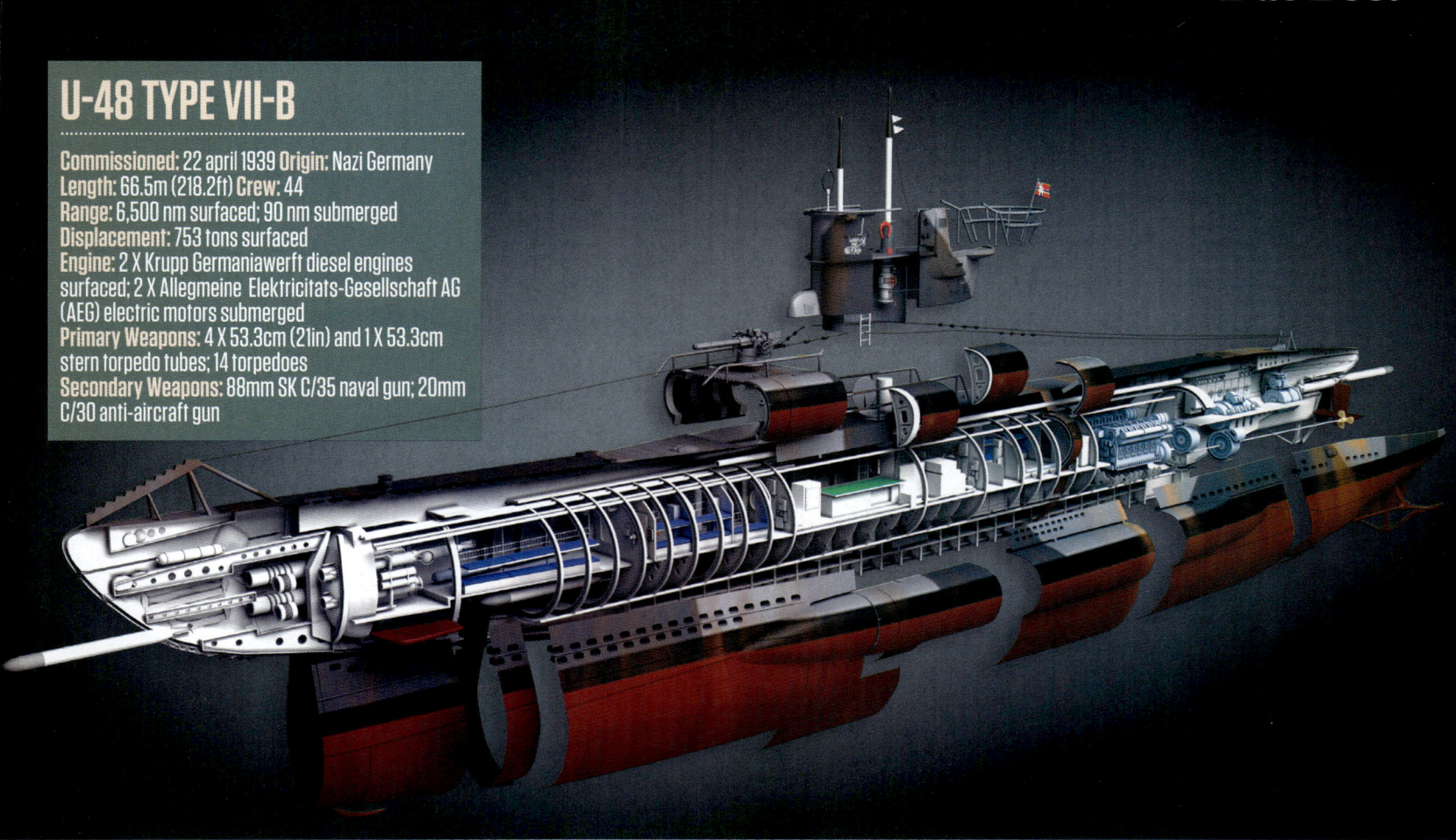

U-48 Type VII-B

The German submarine U-48 was the most successful weapon of its kind deployed during World War II

Despite the fact that unrestricted submarine warfare had brought the British Isles to near collapse during World War I, the German navy of World War II, the Kriegsmarine, had only 56 operational U-boats (Unterseebooten, or undersea boats) when the conflict erupted in September 1939.

Admiral Karl Dönitz, commander of the U-boat service of the Kriegsmarine, realised the potential that a renewed blockade of the British Isles and a concerted effort to interdict trans-Atlantic merchant shipping to the island nation held. If enough U-boats were constructed and deployed, it was suggested, they would be able to strangle Britain into submission, cutting off its resources. Dönitz argued forcefully for a vigorous building programme and the launching of dozens more U-boats to help ensure the ultimate victory. However, when World War II began the Kriegsmarine was woefully short of his goal.

Nevertheless, German submarines indeed wrought significant damage on British shipping once again, and the development of a second generation of modern, sleek undersea hunters had been ongoing during the interwar years. The Type VII series of U-boats was completed in the greatest numbers, with just over 700 launched during roughly a decade of production from 1935-1945. Designated A, B and C, the Type VII U-boats menaced the sea lanes and were responsible for the sinking of millions of tons of Allied shipping.

The most successful submarine of World War II in terms of ships and tonnage sunk was the Type VII-B U-48, launched on 8 March 1939 and commissioned six weeks later. Already at sea when the conflict broke out, the U-48 survived a dozen war patrols under three commanders, served as a training boat and was sunk in the spring of 1945 during the last days of the war – not by enemy action, but scuttled by its own crew to prevent it from falling into Allied hands.

During its 22-month wartime career the U-48 sank or damaged 55 ships totalling 328,414 tons, a record unsurpassed in World War II.

The U-48 operated in two wolfpacks during the early months of the war and survived serious damage in numerous encounters with Allied convoy escort vessels. It spent 325 days at sea and completed its war patrols under three commanders – Kapitanleutnant Herbert Schultze, Korvettenkapitan Hans Rudolf Rösing, and Kapitanleutnant Heinrich Bleichrodt. Each commander received the Knight's Cross, as did officers Reinhard Suhren and Erich Zürn.

The U-48 achieved its first kill on 5 September 1939, just two days after Britain and France declared war on Germany, sinking the 4,853-ton merchant vessel Royal Sceptre with its 88mm deck gun. After sinking the 5,055-ton Winkleigh on 8 September, U-48 dispatched the 4,869-ton Firby three days later and radioed the message, "Transmit to Mr Churchill. I have sunk the British steamer Firby. Posit 59°40'N 13°50'W. Save the crew if you please, German submarine."

During its seventh war patrol U-48 sank the 1,060-ton sloop of war HMS Dundee on 15 September 1940, which was followed on 18 September with a tragic event. With Bleichrodt in command, the U-48 torpedoed the steamer SS City of Benares, which was participating in a programme to evacuate British children to Canada. 90 children were aboard the ship and 77 died.

The U-48 concluded its last patrol on 21 June 1941 and returned to Kiel. It was subsequently transferred to the 26th Bootflotille at Pillau and then to the Third U-boat Lehr Division to be used as a training craft. The boat was scuttled by its crew on 3 May 1945 to prevent it falling into Allied hands.

77

War

THE GREAT ESCAPE

Director: John Sturges **Starring:** Steve McQueen, Richard Attenborough, James Garner **Country:** USA **Year:** 1963

This story of a mass escape from a German POW camp is a screen classic, but should it be locked up for crimes against accuracy?

During the Second World War a group of Allied Prisoners of War hatch plans to escape from their prison camp, all under the watchful eyes of their German guards. While some inmates make daring and foolhardy attempts to escape the camp, a team led by Squadron Leader Roger Bartlett (Richard Attenborough) begins hatching a plan to break out hundreds of inmates.

They begin constructing three tunnels – named "Tom", "Dick" and "Harry" – beneath the camp fences, all the while inventing ingenious ways to conceal their work from the Germans. When "Tom" is accidentally discovered by the guards, American Captain Virgil Hilts (Steven McQueen), a serial escaper, offers to help with the plan. Equipped with fake documents and civilian clothes, dozens of prisoners break out of tunnel "Harry" but their ordeal has just begun as they attempt to evade recapture. Based on a real POW escape during the Second World War, *The Great Escape* is considered a cinema classic. Starring alongside McQueen and Attenborough are other screen legends such as Charles Bronson (as Danny Welinski) and Donald Pleasance (as Colin Blythe).

Donald Pleasence really was a POW during WW2, though he did not escape

VERDICT
- **HOLLYWOOD: A** — This Sixties classic is one of cinema's all-time greats
- **HISTORY: C** — An entertaining retelling that lets a lot of facts slip away
- **OVERALL: B**

01 The film is based on a real mass escape that took place on 24 March 1944 at Stalag Luft III. However, the American-made film exaggerates the role of their countrymen in the story as most were transferred from the camp months before the escape took place.

02 Richard Attenborough portrays Roger Bartlet, the mastermind of the operation, based on Roger Bushell. Sent to the camp for escape attempts, Bushell was also a suspect in the assassination of Reinhard Heydrich, one of the architects of the holocaust.

03 The captured airmen plan to escape via a series of tunnels known as 'Tom', 'Dick' and 'Harry', but Tom is discovered by the guards. However, the film does not explain that Dick proved useless when the camp was expanded. Instead excess soil was deposited here.

04 A number of sequences were added to increase drama and tension. There was no motorbike jump, nor a daring theft of an aircraft. Even dramatic sequences, such as Donald Pleasence's character Colin Blythe going blind, are entirely fictional.

05 76 men escape from the camp, though only 3 are able to get to safety. The film ends on a sour note when 50 were murdered. These executions really took place, though not in the mass manner depicted, on the personal orders of Adolf Hitler.

The Great Escape

POWs were surrounded by high barbed-wire fencing at Stalag Luft III and were closely observed by German guards in distinctive wooden watchtowers

Surviving Stalag Luft III

Bomber Command veteran Air Commodore Charles Clarke OBE was imprisoned at the infamous POW camp and witnessed the legendary 'Great Escape'

Apart from Colditz Castle, no other prisoner-of-war camp of World War II captures the public imagination quite like Stalag Luft III: a vast complex of wooden huts, compounds, barbed wire and guard towers. The camp became most famous for the mass breakout that occurred on 24-25 March 1944 when dozens of Allied POWs escaped through a tunnel. This event later became the stuff of cinematic legend, but for those who were held captive in Stalag Luft III the actual experience of being a POW was a hard endurance test of almost continual suffering.

One of those who survived was Charles Clarke, who was then a teenage pilot officer in RAF 619 Squadron. Now a retired air commodore, Clarke is one of the few men still alive who not only witnessed the 'Great Escape' but also survived a little-known but horrendous forced march through central Europe that killed many Allied prisoners of war, known as the 'Long March'.

Officially known as 'Stammlager Luft III', the famous POW camp was run by the Luftwaffe and primarily held captured Allied air officers. Opened in March 1942, the camp consisted of several compounds where Allied nationalities were separated. British and Commonwealth airmen (of both the RAF and Fleet Air Arm) were imprisoned in North Compound while South Compound was opened for US personnel in September 1943. Although commissioned officers made up the bulk of the prisoners, there were extended compounds for NCOs, and non-airmen were also occasionally held.

Each compound consisted of 15 single-storey huts that could sleep around 15 men per room in five triple-deck bunks. Stalag Luft III eventually grew to 60 acres and was the home of 2,500 British air officers, 7,500 from the US Army Air Force and approximately 900 officers from other Allied air forces.

It was into this large camp that Clarke arrived, after being shot down and captured in Schweinfurt, Germany. before he could settle in he was subjected to one last interrogation. "When we got there we were interrogated (although 'questioned' is probably a better word) by our own people. This was because they were afraid of people infiltrating [the POWs], and I was thrust into a room of 12-16 other people."

The 'infiltration' that the more experienced POW officers were worried about was a security concern, because when Clarke arrived deep progress was being made on preparations for a mass breakout. Three tunnels had been constructed, but only one had been successfully completed. The preparations were detailed, and Clarke had arrived just in time to be a witness to the 'Great Escape'.

In early 1943, Squadron Leader Roger Bushell devised an audacious plan for a mass breakout from Stalag Luft III. Bushell was the head of the camp's escape committee and proposed building three tunnels simultaneously so that 200 men could break out in a single attempt.

The tunnels were codenamed 'Tom', 'Dick' and 'Harry' and over 600 prisoners eventually became involved in their construction. Located at a depth of nine metres (30 feet) and designed to run more than 90 metres (300 feet) into the outside woods, the tunnels were certainly ambitious. However, at only 0.9 square metres (two square feet) in size, they were extremely small, and working underground in sandy subsoil required great courage and ingenuity.

Bed boards were used en masse to prop up the tunnels; candles were made from worn clothing and soup fat, while tin cans could be turned into tools or ventilation ducting. As progress continued, the tunnels became more elaborate. Electric lights were installed and hooked into the camp's power grid, while most famously a small rail system was developed. Rope-pulled wooden trolleys were essential in removing tons of soil over 12 months, and they even had stopping points that prisoners nicknamed 'Piccadilly Circus' and 'Leicester Square' after London Underground stations.

Escape preparations were not just confined to tunnelling. Skilled forgers made maps, false documents, compasses and civilian clothes while dispersers scattered the tunnels' soil around the camp using hidden pouches in their trousers. All of these operations were also covered by an excellent security system. Prisoners became highly adept at distracting the German guards or

79

War

After the war, the RAF Police led an extensive investigation into the Stalag Luft III murders. 72 men were eventually identified, and many were tried, executed or imprisoned

acting as 'Stooges' (including Clarke) who could subtly alert the working escapees of potential enemy approaches or flashpoints.

Despite these intricate plans, the Germans discovered 'Tom' in September 1943 and 'Dick' was abandoned to be used as storage. Only 'Harry' was used for the breakout of 24-25 March 1944, when 76 officers escaped. After the escape, the Germans compiled a list of missing materials, and the statistics were extraordinary. The prisoners had used, among other items, 4,000 bed boards, 3,424 towels, 1,699 blankets, 305 metres (1,000 feet) of electric wire, 180 metres (600 feet) of rope, 30 shovels and 478 spoons.

Clarke soon became aware of the plan. "We quickly knew that there was going to be a big breakout, and the security was remarkably good." Nevertheless, Clarke had arrived late and at 19 was deemed too young to take a prominent part in preparations. "I met the inner circle but didn't know them well. I was a new boy – and I emphasise the word 'boy' rather than a man. All of the planning had been going on for years. Most of the people who went through the tunnel had been prisoners of war for at least a year."

Despite not being given a place in the tunnel, Clarke still played a small part in the

"The escape has since become the subject of many myths"

security for the escape. "I acted as a 'stooge', which was a guard or sentry. One of the things was that they had people scattered throughout the camp who used signals. For example, if you stood up it meant that there was a 'Goon' [German guard] nearby. It was all low-key stuff."

When everything was prepared, the escapees waited for the best time to break out, which was the moonless night of 24-25 March 1944. 200 Allied POWs lined up to escape from the tunnel, although there were no Americans, as Clarke explains: "People often ask why there were no Americans in the camp but the answer is very simple. In the weeks before the Great Escape the Americans had been moved to a new US camp. We were in North Camp, and the move saved their lives of course."

The night of the escape featured an Allied air raid nearby. Clarke recalls the escapees' progress: "Before the air raid there were movements of people within the huts, and it was all done quietly. Those who were going through the tunnel got into Hut 104 so that they could be the first away." Clarke also remembers when the Germans discovered the escape: "When the lights came on after the air raid had finished the escape became obvious to the Germans. We heard a shot and we knew the game was up."

The escape has since become the subject of many myths, not in small part as a result of the hugely popular 1963 film. The incident involving the German gunshot is one that Clarke is keen to clarify: "You hear lots of nonsense. I've heard one chap say, 'I was in the tunnel when they fired the shot. Fortunately there was a curve in the tunnel otherwise I would have been killed.' That was absolute rubbish: your head had to be straight so you could pull the trolleys along. Also, the shot that was fired was above ground, and the guard had fired a warning shot."

The Great Escape

Clarke with Dame Judi Dench and Women's Auxiliary Air Force veteran Igraine Hamilton at the Bomber Command Memorial in London, 21 May 2013

A railway trolley in tunnel 'Harry', photographed by the Germans after the mass breakout

Despite several setbacks, 76 Allied POWs had successfully escaped. Clarke recalls that the Germans' immediate response was severe: "We were kept out in the snow virtually all day the following day while they counted and recounted us. They got no help from us because we kept moving around to confuse them. This went on for several days, and they stopped all rations and lots of other things. We were subjected to harsher treatment after the escape and there was also a huge manhunt."

Eventually, the prisoners learned the awful fate of the escapees. "There were many more searches, and then of course the news came back to the camp commandant that 50 had been murdered. He called the British senior officer in and told him that 50 had been shot escaping. Fortunately, that officer was due to be repatriated the following week due to a gammy leg so he was able to report directly to parliament. It was then that [Foreign Secretary] Anthony Eden said that justice would be asserted."

Although the escape was audacious, Clarke recounts the bleak statistics: "Eventually, two or three escapees came back to the camp, which was surprising. They included Jimmy James, who was a great man and a friend of mine. About 70-odd went through the tunnel; 50 were murdered, two or three successfully escaped and the rest were brought back. After the Great Escape, escaping was forbidden by the British because of the risk that people would be shot again."

A fearful time

The murder of the 50 escapees cast a shadow over the camp, and prisoners feared for their lives. "For the rest of our time at Stalag Luft III we kept wondering what was going to happen to us. After the other prisoners were shot we wondered if we would also be murdered. We even planned to defend ourselves with cudgels – it was really ridiculous because we wouldn't have stood a cat in hell's chance."

With escaping banned, the POWs waited for news on the war. "When the invasion of France occurred we thought we would be released the following week. How naïve we were, because the war went on for months after that, but we followed its progress. We had an illegal radio, and a South African newspaper reporter wrote the news down in shorthand. He would turn out a bulletin and it would be read out in each hut despite there being guards all around us."

Despite possessing the illegal radio, the Germans did not go out of their way to find it. "The Germans had a map that followed things according to their own radio, but it is reputed that the commandant asked our senior British officer how the war was going! He knew damn well we had the radio."

Although camp life was extremely tense, especially after the escape, the prisoners did find creative outlets in staging improvised theatre shows. "The Germans allowed some prisoners to build a theatre, and it was done very well. It amazes me how they allowed these theatricals to take place. I think the Red Cross brought in some clothing, and the plays they put on were out of this world. So many actors started out their careers that way. The camp had so much talent in it and they were a remarkable collection of people."

The theatre was not only a breeding ground for thespian talent, but also a useful location for another hidden tunnel. "It was under a corner of the theatre and used as a store, although it was incomplete. I went down it and it's rumoured that sketches of the camp were hidden there, that were later used as a basis for the film The Great Escape. These drawings were put in a tube, stored and recovered after the war."

War

FURY

Director: David Ayer **Starring:** Brad Pitt, Logan Lerman, Shia LaBeouf, Michael Peña, Jon Bernthal **Country:** USA **Year:** 2014

Does this tense and grisly action flick reflect the horrors of war?

Brad Pitt's return to WWII uniform sees him at the helm of an M4 Sherman tank, nicknamed Fury, in the dying days of the war in Europe. After he and his tank crew are joined by rookie recruit Norman (Logan Lerman), they are soon part of a dangerous offensive into Germany. Norman quickly learns what it takes to survive in the intense confines of the tank, and is also exposed to the horrific nature of a war that has already emotionally scarred his new crewmates.

Upon release, Fury received plenty of criticism from armchair generals, particularly regarding some of its action sequences that were designed more around drama than depicting real battlefield tactics. Nonetheless, the movie provided plenty of realism to a genre that in previous generations had seen the snow-bound Battle of the Bulge re-created in the Spanish mountains.

The tank used in the film was a fully-working M4A2 provided by the Bovington Tank Museum in the UK. At the box office, the movie pulled in a respectable $211 million worldwide, lagging miles behind the likes of Saving Private Ryan in terms of the all-time war movie moneymakers.

★ VERDICT ★
B+ HOLLYWOOD — A dedicated, all-star cast with plenty of compelling action
B- HISTORY — Nit-picking aside, more commitment to realism than most
OVERALL B

The world's only remaining operable Tiger tank is featured in the film

01 During the battle with the Tiger, the Sherman's armour-piercing round could have penetrated the front armour of the Tiger easily at short range. 'Fury' was an 'Easy Eight' Sherman, and its 76mm high-velocity gun would have been a match for most armour.

02 The film lacks any sort of credible infantry tactics on both the US and German sides. The lack of combined arms (artillery and air support, for instance) on the US side and the SS battalion's inability to destroy the immobilised tank are two standout examples.

03 Pitt's character being able to make such regular use of a German StG 44 is highly unlikely. They weren't common and ammo and spare parts would have had to be scrounged from the battlefield. For obvious reasons tankers preferred more compact arms.

04 The myth of the Germans possessing tanks that were vastly superior to anything the Allies could field is a common misconception, and one that is perpetuated by this film. The M4 'Sherman' medium tank was one of the Allies' most effective vehicles.

05 Fury captures the emotional and physical toll experienced by soldiers in war, and the characters exhibit extreme mood swings and PTSD from the horrors they have witnessed. Some veterans have remarked how well the film portrays this on screen.

THE PATRIOT

Director: Roland Emmerich **Starring:** Mel Gibson, Heath Ledger, Joely Richardson **Country:** USA **Year:** 2000

Does this Hollywood depiction of the American Revolutionary War come under heavy fire?

Just a few years after his monumental success hacking into English soldiers in *Braveheart*, Mel Gibson swapped his tartan for a tricorn hat in another historic reimagining, this time set in the Revolutionary War. Following the similar trope of a reluctant warrior driven by revenge and a zeal for liberty, Gibson plays Benjamin Martin, an American war veteran turned farmer who is dragged into the conflict when his son is murdered by British soldiers.

Finding the Continental Army disorganised and on the back foot, Martin lends his marksmanship and brutal close-quarter combat experience to the Patriot forces. At the head of a small militia, he leads a guerrilla campaign against the redcoats, overcoming further tragedy before the climactic British surrender at Yorktown. Similar to Gibson's previous historic epic, *The Patriot* is less concerned with real history and is unapologetic in its flag-waving melodrama. A lot of effort went into its battle scenes, which do a good job of presenting the gritty violence of 18th century battlefields. The resulting healthy box office returns, as well as three Academy Award nominations, perhaps proves that facts really don't care about your history.

VERDICT
- **B- HOLLYWOOD** Unapologetic melodrama at its height
- **E+ HISTORY** Takes a trusty tomahawk to the facts
- **OVERALL C-**

Mel Gibson's character is based on several real-life Revolutionary era soldiers

01 Gibson's Benjamin Martin is based on militia leader Francis Marion, portrayed in the film as a family man and a hero. In reality, Swamp Fox, as Marion was known, was a serial rapist who murdered Cherokee Indians in the name of fun.

02 The film's portrayal of slavery has come under criticism as "a whitewashing of history". In the film Martin doesn't own slaves, but this is unlikely considering his status and the film's era, and even Gibson called this decision "a cop-out".

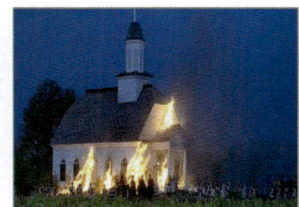

03 One of the film's harshest criticisms is for its portrayal of atrocities committed by the British. The redcoats are shown killing POWs and even burning a church packed with unarmed civilians. This has no factual basis in any 18th-century war.

04 Martin's sister-in-law Charlotte is shown wearing a selection of dresses that at the time would have been considered revealing and scandalous. She is also shown wearing her hair down, which was considered risqué.

05 In the film Cornwallis orders to "Sound the retreat" at the end of the Battle of Guilford Courthouse, while the Americans celebrate victory. In reality, the British won this battle and Nathanael Greene's American army was forced to retreat.

War

BRAVEHEART

Director: Mel Gibson **Starring:** Mel Gibson, Sophie Marceau, Patrick McGoohan **Country:** USA **Year:** 1995

How much artistic freedom was used in this Hollywood retelling of William Wallace's fight for Scottish independence?

It's the 13th century, and Scotland is in the chainmail grip of English tyranny. Taxed, oppressed and harassed, the Scottish people's plight isn't helped by petty Scottish noblemen, unable to unite against their foe – until the arrival of William Wallace (Mel Gibson). Driven by revenge, as well as his quest to free his country, Wallace gathers a rebel army.

Winning victories on the battlefield, Wallace finds an ally in nobleman Robert Bruce (Angus MacFayden), and even Princess Isabella (Sophie Marceau), an envoy from England who is enraptured by Wallace's rugged charm. Hacking and slashing their way through Englishmen in their mission for freedom, the Scottish army eventually faces King Edward I (Patrick McGoohan) in battle. With the odds against him, Wallace is betrayed, taken prisoner, his rallying cries for freedom reverberating around the nation.

Gibson's epic retelling of the celebrated Scottish hero isn't the most faithful to the facts – actually, in parts it takes a massive claymore swing at some of the historical events and characters – but its part Mediaeval hack-and-slash, part revenge romance narrative still resonates with audiences.

VERDICT
- **HOLLYWOOD: B** – "They will never take our freedom! Alba gu bràth!"
- **HISTORY: D** – It's like watching facts be hung, drawn and quartered
- **OVERALL: C**

Most of the filming was shot on location in Ireland

01 Wallace and other Scottish characters are seen wearing belted plaid. No Scots in that period would have worn belted plaids or kilts, as it was not introduced until the 16th century. Additionally, when belted plaid was worn, it was not in the fashion depicted in the movie.

02 Robert the Bruce is shown to secretly side with the English and betray Wallace on the battlefield, but this is not true. He fought and helped to obtain Scottish independence. and the nickname 'Braveheart' was first used to describe Robert, not Wallace.

03 The young Wallace of the film is depicted as a struggling commoner, but it is thought that Wallace's family had minor nobility due to his father. William was a landowner and was also a knight even before the Battle of Stirling Bridge.

04 Wallace is shown having an affair with Princess Isabella, who implies the child she is carrying is Wallace's. The real Isabella was born in 1295 and Wallace was killed in 1305, making her only ten years old at the time. Her child was born in 1312, years after Wallace's death.

05 Edward I Longshanks is shown drawing his final breath before Wallace is executed, making for a bittersweet ending. However, Wallace was executed on 23 August 1305 and Edward I didn't die until 7 July 1307, while leading an invasion of Scotland.

Braveheart

This frieze in the Scottish National Portrait Gallery, with William Wallace in the front row, shows many notable figures from the First War of Scottish Independence

Scotland's fight for freedom
William Wallace

Discover the man behind the myth and his savage guerrilla war to end England's tyranny

Michael Brown is professor of Medieval Scottish history at the University of St Andrews. He is the author of several books including *The Wars Of Scotland, 1214-1371* (2004).

On an autumn morning in 1297, a Scottish army of spearmen, knights, squires, townsmen and peasants looked down from the rocky crag where they were encamped. Below them, the wide River Forth looped through a marshy plain: the only crossing a narrow wooden bridge and causeway. Since dawn the Scots had watched the movements of a large English army assembled on the far side of the river beneath the rock of Stirling Castle. The Scots would have seen the arming of several hundred knights and men at arms, and may have wondered how a mob of poorly trained footmen could withstand the charge of heavy horses and riders. They had witnessed their leaders, the young nobleman Andrew Moray and the fearsome 'commoner' William Wallace, reject an English call for their surrender. "Go back," Wallace told the English envoys, "we did not come here for the good of peace but you should know that we are ready to fight for vengeance and for the freedom of our kingdom." As the English vanguard filed slowly across the bridge, Wallace and Moray ordered their men to prepare for a battle that would determine the fate of Scotland.

The men who stood with Wallace and Moray at Stirling Bridge had been driven to take up arms by the disasters that had overtaken their homeland. These disasters began with a series of deaths that ended a period of relative peace and prosperity between King Edward I of England and his brother-in-law, Alexander III, king of Scotland. To Medieval writers, the royal dynasty was the golden thread that held the kingdom together, but in March 1286, that thread began to fray when tragedy struck.

Alexander had been riding at night to visit his queen when he was thrown from his horse and killed. His only living descendant was his three-year-old grandchild, Margaret, daughter of the king of Norway. As she was so young, parliament chose six guardians to rule Scotland in the name of their absent queen. These guardians turned to King Edward I of England – a neighbour and apparent friend – for help. It was agreed that Edward's son would marry Margaret – a match that would have united Scotland and England under a single dynasty – but the plan was foiled by Margaret's untimely death in 1290. The golden thread had snapped.

Scotland was left with no clear successor – a period known as the 'Great Cause' – with several ambitious families fighting over the throne, foremost among them the Balliols and Bruces. Facing civil war, the guardians once again turned to Edward, asking him to judge between the claimants. Before he agreed, the cunning king demanded that he be recognised as overlord of Scotland, and feeling they had no choice, they relented. Edward judged this Great Cause, choosing John Balliol as king in 1292. During the next three years, the English king asserted his rights over Scotland to the full. Though Balliol found it impossible to stand up to Edward, by 1296, many Scots were prepared to defy him. They allied with the French king, and in the face of this rebellion, Edward geared up for war.

The Scots were disastrously unprepared. From the outset, King John had no stomach for the fight, while his army, led by a group of nobles, manoeuvred ineffectively. At Easter 1296, the English king directed a huge force against the largest Scottish town, Berwick. Despite being defended only by a ditch and a timber palisade, the townsfolk defied the tall figure of the king, bombarding him with insults.

Edward's response was to send his host to storm the town and put many of its inhabitants to the sword. A month later, the Scots suffered a second lesson in warfare. The leader of King Edward's army, John de Warenne, earl of Surrey,

85

War

caught the main Scottish host outside Dunbar Castle. The Scots advanced without caution and were routed. While large numbers of footmen were cut down, most of the nobles were able to flee to the castle where more than a hundred surrendered to the English.

In the face of these disasters, the will of the Scottish king and nobles to resist collapsed. Lords hurried to make peace with the English king as he advanced through Scotland. John Balliol had failed to lead his people in this time of crisis and for this he earned a reputation as a weak, ineffectual monarch. His nickname – 'Toom Tabard', or 'empty coat' – was derived from Balliol's surrender at Brechin in early July 1296. Edward had the hapless Balliol stripped of his surcoat bearing the lion rampant arms of Scotland's kings. He was imprisoned in the Tower of London, and the Stone of Destiny – the seat on which Scottish monarchs were enthroned – was captured. To cement his rule, Edward held a parliament in the wreckage of Berwick, forcing Scottish nobles – knights, bishops, and claimants to the throne – to pledge obedience to him. Nearly 1,900 names were scrawled on the infamous document: the Ragman Rolls.

Most of the leading nobles were held in custody in England, while the government of the country was left in the hands of ambitious English bureaucrats, such as the hated treasurer Hugh Cressingham. To ordinary Scots, used to being governed by compatriots who understood their laws and customs, this was a shock and an insult. Across the kingdom, Scottish townsmen, freeholders and peasants experienced this new regime through the orders of English sheriffs backed by soldiers based in local castles. These 'middle-folk' may have regarded the war of 1296 as a matter of rival kings, but now they witnessed the humiliation of their country. They were also forced to endure the demands of the English administration. To aid Edward's war against the French, he seized the goods of Scottish farmers and merchants, and it was feared that ordinary Scots were to be force to serve in his army.

Amid this tense atmosphere emerged William Wallace. His origins remain mysterious, but the English denounced him as a brigand and scoffed when he was knighted that the Scots had tried to turn a raven into a swan. In reality, Wallace was the brother of a knight and was trained to carry weapons, but he was young and landless. Hence it would be his deeds and ability to inspire support, rather than his birth or rank, that turned him into a leader of his people.

In early 1297, Wallace and a band of men ambushed and killed the sheriff of Lanark, William Heselrig. Though romanticised in later stories as an act of vengeance for the murder of his wife, Wallace's action was planned as a blow by local men against foreign rule. It would be the start of open rebellion.

In the weeks after his slaying of the sheriff, Wallace's supporters grew into an army of men

William Wallace rejects English terms shortly before the battle of Stirling Bridge

Wallace's trial in Westminster Hall. He was forced to wear a garland of oak leaves to suggest he was 'king of the outlaws'

from the 'middle folk' and peasants of south-west Scotland, but these events were part of a wider insurrection. Andrew Moray – a noble that had been imprisoned in England – managed to engineer his escape from Chester Castle and return to his home in northern Scotland.

Like Wallace, Moray was young and determined, however, his father owned extensive estates and many of his tenants rallied to join his son in arms. In late May 1297, his band of followers – in alliance with the townsfolk of Inverness – expelled the English garrison and attacked Urquhart Castle on Loch Ness.

The English quickly rounded up the nobles who had risen in support of Wallace, but then, in the words of Hugh Cressingham, "The English had gone to sleep." Wallace and his band had slipped away from the west into the hills of Ettrick Forest, where men continued to flock to his banner. Meanwhile, more than 300 kilometres to the north, Moray was also winning ground, picking off isolated English garrisons.

Braveheart

Prior to his execution, Wallace was dragged naked through London

No contemporary images exist of Wallace, so we must rely on artistic interpretation

> "The rebellion had recovered Scotland and it also created an army. William Wallace was now its commander"

King Edward in London and his officials in Berwick could only write letters asking Scottish lords to stop Moray. By August, English authority north of the Tay had collapsed and Wallace was able to lead his followers north to join forces with Andrew Moray's band outside Dundee. Faced with this crisis, the Earl of Surrey took charge. He assembled an army of perhaps 5,000 infantry and 500 heavy cavalry from northern England and led it towards Stirling castle.

This location was the strategic key to Scotland. It was no accident that three of the major battles of the Scottish wars were fought within sight of the castle. Perched high on its rock, this stronghold commanded Stirling Bridge, which provided the only land route for an army seeking access to northern Scotland. If he was to win back the north for his king, Surrey had to cross. His enemies knew this, too. By the morning of 11 September, Moray and Wallace were encamped with their men on Abbey Craig, a rocky outcrop to the north of the bridge that gave them a commanding view of the plain below. They may have led a similar number of men to Surrey but had few or no horsemen.

The Earl of Surrey clearly despised the Scottish army and its leaders. Remembering the previous year, he expected them to submit or melt away. He rose late from bed and called back some of his vanguard who had already crossed Stirling Bridge. The earl then knighted some of his followers and sent the envoys to offer mercy to the Scots. Finally, he made ready to move. At a council of war, a Scottish knight in his army warned Surrey. "If we cross the bridge, we are dead men. For we cannot cross except two by two. Our enemies are in the open and their whole force will fall upon us." He offered to lead a force across a ford upstream and outflank the Scots but the treasurer Cressingham, "a pompous man," rejected this plan and demanded an immediate advance across the bridge to end the war and save money. The delays had given Moray and Wallace time to lead their men onto the low ground north of the bridge and form them up for battle. When, at 11am, the English vanguard began to file across the narrow bridge, the Scots were ready.

Stirling Bridge must have been choked with men and horses moving to the north side of the river. Wallace and Moray waited for the best moment. When about a third of the English army was across, they struck. The Scottish spearmen surged forward, making their strongest attack against the north end of the bridge. The English vanguard did not have time to form up and were pushed back at once. The bitterest fighting was probably for control of the bridge and causeway where many were thrown into the river and drowned. Once the Scots secured this, the English who had already crossed were cut off from the main body of the army.

With the end of the bridge held by the enemy, the Earl of Surrey could only watch in horror as his vanguard met its fate on the far bank of the Forth. Though one English knight, Marmaduke Tweng, managed to force his way back across the bridge, carrying his wounded nephew to safety, his comrades were penned into a loop of the river. Some unarmoured Welsh bowmen escaped by swimming, but the heavily equipped men at arms faced drowning or death in battle. Outnumbered, they were cut down by the triumphant Scots. Among the dead was Cressingham, whose body was skinned to make trophies.

Having seen the fate of his army, Surrey's nerve cracked. He fled the field and rode south to Berwick. Behind him, Stirling Castle and much of southern Scotland surrendered to the victors. However, the Scottish army had suffered losses in the fighting. Andrew Moray was wounded and, though he survived for several months, by the end of the year the daring northern leader was dead. The rebellion had recovered Scotland and it also created an army. William Wallace was now its commander, and after Moray's death was named sole guardian of the kingdom. Through the winter he continued to train the army and ready Scotland for the coming storm.

War

DUNKIRK

Director: Christopher Nolan **Starring:** Fionn Whitehead, Tom Glynn-Carney, Jack Lowden, Harry Styles, Aneurin Barnard, James D'Arcy, Barry Keoghan, Kenneth Branagh, Cillian Murphy, Mark Rylance, Tom Hardy **Country:** UK **Year:** 2017

Did Batman Begins director Christopher Nolan compromise historical fact to make his World War II blockbuster?

Already one of Hollywood's most sought after directors off the back of his *Dark Knight* series, Christopher Nolan's much anticipated WWII drama recounts the evacuation of over 300,000 Allied forces from the French beaches, in the Summer of 1940. Split between action on the beaches, at sea and in the air, Nolan attempts to do justice to the enormous task faced by all branches of Britain's military, in their most desperate hour.

Perhaps even more memorable than the stellar performances from Kenneth Branagh, Tom Hardy, Mark Rylance and others, is the film's score by Hans Zimmer, which binds together the tension running through the narrative as time begins to run out for the thousands of men stranded on the beach. Though Nolan narrowly missed out on his own first Academy Award, the film did receive three Oscars for film editing, sound mixing and sound editing. Globally, it surpassed half a billion dollars in gross earnings, making it one of the most profitable World War II movies ever.

Some of the ships that appear in the film are the real vessels from 1940

VERDICT
A HOLLYWOOD — One of the all-time great filmmakers at his best
B HISTORY — Immersive and painstakingly detailed
OVERALL A

01 At the beginning of he film, the Luftwaffe drop thousands of propaganda pamphlets onto Dunkirk's beaches, urging the Allied troops surrender. While this did actually happen in real life, the design of the pamphlets used in the movie is inaccurate.

02 The film's characters are fictional but some of their stories are rooted in fact. Commander Bolton is a composite character with some of his actions based on the real-life story of piermaster James Campbell Clouston. He died during the evacuation.

03 While its hard to imagine civilian boats being used in a rescue mission of this scale, around 700 'Little Ships of Dunkirk' did sail to save soldiers, alongside 43 Allied destroyers. These were either British or Canadian ships, but the one used in the movie is French.

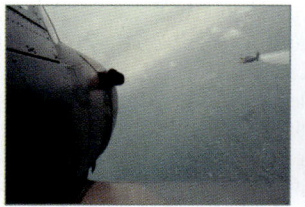

04 Just like in the film, there really were dogfights between the British Spitfires and the German Messerschmitt Bf 109s. However, the German planes are depicted with yellow noses when in reality they were not painted that colour until a month after Dunkirk.

05 The troops at Dunkirk truly believed the RAF had abandoned them because they could not see the Allied aircraft — in the film, a desperate soldier demands to know where they are. Of course, the RAF was actually fighting the Germans across the Channel.

Dunkirk

Allied troops line up on the beach at Dunkirk to await evacuation

The Spirit of Dunkirk

Social historian Henry Buckton says that Dunkirk has been woven into the British identity, but experts view it differently

How have historians' perspectives on the evacuations changed?
Dunkirk is perhaps unique because it has been written and spoken about in the same exalted company as Agincourt, Waterloo and the Normandy Landings for decades. However, it was, of course, a defeat. Yes, it was a logistical victory and did wonders for public morale, but militarily it was a disaster. I think today the perspective in the eyes of the public has changed to appreciate this point; historians have largely always understood it.

Why were Allied forces so badly beaten in France that they had to retreat?
The Germans launched a new type of warfare: it was fast-paced and direct, and took the Allies by complete surprise. They were digging in expecting a long drawn-out campaign similar to the trenches of the First World War but the Nazis had other ideas.

How would you describe the impact of the little ships fleet?
Immense! This was a remarkable and typically British response to a disaster that very few other nations would even have contemplated. It is doubtful that the Royal Navy would have been able to rescue the vast numbers achieved without the help of the little ships. Time would have been against them and many more Allied soldiers would have been left behind and taken prisoner.

How did the public react to the evacuations?
Most people in Britain knew absolutely nothing of what was occurring – in fact, they believed the army to be invincible – so when word got around Bristol that they were bringing soldiers back, people were confused. Women and children in their droves went down to Stapleton Road station to cheer them on and wave flags. The sight that met their eyes was not at all what they had expected: train after train unloading men that were dirty, unshaven and desperately tired. Some were on crutches, others wearing dirty, blood-stained bandages.

What effect did Dunkirk have on the rest of the war?
In reality, it probably had very little impact militarily. Even if the BEF had surrendered, Britain would have remained free and was able to build new armies and in time provide a training ground for the armies of America and Canada as well as a springboard from which to launch the reconquest of occupied Europe in 1944.

Why does Dunkirk still resonate so strongly with Brits today?
Probably because the very word 'Dunkirk' has become part of Britain's identity and DNA. It is used to describe perceived traits of the British character like defiance, bravery, stoicism, all pulling together to overcome adversity: the so-called Dunkirk spirit.

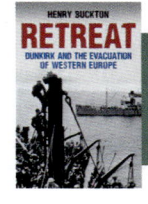

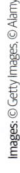

Henry Buckton is an author, social historian filmmaker and songwriter based in the UK. He has multiple bestselling books, including Retreat: Dunkirk and the Evacuation of Western Europe *(2017), coinciding with the Christopher Nolan film.*

HENRY BUCKTON'S NEW BOOK RETREAT: DUNKIRK AND THE EVACUATION OF WESTERN EUROPE IS OUT NOW.

War

PEARL HARBOR

Director: Michael Bay **Starring:** Ben Affleck, Josh Hartnett, Kate Beckinsale, Cuba Gooding Jr **Country:** USA **Year:** 2001

It was a hit at the box office, but how on target was its historical accuracy?

President Roosevelt aptly referred to the 1941 bombing of Pearl Harbor as a 'date which will live in infamy'. Some six decades later, Hollywood executives could not have predicted the infamy their big-screen retelling would earn. Like any historical disaster film (it has several times been described as the *Titanic* of war movies), we know where the plot is inevitably headed – a romance sideshow and character backstory plod along until the Japanese planes loom on the horizon.

It's when the bombs start falling that audiences get a glimpse of what would later become director Michael Bay's signature style in his *Transformers* series – big action, with big CGI effects. Seeing the mass of computer-generated fighter-bombers swarming over stricken US Navy ships below was certainly impressive to early-Noughties audiences. There is even a point-of-view shot that follows a torpedo on its path into the side of a hull. Like many of Bay's later movies, *Pearl Harbor* wasn't short of criticism for prioritising style over substance, and certainly when the big effects start flying there is little room for much else.

VERDICT
- HOLLYWOOD: D — Earned its money, but also its infamy
- HISTORY: D — Sends the facts to the bottom of the ocean
- OVERALL: D

The real attack on Pearl Harbor lasted for less than two hours

01 The Japanese torpedo bomber planes attack the Pearl Harbor military airfield, where one of the film's main characters is taking shelter. But why would torpedo bombers take a large detour to attack an airfield? How would they be effective? What would they torpedo there?

02 Franklin D Roosevelt discusses the possibility of the Japanese invasion of the United States mainland, and then pulls himself out of his wheelchair to make a point. This is out of character for Roosevelt and besides, Japan had no such lofty ambitions.

03 The characters played by Ben Affleck and Josh Hartnett, based on real-life pilots George Welch and Kenneth Taylor, are sent on a Tokyo bombing raid by Lieutenant Colonel James Dolittle – but he would have needed bomber pilots, not fighter pilots.

04 Following the first wave of attacks, a naval officer is handed a telegram stating: "Be on alert. Attack by Japan considered imminent." The Navy was actually warning all its officers as early as 26 November that Japan was going to attack, they just didn't know where.

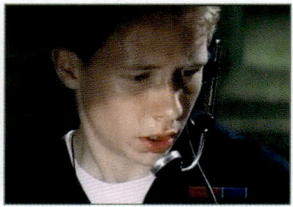

05 Several scenes show pilots communicating easily with the control tower and at one point a radio operator listens to the dogfighting via pilot radios hundreds of miles away in Hawaii. This wasn't possible with the radio technology of the Forties.

90

THE KILLING FIELDS

Director: Roland Joffé **Starring:** Sam Waterston, Haing S Ngor, John Malkovich **Country:** USA **Year:** 1984

A powerful tale of friendship and conflict journalism in Cambodia

The Cambodian Genocide was one of the worst atrocities of the late 20th century, with approximately two million people killed at the hands of Pol Pot's Khmer Rouge government. This 1987 drama is based on the real experiences of *New York Times* reporter Sydney Schanberg (played by Sam Waterston) and Cambodian interpreter and journalist Dith Pran (Haing S. Ngor).

The pair witness the takeover of the Khmer Rouge once the American military has pulled out of the country, and narrowly escape execution at the hands of the new regime. Fearing for his life, Schanberg eventually escapes, while Pran is forced into a brutal cycle of forced labour and 're-education'. Upon escaping, he uncovers the resting place of countless victims of the government's "Year Zero" killings. Based on Schanberg's 1980 book *The Death and Life of Dith Pran*, the film received critical acclaim in the US, and raised greater public awareness of the atrocities in Cambodia. It picked up three Academy Awards, with best supporting role going to Haing S. Ngor.

VERDICT
- **HOLLYWOOD: B** — A difficult but important piece of cinema
- **HISTORY: A-** — Incredible accuracy and commitment to detail
- **OVERALL: B+**

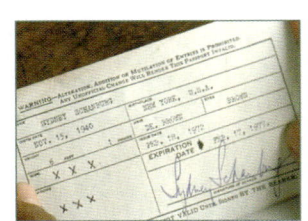

Haing S. Ngor was himself a survivor of the Cambodian Genocide

01 The film follows *New York Times* journalist Sydney Schanberg (Waterston) and his fixer in Cambodia Dith Pran (Ngor) as they cover American actions in the country. Attention to detail was paramount - even the typeface in Schanberg's visa is correct.

02 The Khmer Rouge launched a coup, forcing foreigners to leave. Schanberg attempts to get Pran out with a forged passport. This is true, although dramatised with a desperate scramble for a photo. In reality, it was just a bad forgery and Pran remained in Cambodia.

03 Time is compressed here, with Pran quickly put to work in the fields of the new collective farms. At first he actually disguised himself as a taxi driver for a while. Schanberg, meanwhile, won a Pulitzer Prize, depicted in the film as an AIFPC award.

04 Not shown in the film are Pran's many jobs from 1975 to 1979, which included being a chief in his old home town for a short while. His journey to this region is compressed and includes the titular killing fields he described, recreated pretty accurately by the film.

05 Schanberg described the guilt he felt in his book *The Death and Life of Dith Pran* and how he spent years looking for information on Pran's whereabouts. He eventually gets word he's reached a refugee camp and they are reunited, just as the film shows.

War

KINGDOM OF HEAVEN

Director: Ridley Scott **Starring:** Orlando Bloom, Eva Green, Ghassan Massoud **Country:** USA **Year:** 2005

Does Ridley Scott favour action over accuracy in this Crusader epic about the Siege of Jerusalem?

Director Ridley Scott's anticipated return to historic drama follows the story of Balian (Orlando Bloom), a widower blacksmith of mysterious origins who journeys with a band of knights to the Kingdom of Jerusalem. After implausibly inheriting a land and title in the Holy Land, Balian becomes embodied in the power struggles and court politics of the realm. Outnumbered by a Saracen army and with treacherous crusader princes conspiring to seize the throne, Balian finds himself as the last honourable defender of Jerusalem.

Burgeoning from his breakout role as Legolas in *The Lord Of The Rings* and Will Turner in *Pirates of the Caribbean*, Bloom's star power was no doubt brought on board to guarantee ticket sales. In the end, his performance doesn't carry the weight of the epic, and worse still for executives, his name wasn't enough to prevent the movie flopping in the US. Nonetheless, Scott delivers a considered and nuanced portrayal of the Saracen forces, and does a credible job unravelling the complex world of the Holy Land during the 12th century. There are also memorable performances from legends such as Jeremy Irons, David Thewlis, and Liam Neeson.

The real Balian of Ibelin was a nobleman born in the Kingdom of Jerusalem

VERDICT
- **HOLLYWOOD: D** — An uninspiring narrative at the centre of some epic worldbuilding
- **HISTORY: C** — Though not completely inaccurate, Scott uses a lot of artistic licence
- **OVERALL: C-**

01 Balian of Ibelin, played by Orlando Bloom, was indeed a real-life knight who served in Jerusalem during the Third Crusade. However, unlike in the movie, at no point did the nobleman work as a blacksmith as penance for his wife's suicide.

02 King Baldwin IV, played by Edward Norton, really did suffer from leprosy - although he did not wear a silver mask to hide it, as in the film. It is also true that he defeated Saladin's forces at the Battle of Montgisard, when he was just 16 years old.

03 Although the film portrays a romance between Balian and Princess Sibylla, in real-life no such relationship existed. However, Sibylla was married to Guy de Lusignan, the main antagonist of the movie, who became king of Jerusalem through their marriage.

04 As depicted in the film, the Crusaders did wander in the desert for three days without water before they were ambushed, sparking the Battle of Hattin. It is also true that Saladin's forces crushed the Crusaders at Hattin before he marched to Jerusalem.

05 While Balain defends the city of Jerusalem as Saladin's forces approach, the reality was far different. Balain barely escaped Hattin with his life and he only went to Jerusalem to get his wife and children - and only stayed after the people begged him to.

Kingdom of Heaven

Daily Life of a Templar

Inside the routines and rituals of the Crusaders

What do you think is the biggest misconception about the Templars?
There are so many misconceptions about the Templars that I could simply say, 'Almost everything you think you know about the Templars is wrong', but that would be unfair to those who do know something about the historic Templars. To choose just one misconception, there is a misconception that Templars were burned at the stake and their organisation was dissolved because they were found guilty of heresy.

The Templars who were burned at the stake (in France) were burned because they confessed to heretical beliefs under torture, and then later went back on those confessions and declared themselves innocent. An accused heretic who confessed and then recanted their confession was regarded as having returned to their crime, so these Templars were burned at the stake. The pope did not find the Order of the Temple guilty as charged....

How similar were living conditions from one Templar estate to another?
Some Templar estates were on much better land and so were much wealthier than others. The wealthier houses had well-equipped chapels with fine altar-cloths, silk banners, silver candlesticks, lovely reliquaries containing holy relics, and beautiful service books. The poorer houses had very little equipment in their chapels and perhaps just one service book. Some houses had many farm workers, a maid in the kitchen, clerks assisting to keep records and many associate members with the right to eat in the Templars' dining hall.

Would daily life have been very close to that of a monk of this time?
Monks and Templars followed a daily routine of work and prayers set out in their regulations, their official 'Rule' approved by the Church. But monks' work was focused in the monastery, and they did not normally do physical work: typically they studied, copied books, and composed books. Their social function was to pray: they were contemplatives. They might have to go out of the monastery on the monastery's business, but their regulations expected them to live an enclosed life in the monastery. Templars (and Hospitallers, and friars) did not live enclosed lives, and their social function was to be active in the community. The Templars fought against the enemies of Christendom (on the frontiers of Christendom) or raised money for their work (everywhere else); the Hospitallers did that, and also operated hospitals; the friars preached.

However, in practice monks did not stay in their houses but went out and about in the community, and Templars who were running their estates would have to stay in their houses and work there. So in practice, they could be living similar lives.

To what degree did Templars appear to integrate themselves with the community?
They appear to have integrated closely with the local community. They were significant employers, they bought and sold produce, they operated parish churches and appointed parish priests. They also encouraged ordinary people to join their confraternity, ie become associate members. In return for a few pence a year, they would be part of the Templars' prayer community, could claim the same legal exemptions that the Templars enjoyed, and would be buried in the Templars' cemetery. In addition, in return for a larger donation, individuals and married couples could claim the Templars' support for the rest of their lives. This was a sort of pension scheme, called a corrody, but it wasn't necessary to be old to have a corrody and live at the Templars' expense for the rest of your life. Some donors also passed on this right to their children.

What happened to these communities when the Order of the Temple was dissolved?
Initially the royal officials who took over the Templars' estates and managed them kept on the employees, but they didn't pay out the corrodies. The corrodians had to appeal to the king to get their rights and anyone who had been a member of the confraternity lost their rights and was even in danger of being called into court to give evidence against the Templars. The royal estate managers set about making as much money out of the Templars' estates as they could, as quickly as they could, so they laid off most of the workers...

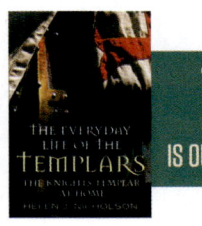

Prof Nicholson is a world-leading scholar of the history of military religious orders and the Crusades, who currently works in the school of History, Archaeology and Religion at Cardiff University. She is also a Fellow of the Royal Historical Society and a Fellow of the Learned Society of Wales.

THE EVERYDAY LIFE OF THE TEMPLARS IS OUT NOW FROM FONTHILL MEDIA

93

War

DOWNFALL

Director: Oliver Hirschbiegel **Starring:** Bruno Ganz **Country:** Germany **Year:** 2004

As the Soviets march on Berlin, the Nazi leader loses control of the war and his commanding generals, in the confines of his bunker

April, 1945: the final days of Adolf Hitler (Bruno Ganz), and the Third Reich are played out in the dingey confines of the Führerbunker, deep underground in Berlin. With the battle for the capital raging, Hitler and his generals frantically pore over increasingly alarming maps, as the Red Army closes in.

Flipping between depressed resignation, enraged outburst and delusional enthusiasm, Hitler gives orders to fantasy regiments, and shares his dreams of rebuilding a new Berlin 'after the war is won'. Witnessing this, the bunker's occupants gradually reach the grim realisation that the war is lost. While some flee, or drown their grief in liquor, some pledge to remain with Hitler until the end – among them is Traudl Junge (Alexandra Maria Lara), Hitler's typist. After the deathly endgame in the Führerbunker, we follow her journey through the desolated city.

Ganz's award-winning portrayal of an ailing, flailing Hitler was widely acclaimed, as was the screenplay, partly based on Traudl Jung's memoirs. After premiering in Germany, the movie earned multiple foreign language film awards around the world and was nominated for an Academy Award.

The film was largely shot in St Petersburg, Russia

VERDICT

HOLLYWOOD: B− Critically acclaimed, with compelling performances

HISTORY: B+ Impressive accuracy brings to light a dark but impactful story

OVERALL: B

01 Albert Speer has a brief conversation with Traudl Junge about whether she plans to stay in the bunker or escape and survive. This conversation is never mentioned in Speer's own recollections, nor by others who were in Hitler's bunker at the time.

02 SS Obergruppenführer Tellermann oversees the evacuation of Schenk's building as Operation Clausewitz begins. While it's likely a German officer was assigned that duty, Tellermann was a character was created specifically for *Downfall*.

03 SS Obersturmbannführer Stehr kills himself along with Walther Hewel after hearing the Nazis have surrendered. In reality, while Stehr did take his own life with a pistol, he actually shot himself before hearing about the surrender to the Soviets.

04 Peter is believed to be based on a composite of Hitler Youth members but mostly inspired by the story of Alfred Czech, who won the Iron Cross. A key difference between Peter and Alfred is that Czech won the Iron Cross for saving wounded soldiers.

05 *Downfall* ends with Traudl Junge leaving the bunker and narrowly evading capture by Russian soldiers thanks to the intervention of Peter. However, we know Peter doesn't exist, so what really happened? Unfortunately, the truth is Traudl was captured.

Downfall

Hitler named Admiral Karl Dönitz as his successor following his death. Dönitz subsequently became president of what remained of the Third Reich between 30 April-23 May 1945. For most of his tenure, the naval officer was based at Flensburg on the German-Danish border until he was arrested

The famous headline announcing Hitler's death for the American military newspaper The Stars And Stripes, 2 May 1945

Inside the Führerbunker

Dr Luke Daly-Groves the author and historian reveals how the leader of the Third Reich met his end among the ruins of his genocidal regime

Dr Luke Daly-Groves is an historian, author, Fellow of the Royal Historical Society and lecturer at the University of Manchester. His book *Hitler's Death: The Case Against Conspiracy* was published by Osprey Publishing in 2019.

Although the war in Europe did not officially end until 8 May 1945, the death of Adolf Hitler a week before dramatically brought about its swift conclusion. Hitler's suicide in his own specially-built bunker in Berlin made international headlines but it was almost immediately accompanied by rumours of his escape.

Luke Daly-Groves has extensively studied Hitler's last days and survival theories in his book Hitler's Death: The Case Against Conspiracy. He discusses the overwhelming evidence for the Führer's demise, Joseph Stalin's role as the first conspirator and some of the wilder claims about the tyrant's alleged whereabouts.

How did Hitler commit suicide and what then happened to his body?
Historians can't agree exactly how Hitler committed suicide. His method of death became a Cold War political issue as the Soviets insisted he took poison (which was considered a cowardly death) but Western historians were convinced he shot himself. Some argue he did both, but I find this unconvincing due to how quick cyanide acts. From the evidence I've seen, I'm certain that he shot himself. All the key eyewitnesses concur due to the blood on his corpse and on post-war photographs you can see blood splattered on his sofa. Hitler's body was doused in petrol and set on fire outside the bunker.

After the war, the Soviets found all that was left of him. They sent his jaw and teeth to Moscow. Eventually, in 1970, they incinerated the rest of his remains, scattering them in the river Ehle near Biederitz in Germany.

What happened when the Soviets entered the Führerbunker and confirmed that Hitler was dead?
The first Soviets to enter were a group of women from the medical corps who stole lingerie belonging to Hitler's wife, Eva. This set the semi-farcical tone for what happened next. When the SMERSH unit who had been ordered to find Hitler's body arrived, the corpses of Hitler and Eva were briefly exhumed and then reburied. This is because the Soviets initially mistook a poor lookalike corpse to be the Führer himself. Realising their mistake, the actual corpses were re-exhumed and sent for autopsy. They were convincingly identified by dental assistant Käthe Heusermann and dental technician Fritz Echtmann who had both worked on Hitler's teeth.

To what extent did Stalin begin conspiracy theories that Hitler had escaped?
The international explosion of Hitler survival

War

SUICIDE — WHILE OF UNSOUND MIND

HITLER'S DEATH: THE CASE AGAINST CONSPIRACY by Luke Daly-Groves is published by Osprey Publishing. To purchase a copy visit: www.ospreypublishing.com

A cartoon from October 1939 that eerily depicted Hitler committing suicide in the face of world opinion

rumours that began in the summer of 1945 can be largely blamed on Stalin. Prior to Stalin's statement in June 1945 that Hitler was still alive – and his later claim at the Potsdam conference that Hitler could have escaped to Spain or Argentina – there is little evidence of British or American intelligence organisations being swamped by such rumours. There may have been some local rumblings on the ground in Germany as the situation after such a catastrophic war was understandably confused. However, it is only after Stalin's statements that the intelligence files filled up with escape rumours. Most historians now agree that Stalin likely had political reasons to make these false claims, but modern conspiracy theorists still reproduce them as fact.

What were some of the most outlandish theories about Hitler's survival?
To me, they are all outlandish but it has become something of a sport for historians to mention the silliest ones. Some of the strangest I have read describe Hitler disguised as a monk and a woman!

A particularly daft one is that he converted to Islam in Egypt. There were several 'sightings' in America of poor people who looked a little bit like Hitler or sounded like him. In 1948, two FBI agents boarded a train near New Orleans to investigate a claim that Hitler and Eva were on board, but the two individuals looked nothing like them. What is important to note about such theories is that they all strengthen the evidence for Hitler's suicide because they were investigated and disproved by numerous intelligence organisations.

What is the scientific proof that Hitler died on 30 April 1945?
Hitler had very unique dental work due to the poor state of his teeth, which was the product of his liking for sugary treats. Consequently, two dentists who had worked on his teeth had no trouble identifying them in 1945. In the 1970s, forensic scientist Reidar Sognnaes published a detailed article comparing recently published Soviet evidence with Hitler's medical information in American archives. He convincingly confirmed that the Soviets did in fact find Hitler. In 2018, Professor Philippe Charlier published a modern forensic analysis of Hitler's teeth reconfirming, with detailed images, that they are in fact Hitler's. They even show signs of vegetarianism. The Soviets bolstered this evidence in 1946 when they tested the blood on Hitler's sofa and confirmed it was his type.

What would have happened to Hitler if he had been captured alive by the Soviets?
During my research I haven't come across any plans detailing what the Soviets would like to have done with Hitler had they captured him alive. It certainly wouldn't have been pleasant. Hitler knew and feared this. Several eyewitnesses in the bunker recall him expressing horror at the idea of being captured by the Russians and potentially displayed in a 'monkey cage' in Moscow. He implicitly refers to this in his private will, essentially a lengthy suicide note, in which he says that both him and Eva "in order to escape the disgrace of deposition or capitulation – choose death".

What is it about Hitler's final days that are so compelling for historians?
Hitler's last days represent a grim, unique moment in world history when an entire world came to an end and so much rested on the shoulders of one sick, evil man. Studying them reveals much about the Nazi regime, Hitler's world view and what all that stood for. Magda Goebbels was willing to murder her children because she did not wish them to live in a world without Nazism. It's easy to see how people with such opinions could support the Holocaust. Studying the lives of those in the bunker helps us to better understand Nazism and to help make sure it doesn't happen again. These people weren't supernatural-style monsters – they were human beings with terrible ideas, capable of love and friendship but also despicable evil. It is that which makes studying Hitler's last days so interesting. It reveals much about the evil human beings are capable of.

INSIDE THE FÜHRERBUNKER

Hitler's last hiding place was bomb-proof and blast-proof, but couldn't shield the dictator from the disaster that was overtaking his capital city

Originally built as an air-raid shelter for the Reich Chancellery, the first phase of the bunker's construction, the Vorbunker, was buried five feet under a cellar in the old Chancellery building and completed in 1936 – the year of the Berlin Summer Olympics. Once the bombing of Berlin by the Anglo-American forces became more frequent as the war progressed, the decision was made to construct a far bigger and more secure level: the Führerbunker. This would be connected to the Vorbunker by a steel blast door and a flight of stairs, but would have a concrete roof some three metres thick and would comprise of 30 rooms branching off a long corridor. Several of the rooms were for Hitler and Eva Braun's personal use, including a sitting room, a study (in which hung a large portrait of the Prussian king Frederick the Great), a bedroom for Eva Braun and another for Hitler himself. Communications with the outside world were via a telephone switchboard, a telex machine, a military radio set complete with an antenna running to the surface, and by personal messenger. Ventilation was not great and, combined with the damp, the atmosphere in the bunker was both claustrophobic and depressing. Despite its size the bunker was crowded, particularly towards the end with the arrival of Joseph and Magda Goebbels and their six children.

BRIEFING ROOM
It was from this room that Hitler and his top officials planned and submitted orders for the final few months of the war.

HITLER'S ROOM
This sparsely decorated room took furniture from the Chancellery around February as the bunker became the Führer's permanent residence.

DEATH PLACE
Hitler's study featured an oil painting of Frederick The Great. This was the room in which he and Eva Braun committed suicide shortly after being married.

TO THE GARDEN
As per his instructions, Hitler and Braun's bodies were taken via this exit into the Chancellery gardens to be burned not long after their bodies were found in his study.

HITLER'S PHYSICIAN
This was the quarter's for Hitler's personal physician, originally Ernst-Robert Grawitz, who committed suicide in April. He was replaced by Ludwig Stumpfegger.

WAITING ROOM
This was the lower level of the bunker, with an additional level of security to access. Staff would gather and wait in this area to access their superiors.

War

ENEMY AT THE GATES

Director: Jean-Jacques Annaud **Starring:** Jude Law, Ed Harris, Joseph Fiennes **Country:** USA **Year:** 2001

Is this a fair representation of one of the most pivotal battles ever?

When an actor adopts a different accent – or fails to do so – as part of their role, it can produce a truly memorable performance, either positive, or positively laughable. Perhaps topping Kevin Costner's notoriously 'American Robin Hood' is Jude Law's English dialect as Red Army sniper Vassili Zaitsev. However, if the viewer can zoom in past this potentially jarring aspect, *Enemy at the Gates* presents a perfectly passable if skewed Second World War drama.

In the dark days of the Battle of Stalingrad, Zaitsev earns fame as a deadly sharpshooter, and is promptly promoted as a hero by Commisar Danilov (Joseph Fiennes) in order to boost morale among the dispirited Soviets. However this notoriety quickly gains the attention of the Germans, who send Major Erwin König (Ed Harris) to hunt down the young soldier. The pair engage in a deadly game of cat-and-mouse, among the ruins of the city. While historians may feel a little shortchanged at one of the most significant battles of the 20th century being relegated to scene setting, there is plenty of tension and entertaining action sequences.

★ VERDICT ★

C+ HOLLYWOOD — Not wide of the target for entertainment

E+ HISTORY — Truth was the first, second and third casualty in this war

OVERALL D

The real Vasily Zaitsev was credited with 225 kills

01 The film gets off to a poor start with a map that shows Switzerland under the banner of the Third Reich despite the country being neutral throughout WWII. Hitler did have plans to invade Switzerland, but Operation Tannenbaum never came to fruition.

02 While Khrushchev is showing Zaytsev around the banquet, the Soviet national anthem can be heard playing. This is wrong, as the anthem was not first performed until January 1944 and adopted in March of that year – long after Stalingrad had ended.

03 It was popular slang in the US military, but the term 'dog tags' was not used by the Soviet troops. Therefore, when Major König is asked for his, it would not have been referred to as such. It's also debated whether König was actually a real person.

04 Zaytsev is portrayed as being far more important than he was, as duels would not have greatly changed the course of Stalingrad. The scarcity of rifles is exaggerated and it is unproven that the shortages were as bad as one weapon to every two men.

05 Even though his role in real life wasn't as great as is portrayed in the film, future leader of the Soviet Union Nikita Khrushchev did serve in the Red Army in Kiev. As well as this, superiors of his ilk were quite happy to throw men at the Germans.

Enemy at the Gates

Snipers of the Eastern Front

Meet the patient sharpshooters who delivered death from afar

LYUDMILA PAVLICHENKO

Allegiance: Soviet Union
Length of service: 1941-53 **Kills:** 309

When Germany invaded the Soviet Union, Lyudmila Pavlichenko rushed to join up. She rejected the recruiting officer's suggestion that she become a nurse and insisted that she become a sniper due to her childhood years on the shooting range.

Any hesitation that Pavlichenko might have had in taking another life evaporated when a fellow soldier was shot as he hid in her sniper's nest at the Siege of Odessa. "After that, nothing could stop me," Pavlichenko later wrote. She got the first of her kills later that day when she shot two German scouts. During the next two months Pavlichenko claimed more than 100 other victims. After Axis troops overran Odessa, she was withdrawn and sent to a second city under siege: Sevastopol.

The Germans feared the enemy they named Lady Death. Wehrmacht snipers were despatched to take her out, but Pavlichenko was successful in 36 tense duels. Some lasted for days until her opponent made a false move. Pavlichenko was pulled from the front line after being hit by shrapnel, but the Germans still wanted revenge. They broadcast messages over loudspeakers threatening to tear her into 309 pieces after they captured the city. "They even know my score!" the delighted sniper exclaimed.

Image: Wiki / PD / Gov

VASILY ZAITSEV

Allegiance: Soviet Union
Length of service: 1937-45 **Kills:** 225

When Germany invaded, Vasily Zaitsev was serving as a clerk in the Pacific Fleet on the far side of Russia. He requested a frontline posting and arrived in time for the Battle of Stalingrad. It was a move that paid off handsomely: Zaitsev killed 32 enemy soldiers with a standard-issue rifle, and his kill-count increased rapidly after he was given a sniper rifle and optical sight.

He excelled amid the burned-out buildings of Stalingrad. In two bloody months he killed 225 enemy soldiers from concealed positions. As his reputation grew, Zaitsev was given command of multiple snipers and ordered to defend several open areas. He developed a strategy in which three snipers worked together from three different positions, each supported by an observer.

Posthumous Hollywood fame came in 2001 with the release of Enemy at the Gates, a film based on a sniper duel between Zaitsev and the head of a German sniper school brought to Stalingrad to eliminate the Soviet marksman. Whether this duel actually took place is debated by historians, although Zaitsev is credited with killing 11 German snipers. A mortar attack damaged his eyesight, but the Hero of the Soviet Union recovered sufficiently to return to the front line in 1945.

Mosin-Nagant Rifle

Russian snipers used a durable weapon that was initially designed in the 19th century but was still the best weapon for marksmen on the Eastern Front

Known in the West as the 'Mosin-Nagant', Zhukova's principal weapon was the Obr. 1891/30-type infantry rifle.

By WWII, the Mosin-Nagant was an old design that had been first adopted in 1891. It was updated by the Soviets to include a telescopic sight for snipers from 1931 and gained a reputation for its simplicity and high reliability.

Other rifles, such as the Mauser Kar. 98k, would seize up in the often freezing conditions of the Eastern Front. By contrast the Mosin-Nagant would always work even in temperatures as low as -30 degrees Celsius. Snipers also benefitted from the PU telescope sight, which had higher quality lenses than the Germans whose sight adjuster drums could jam in the extreme cold.

Zhukova largely praises the Mosin-Nagant although she reveals that it was not faultless, "As soon as we learned to handle our weapons more or less tolerably, our ordinary rifles were replaced by snipers' models with the telescopic sights. We instantly appreciated the advantages of these new weapons, which would accompany us to the front. The Mosin sniper rifle was perfect for point shots at long-range single targets with a telescopic sight providing a range of up to 1,300 metres. However, the design of the optical sight meant that you could only insert one cartridge at a time. Therefore the responsibility of each sniper's shot was dramatically increased."

Biopic

100

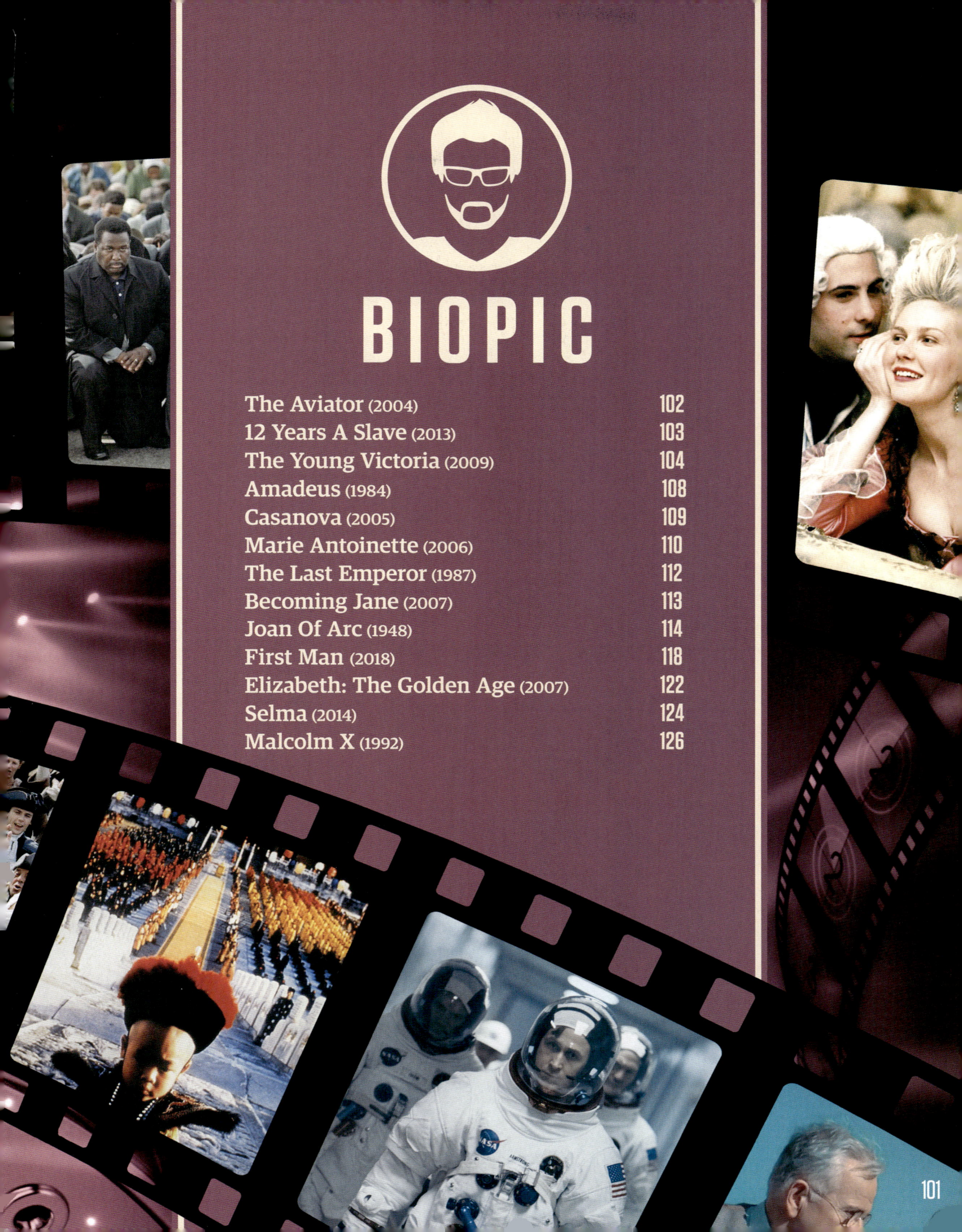

BIOPIC

The Aviator (2004)	102
12 Years A Slave (2013)	103
The Young Victoria (2009)	104
Amadeus (1984)	108
Casanova (2005)	109
Marie Antoinette (2006)	110
The Last Emperor (1987)	112
Becoming Jane (2007)	113
Joan Of Arc (1948)	114
First Man (2018)	118
Elizabeth: The Golden Age (2007)	122
Selma (2014)	124
Malcolm X (1992)	126

Biopic

THE AVIATOR

Director: Martin Scorsese **Starring:** Leonardo DiCaprio, Cate Blanchett, Kate Beckinsale **Country:** USA **Year:** 2004

This biographical epic won five Oscars, but does it fly high in terms of historical accuracy?

The eventful life and career of Howard Hughes would have been consigned to historic obscurity were it not for this 2004 Martin Scorsese production. In the titular role, Leonardo DiCaprio puts on a critically acclaimed portrayal of Hughes, in all of his many guises including filmmaker, engineer, pilot, socialite and more. The narrative recounts the highs and lows of Hughes' many aviation business ventures, film productions, as well as his daring record attempts as a pilot.

Overcoming setbacks and disasters, Hughes also has to contend with his own obsessive compulsive disorder, and extreme germ phobia, which renders him unable to function in public. Tragically, his mental health leaves him tragically isolated from the world and his grand projects end in failure.

Although only achieving moderate success at the box office, the film did receive widespread praise from critics. The film received a staggering 11 Academy Award nominations, with Cate Blanchett winning best supporting actress for her role as Katherine Hepburn, with whom the real Hughes had a fraught romantic relationship.

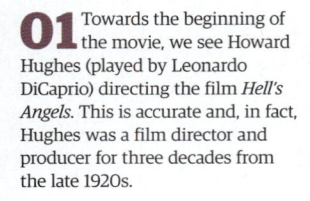

Hughes' 1930 movie Hell's Angels cost $4 million to make

VERDICT
- **A-** HOLLYWOOD — A fitting tribute to an overlooked Hollywood legend
- **C** HISTORY — Not quite the soaring triumph for the truth
- **OVERALL B**

01 Towards the beginning of the movie, we see Howard Hughes (played by Leonardo DiCaprio) directing the film *Hell's Angels*. This is accurate and, in fact, Hughes was a film director and producer for three decades from the late 1920s.

02 Hughes – an eccentric man – demands that Professor Fitz, played by Ian Holm, find him some clouds for the *Hell's Angels* movie. While the majority of the characters in the film are real people, Professor Fitz is a completely fictional character.

03 The film depicts Hughes' busy romantic life, including relationships with Katharine Hepburn (played by Cate Blanchett) and Ava Gardner (Kate Beckinsale). However, it does not show the extent of his promiscuity or the fact that he actually married twice.

04 As the name of the film would suggest, Hughes' obsession with aviation and his role as a pioneer in the field are accurately portrayed. It also depicts the crash in 1946 that almost killed him, while he was test flying the Hughes XF-11 aircraft.

05 Throughout the movie, we watch as Howard Hughes' OCD and germ phobia gets increasingly worse. Hughes really did suffer from these conditions in real life and they eventually dominated his later years as he became a recluse.

12 YEARS A SLAVE

Director: Steve McQueen **Starring:** Chiwetel Ejiofor, Michael Fassbender, Lupita Nyong'o **Country:** USA **Year:** 2013

A case of fact being horrific enough without the need for fiction

When Solomon Northup (Chiwetel Ejiofor), a freeborn African-American, is kidnapped into slavery, he undergoes years of hard labour and suffering under a number of plantation owners and enslavers. Sold under the slave name Platt, Northup spends years on the property of the sadistic Edwin Epps (Michael Fassbender). After he encounters Samuel Bass (Brad Pitt), a white labourer, he persuades him to secretly send a letter to his friends in New York, who eventually have him freed.

The real Northup was liberated from the Epps estate in 1853 and in the same year he released his memoir, *12 Years A Slave*, on which this 2013 film is based. In it, Northup recounts his horrific experiences, as well as the barbarity he witnessed inflicted upon the plantation slaves. He later joined the growing abolitionist movement, giving lectures on his experiences, and there is suggestion he assisted the Underground Railroad, helping freed slaves escape into Canada. At the Academy Awards the film was named best picture, while Lupita Nyong'o was awarded for her debut supporting role as Patsey.

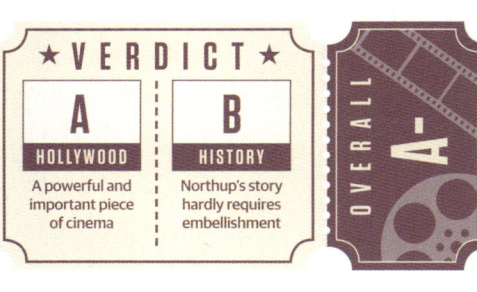

After his freedom, Solomon Northup mysteriously disappeared in 1857

VERDICT
A HOLLYWOOD — A powerful and important piece of cinema
B HISTORY — Northup's story hardly requires embellishment
OVERALL A-

01 Solomon Northup (Ejiofor) is a free man and violinist who is drugged by gentlemen named Brown and Hamilton while having a drink with them in Washington DC. Northup wasn't certain about being poisoned until a witness was able to corroborate his story years later.

02 Northup's first master is William Ford (Benedict Cumberbatch). Northup actually found Ford to be a much more empathetic figure than the film does, calling him kind and noble. However, he was brutalised by a carpenter named John Tibeats.

03 Northup is sold to Edwin Epps (Fassbender), a brutal and sadistic plantation owner, who is introduced reading a passage from the Bible. In Northup's book, it was Ford's brother-in-law, Peter Tanner, who did this. However, Epps' violent actions are accurate.

04 Enslaved woman Patsey (Nyong'o) is whipped by Epps at the encouragement of his wife, who is jealous of his attention towards her. Patsey then asks Northup to kill her. The whipping is accurate to the book, but there is no mention of a plea for death.

05 Brad Pitt appears as an abolitionist named Samuel Bass who challenges Epps' views on slavery. As a producer on the film, one might imagine Bass was an invention, but actually he was real and his speech is taken directly from Northup's recollection of events.

Biopic

THE YOUNG VICTORIA

Director: Jean-Marc Vallée **Starring:** Emily Blunt, Rupert Friend, Paul Bettany **Country:** UK, USA **Year:** 2009

Would Queen Victoria proclaim herself amused by this award-winning depiction of her early life?

The ultimate royal 'coming of age' tale of history's most famous monarch sees Emily Blunt at her very best as Queen Victoria. Even before ascending the throne, Princess Victoria finds herself the subject of a bitter power struggle, with her domineering mother Duchess of Kent (Miranda Richardson) and Sir John Conroy (Mark Strong) attempting to secure power as regents. While her cousin Prince Albert (Rupert Friend) also attempts to win Victoria's favour - as well as her heart - the princess finds a confidant in the Lord Melbourne (Paul Bettany), who counsels the young royal.

Plenty of period drama frills and court intrigue make up for some of the historical faux pas in this biopic, which gives insight into a lesser known side of the sovereign, who later in life gained the reputation of an austere and reclusive widow. The work of renowned designer Sandy Powell was deservedly crowned with an Academy Award for costume design, with the film also receiving nominations for makeup and art direction. Blunt's portrayal of the young, rebellious queen received resounding praise and several award nominations.

★ VERDICT ★
B HOLLYWOOD — Flush with regal setpieces and palace drama
D HISTORY — Certainly not a crowning triumph for facts
OVERALL C

Emily Blunt had access to the queen's private diaries in preparation for the role

01 Lord Melbourne, portrayed by Paul Bettany, appears to be a similar age to Victoria, but the real Melbourne was 38 years older than her. The flirtation between them is also an exaggeration, as Victoria is known to have compared Melbourne to a father figure.

02 The portrait Albert is given of Victoria before he meets her features an image of the young queen in a white dress with a tiara. In fact, the portrait referenced was not commissioned until 1842, and Albert himself designed the tiara placed in her bun.

03 The backs of the women's dresses show the thin seam line of a zipper. The first zipper wasn't patented until 1851. Victoria married Albert in 1840 so there's no way her dresses or those of any other ladies of that period would feature zippers.

04 A sequence shows a bloodied and injured Albert carried to the palace after being shot in an assassination attempt. There were many attempts to kill Victoria and Albert, but they were unsuccessful and both emerged uninjured from all of them.

05 Many characters mention and speak to Albert about Germany, but Germany was not a unified country until 1871 - long after he met Victoria in 1836. Albert lived in and was Prince of Saxe-Coburg and Gotha, which is how it would have been referred to.

The Young Victoria

Victoria and Albert would go on to have nine children

The Rise of Victoria

Celebrated today as one of Britain's most beloved monarchs, Victoria overcame schemes, scandal and her own emotions to secure her place as the nation's queen

When Victoria was born, the monarchy was in the midst of a mild ascension crisis. George III had plenty of children, 15 to be exact, but the untimely death of his heir, George IV's only child, the beloved Princess Charlotte, had left the future of the monarchy in some disarray. There were three older sons in line before Victoria's father, Edward, duke of Kent, but all bar one were aging rapidly and had no legitimate surviving heirs. Upon her birth, Victoria became fifth in line for the throne, and the first in line of the next generation.

The prince regent loathed his brother Edward so much that he found the thought of a child of his inheriting the throne utterly detestable. Although he agreed on the surface, standing in as godfather at her christening, he used his power to forbid any pomp or ceremony and also made a blacklist of 'unacceptable' names for the newborn – all of which happened to be used by the royal family. When the archbishop enquired what name she could be given, the regent reportedly retorted, "Alexandrina." This instance at the young child's christening, and her very name itself, began a tradition that Victoria would have to endure for many years: being pushed and led by men who wished to control her life. The prince wanted this child to garner no attention, he wanted her quietly and invisibly tucked away in a manor house until she could marry a foreign prince, and for a while, he would have his way.

Victoria's father adored his daughter, and to the chagrin of his brother was quick to show her off at any fitting occasion. Unfortunately Edward died just eight months after her birth, leaving her with her mother, the Duchess of Kent, and excessive debt. With Victoria only third in line to the throne, the displaced mother and daughter were offered just a suite of rooms in the dilapidated Kensington Palace to live in. The duchess had a choice – return to her native Coburg with assured income from her first marriage, or take a chance on Victoria's possible ascension. However uncertain it may have been, she chose the latter. From the beginning, the duchess believed her child was fated for greatness. She was still young, beautiful and full of life, but she put all that aside and settled for a life of quiet retirement and devotion to her daughter.

The duchess was encouraged in no small part by her constant companion – John Conroy. He had served as Victoria's father's equerry, and after

Biopic

Edward's death became a close confidant and adviser to her mother. Conroy was a soldier who had attracted disdain through his skill to expertly dodge any actual battles. Although Conroy had been set up with a marriage designed to raise his position in society, he judged this inadequate and viewed Edward and his family as his ticket to power.

Victoria's father was likely wary of him, as he refused, despite much begging, to name Conroy his daughter's legal guardian upon his death. Although he was unsuccessful in obtaining guardianship of the young royal, his power over her mother meant that he was able to exert his will upon Victoria. Together they created an immensely strict set of rules known as the Kensington System that Victoria was expected to obey every day. Conroy was aware of the duchess's unpopular reputation, and worked hard to paint her as a doting, caring mother while whispering warnings in her ear about members of the royal family, fuelling her paranoia.

Though she was a bright, affable girl, Victoria's childhood was constrained and melancholy. Secretly Conroy would bully the young girl, insulting and mocking her at any opportunity, and his power over her mother prevented her from socialising with other children. The duchess likely didn't mean any ill will towards her daughter, but at a very young age she had lost the man she adored. As a lonely, fragile soul, she quickly fell for the whims of an ambitious man who wanted to use her for his own ends, and it seems she was reluctant to believe the truth. Either way, the situation meant that every aspect of Victoria's life was controlled and, though in line to the throne, all power was taken from her.

The young Victoria had accepted her fate, but as she matured, her will began to harden. She was lively, effervescent, and growing acutely aware of her position in society and the duty that may one day fall upon her. When Victoria was 13, Conroy arranged for her to take a tour of the midlands in order to show her off to the public. King William IV, Victoria's uncle, disliked the trips, stating they portrayed the young girl as his rival rather than his heir, and Victoria shared his opinion.

She complained that the constant appearances were exhausting and she quickly fell ill. Conroy dismissed this illness, but when Victoria contracted a fever, he was quick to try and take advantage of her weakened state by pressing his candidacy as her personal secretary. However, Victoria, after years of control by a cruel man, told him no. From this day on the princess grew more stubborn, though she did not portray it outwardly, and remained the vision of a perfect Georgian lady. In private, she poured her frustrations into journals and waited for the day she could finally take control of her own life.

Although the duchess had fallen for them, Conroy's schemes didn't fool everyone. At what would be his final birthday banquet in 1836, William IV proclaimed to all - Victoria and her mother included - that he would live at least nine months longer in order to see his beloved niece on the throne, preventing her mother acting as regent and describing her as "surrounded by evil advisers". Victoria was so shocked she burst into tears. Nine months later, as promised, he was dead. Victoria had turned 18 just weeks before. Unfortunately for Conroy, the old man's sheer will had won out.

On the very morning of William's death, Victoria, wearing only a dressing gown, was informed she was queen. Her first request as monarch was for something that she had never before experienced - an hour alone. At 9am that morning, she received Lord Melbourne, the prime minster, "quite alone" in her room, where he kissed her hand repeatedly and spoke with her at length. Later that day at 9pm, she saw him again, writing, "I had a very important and a very comfortable conversation with him." Conroy had spent 18 years trying to control Victoria with manipulation and savagery; Melbourne, however, had won her heart with kind words and charm in under an hour.

Conroy had placed his bets on a malleable figure, but in Victoria he had looked in the wrong place. Upon moving to Buckingham Palace, Victoria did everything in her power to keep Conroy and her mother far away from her, denying the ambitious servant of the power and place in her court he so desired. When her mother

Victoria was named Alexandrina after one of her godfathers, Emperor Alexander I of Russia

"As a lonely, fragile soul, she quickly fell for the whims of an ambitious man who wanted to use her for his own ends"

The Young Victoria

This sketch of Victoria is dated to 1837, the year of her ascension to the throne aged just 18

Queen Victoria's wedding cake reportedly weighed 300 pounds

objected, Victoria responded, "I thought you would not expect me to invite Sir John Conroy after his conduct towards me for some years past." It's easy to see why Conroy may have thought her a soft touch - she was a tiny, plain girl, somewhat shy and wholly inexperienced - but beneath her mild exterior she harboured a will of fire, and for the first time Victoria made it clear that she was not to be pushed any longer. Conroy was expelled from the queen's household.

Victoria was the first monarch to live in Buckingham Palace and, far from the splendour we associate with the building today, it was in a terrible state of disrepair. The lavatories were not well ventilated and hundreds of the windows were impossible to open. Just a teenager, Victoria was alone in a new place without the two people, however much she despised them, who had been the strongest influences on her life thus far, and to top it off, faced the most monumental role any individual could play. It is likely that this fear encouraged Victoria to attach herself so fiercely to her most beloved companion, Melbourne.

She wasn't used to kindness, especially not from men, and Melbourne was not only considerate but he flattered her - he assured her that all her insecurities - her size, inexperience and shyness - were advantages. He treated the young woman with a tenderness she had seldom felt, spending hours every night writing to her, and for this she admired and loved him greatly. When Victoria held her first privy council, hours after being told she was now queen, she was an 18-year-old surrounded by the most influential and experienced men in British politics. Even if she did later proclaim herself "not at all nervous", she must have felt comfort in the assurance that, from now on, she could steady herself on Melbourne's arm.

The two quickly grew inseparable. Melbourne, 40 years her senior, was a childless widow, and it is likely he saw Victoria as a kind of surrogate daughter. As the diarist Charles Greville wrote, he was "...passionately fond of her." What this relationship meant to Victoria, however, is up for debate. It is of no doubt she lacked a father figure in her life, and she herself proclaimed to have loved him "like a father," but it's possible the young woman's feelings were complex. She was new to the realm of romance and, as demonstrated in her later life, easily wooed by charismatic men.

Greville too suggested that the young queen's feelings may have been romantic, "...though she did not know it." Victoria was, after all, incredibly professional and dictated by her duties. Even if she did feel some attraction to her witty, adoring minister, it is unlikely she would have acted upon it.

A year after she ascended the throne, Victoria was officially crowned at Westminster Abbey, attracting unprecedented crowds. For the people watching, there was much at stake - the monarchy had fallen out of favour thanks to the excessive extravagance and general unpopularity of her uncles, and in a way, a youthful woman with silent professionalism was a breath of fresh air. At one point in the ceremony, the 82-year-old Lord Rolle fell down the steps and Victoria immediately advanced towards him to prevent him hurting himself further. This simple act of kindness caused a sensation in the public who had never witnessed such naiveté and good-naturedness in their monarch before. Victoria wasn't excessive, she was a tiny, dignified lady with a strong presence and the public instantly adored her. Melbourne adored her too; he stood by her side for the entire ceremony.

Biopic

AMADEUS

Director: Milos Forman **Starring:** F Murray Abraham, Tom Hulce, Elizabeth Berridge **Country:** USA **Year:** 1984

An exuberant celebration of genius, but not necessarily of historical fact

From Czech director Miloš Forman, this multi-award winning biopic of Wolfgang Amadeus Mozart told from the perspective of creative rival Antonio Salieri is a rightly celebrated work. Forman came to this picture with a strong background in mixing comedy and tragedy in movies like One Flew Over the Cuckoo's Nest (1975) and in musical films, like Hair (1979). He made a number of bold choices in the production of this film too, such as using a largely American cast and allowing them to speak in their native accents, emphasising performance over accuracy.

In some ways that speaks to the movie as a whole. Salieri claims to have been responsible for Mozart's death while also being captivated and in awe of his genius. There is no proof of any such rivalry between them, but it plays well in the film. Performances feel like rock concerts and Hulce's Mozart sometimes seems possessed by his music, making it a compelling watch. Critics and audiences seemed to agree as it made $90 million on an $18 million budget and picked up eight oscars including Best Picture, Best Director, Best Actor (Abraham) and Best Screenplay.

The Don Giovanni scene was filmed on the stage where the opera made its debut in 1787

VERDICT

A- HOLLYWOOD — An energetic and engrossing celebration of genius and creativity

D HISTORY — Plays pretty fast and loose with the historical facts

OVERALL: B-

01 In the film, Italian composer Antonio Salieri (Abraham) confesses to the murder of Wolfgang Amadeus Mozart (Hulce). This idea originated from a play by Alexander Pushkin that made the accusation five years after Salieri died, but there is no evidence it's true.

02 Mozart is depicted as childish, foul-mouthed and crude with an annoying laugh. This might be true. Based on his letters to family and friends, he often expressed a crude sense of humour and others wrote his laugh was frequently loud and aggravating.

03 We see a child Mozart being taken around the powerful courts and palaces of Europe as a prodigy by his father. This really happened, although the ages Salieri gives are a little off. He had him writing a concerto aged four, but it was more likely aged 11.

04 The film claims Salieri made a vow of chastity as a bargain with God for his talent. In reality, he was married with several children. He was also much more successful as a composer and teacher than the film suggests, with Beethoven being one of his students.

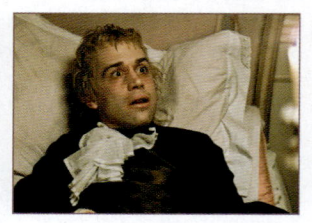

05 A dying Mozart is commissioned to write a requiem by a masked stranger. The anonymous commission is real, but it was from Count Franz von Walsegg, not a disguised Salieri, and it was finished by Mozart's student Franz Xaver Süssmayr.

CASANOVA

Director: Lasse Hallström **Starring:** Heath Ledger, Sienna Miller, Jeremy Irons **Country:** USA **Year:** 2005

Did this retelling of the legendary lover's life woo the history critics?

One of history's most famous figures, Giacomo Casanova's endeavours, including as a soldier, scholar, adventurer, musician, gambler, have been overshadowed by his numerous self-reported romantic liaisons. The latter reputation is perhaps inevitably at the heart of this 2005 Hollywood retelling, starring Heath Ledger as the Venetian lothario.

Leading a rakish, libertine lifestyle, Casanova is forced to either marry or be exiled from the city. Though he does become engaged to Victoria (Natalie Dormer) his eye wanders a fellow free spirit, Francesca (Sienna Miller), who is secretly the author of feminist fiction. Several further love triangles, disguises and conspiracies converge into a veritable maze of subplots, leaving Casanova and Francesca on the point of execution, accused of heresy.

This 21st century attempt to recount the complex life of the real Casanova is far less effective than the 1976 production starring Donald Sutherland in the lead. The box office agreed – a flop worldwide and lukewarm reception from critics hardly living up to the mythological much less the real Casanova.

★ VERDICT ★
D+ HOLLYWOOD — Some fine actors try their best to inject a little passion
E HISTORY — Not a lot here for history lovers
OVERALL: D-

Some plot points are lifted from Shakespeare's Merchant of Venice

01 An elderly Casanova says in a voiceover: "10,000 pages [...] about one woman for every page." But Casanova's real memoirs were a mere 3,800 pages long and featured liaisons with 136 women, hardly the 10,000 his film equivalent claims to have bedded.

02 Although the real Casanova did write about his encounters with a nun, the chase that ensues with the Inquisition in the film is not accurate. The real Inquisition disapproved of Casanova more for his beliefs about astrology and Kabbalah than his sex life.

03 As Casanova races through Venice he hides in a university auditorium where he spies his one true love, Francesca Bruni. This building is the Teatro Olimpico, which is not in Venice at all, but in Vicenza, 74km (45mi) away from the city.

04 The film paints Casanova as smitten by feminist writer Francesca Bruni, likely inspired by a single line in his memoirs. This line was most likely added by his editor Jean Laforgue who modernised his original text and added lines favourable to the French Revolution.

05 When Casanova and Francesca take to the skies of Venice in a hot-air balloon, it would have been 30 years prior to the first real flight. The Montgolfier brothers, Joseph-Michel and Jacques-Étienne, manned the first flight of a hot-air balloon in 1783.

Biopic

MARIE ANTOINETTE

Director: Sofia Coppola **Starring:** Kirsten Dunst, Jason Schwartzman, Rip Torn **Country:** USA **Year:** 2006

Is this film a revolutionary new look at the life of the French queen?

The film was shot on location at the Palace of Versailles

There are few monarchs as controversial as Marie Antoinette. She was certainly not remembered kindly by the French Revolutionaries as a representative of a decadent, self-serving and uncaring regime and their image of her was the one that dominated for many years. However, more recent reevaluations of the monarch have cast her in a different light and it's here that director Sofia Coppola stepped in.

Working with longtime collaborator Kirsten Dunst as the titular queen, Marie Antoinette paints a picture of a young woman way out of her depth and isolated from the comforts of her upbringing, in line with the assessment of some experts. The movie deliberately veers into the anachronistic, however, with pop and punk music blowing away any of the historical cobwebs. It's a very modern take, which is an approach that has seen many imitators in films that followed.

It didn't go down very well at the Cannes Film Festival, however, with some French critics allegedly booing the film following a screening. It performed well when released, however, around $61 million on a $40 million budget.

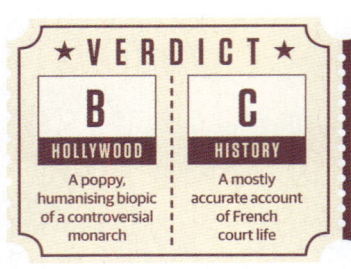

★ VERDICT ★
B HOLLYWOOD — A poppy, humanising biopic of a controversial monarch
C HISTORY — A mostly accurate account of French court life
OVERALL B-

01 Marie and Louis are depicted as having three children, as seen in the painting. Their youngest daughter did die as insinuated by the changing picture. But they actually had four children, and in the original painting Louis-Charles was on Marie's lap.

02 Treating Marie and Fersen's affair as fact in the film is not necessarily a sin, as historians argue about this. Fersen remained a very key part of the queen's life. In the movie he disappears after going to war and is only glimpsed in the queen's daydreams.

03 We can only assume that Louis and Marie's bedroom rendezvous were as awkward as the movie depicts, the evidence being the lack of an heir for seven years. But they almost certainly did not share a bedchamber, as is witnessed frequently in the film.

04 The depiction of the queen is a little off the mark. Yes, she was a foreign princess thrust into French court life, but she was a quick learner and a determined woman. The film's depiction of a naïve girl is more inspired by the stories in the libelles than fact.

05 The scene where Marie is 'delivered' to the French and stripped of every piece of clothing then redressed in the French style is accurate. This was common for any noble that wished to ingratiate themselves into French life, and was expected of a dauphine of France.

Marie Antoinette

GOOD DEEDS
The kind acts that the libelles tried to hide

HOUSING THE HOMELESS
The construction of Hameau de la Reine was criticised as the queen playing at being a peasant, but she allowed several peasant families to live at the site, building cottages for them.

THE BELOVED COUPLE
When Marie and Louis were married in 1774, people were killed in a stampede during the firework display. The newlyweds donated all their private spending money for a year to the suffering victims.

A SYMPATHETIC QUEEN
Marie never said "let them eat cake," in response to bread shortages. When hearing about the famine she replied: "We are more obliged than ever to work hard for their happiness."

CHARITABLE MONARCH
The king and queen both supported a number of charities. Marie was patron of a society that helped the elderly, blind and widowed. She also started a home for unwed mothers.

SACRIFICE FOR THE NATION
During the famine of 1787-88, Marie's family sold a lot of their flatware to buy grain for the poor. Also, every Sunday Marie took a collection from the rich courtiers living at Versailles.

A QUEEN'S FAVOURITE THINGS
The extravagant purchases that drove a nation to loathing

WARDROBE
258,000 LIVRES A YEAR

Officially, Marie had a fixed allowance of 120,000 livres for clothes and accessories. However, she often exceeded this quite considerably. Although she was supposed to restrict her orders to 36 dresses for summer and another 36 for winter, for the fashionable queen this simply wasn't enough. Combined with the 18 pairs of gloves and four pairs of shoes ordered for her on a weekly basis, Marie's wardrobe filled three separate rooms at Versailles.

HAMEAU DE LA REINE
500,000+ LIVRES

Marie, constantly surrounded by the rigid structure and responsibility of court life, ordered the construction of this hamlet as a place of escape. Hameau de la Reine was a working farm designed in rustic, pastoral style. There, Marie, her children and friends would dress up as simple peasants, milk the cows and sheep and enjoy the simplicity of the fantasy retreat, while outside the starving and struggles of real French peasants continued.

CHÂTEAU DE SAINT-CLOUD
6-10 MILLION LIVRES

After falling pregnant again in 1784, Marie convinced the king to purchase this extravagant palace for her on the premise that the air of the commune would be beneficial to her children. As well as the substantial 6 million livres price tag, Marie poured money into redecorating and rebuilding parts of the building and gardens. The French people were shocked, not only at the irresponsible spending but also at the prospect of a queen independently owning her own residence.

Expert Opinion

Historian and author Melanie Clegg discusses whether the queen was wrongly blamed for France's misfortunes

Melanie Clegg is the author of a number of historical novels and is also a regular magazine contributor and her own women's history blog Madame Guillotine. Her first biography, *Marie Antoinette: An Intimate History* was published in 2015 and her second biography, *Scourge of Henry VIII: The Life of Marie de Guise*, was released the following year.

Was Marie really to blame for the French Revolution, or was she simply a scapegoat?
Although the image of the flaunting, extravagant queen causing the French Revolution with her careless profligacy is a potent one, the fact is that the revolution was ultimately the result of centuries of fiscal and social inequality. A series of poor harvests and the ruinously expensive involvement in the American Revolution acted as the catalyst in 1789. Marie Antoinette, the unpopular foreign queen who was commonly believed to be the power behind the throne, while at the same time in league with the Austrians, was a convenient scapegoat for all – for the aristocracy, who had no wish to lose their privileges; the middle classes, who resented the power and privilege of the upper classes; and the lower orders, who believed the scurrilous lies and exaggerations being spread by disaffected members of the aristocracy and even the royal family about the queen's personal life and spending habits.

Biopic

THE LAST EMPEROR

Director: Bernardo Bertolucci **Starring:** John Lone, Joan Chen, Peter O'Toole **Country:** USA, Italy **Year:** 1987

This lavish historical epic won every Academy Award it was nominated for, but does it win any points for accuracy?

The life of Aisin Gioro Puyi, emperor of China, coincided with one of the most turbulent periods in his country's history. Ascending the Dragon Throne at the young age of three, Puyi grows up in the splendour of the Forbidden City, with only eunuchs and courtiers for company. The young emperor is swept along with the rapid changes in China, which after the 1911 revolution cast off its ruling Qing dynasty in favour of a republic.

As he comes of age Puyi (John Lone), embraces his Western education, and eventually is able to leave the imperial palace. From the devastating wars with Japan, to the civil war and the Communist Cultural Revolution, Puyi is reduced to being a mere witness to the violent transformation of the nation he once ruled. While narrating several decades can never entirely cover the full timeline, and much is left out of what is still a lengthy run time, director Bernardo Bertolucci's epic is a monumental achievement in historical storytelling. The result was recognised with a staggering nine Academy Awards including for best picture and best director.

★ VERDICT ★
A HOLLYWOOD — Some visually stunning scenes and epic storytelling
B HISTORY — A fairly balanced portrayal of Puyi's fascinating life
OVERALL A-

Filming was permitted on location inside the Forbidden City

01 Near the beginning of the film, Puyi attempts to commit suicide after he is taken as a political prisoner by the People's Republic of China. While Puyi was a prisoner, he never attempted to kill himself and so this particular scene is fictional.

02 The film accurately depicts Empress Dowager Cixi choosing young Puyi to succeed her on the Dragon Throne, taking him away from his biological mother. The decision was made on her deathbed after her nephew, the Guangxu Emperor, died the day before her.

03 Puyi's Scottish tutor Reginald Johnston, played by Peter O' Toole, really did exist. It is also accurate that Puyi planned to escape the Forbidden City and go to Oxford University, where Johnston had studied, only to be stopped by his tutor.

04 The emperor did have two wives, Empress Wanrong and his concubine, Wenxiu. After he was expelled from the Forbidden City, Puyi moved with his wives to Tianjin, where Wanrong descended into opium addiction and Wenxiu filed for divorce.

05 Following his release from prison, Puyi found work as a gardener, which is correctly portrayed in the film. It also depicts the former emperor visiting the Forbidden City as a tourist, something that Puyi was known to have done.

BECOMING JANE

Director: Julian Jarrold **Starring:** Anne Hathaway, James McAvoy, Julie Walters, James Cromwell, Maggie Smith **Country:** UK **Year:** 2007

Did Jane Austen really plan to elope, or is Becoming Jane more historical fiction than hard fact?

Centuries before *Bridgerton*, Jane Austen was enthralling readers with her stories, delving into the romance and intrigue of 18th century high society. However, this 2007 period drama turns the focus on the author herself before she first lifted her quill, and her experience navigating the tricky world of 'matchmaking'. A young writer with aspirations of marrying for love, Jane (Anne Hathaway) parries the advances and proposals of several suitors, before falling in love with a young roguish lawyer, Thomas Lefroy (James McAvoy). However fate, circumstance, social standing and sensibilities all conspire to prise the pair apart, when their proposal for marriage is rejected, leaving Jane heartbroken.

Off the back of the hugely successful *Pride and Prejudice* (2005), this retelling of Austen's early life certainly piles on more fiction, but nonetheless serves as a reminder of women's lack of power and autonomy during this period. Behind the titillating society gossip and scandal in this story is a meaningful social commentary on the world in which Austen lived, as well as a window onto her own tragic tale of love and loss.

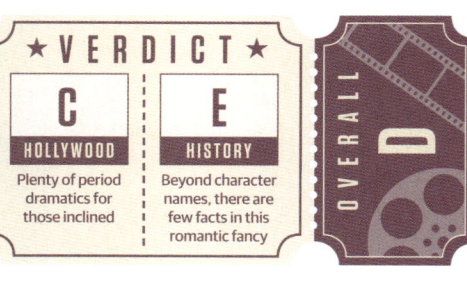

Anne Hathaway read all of Jane Austen's books in preparation for the role

★ VERDICT ★
- **C HOLLYWOOD** — Plenty of period dramatics for those inclined
- **E HISTORY** — Beyond character names, there are few facts in this romantic fancy
- **OVERALL: D**

01 Jane Austen and Thomas Lefroy did meet at Christmas in 1795. Taking a break from his legal studies, the young Irishman and the budding author danced together at three balls. Jane wrote to her sister to let her know how much she enjoyed their encounters.

02 There was no sensitive, awkward Mr Wisley in real life. Although Jane did receive and reject a proposal from a gentleman named Harris Bigg-Wither, Mr Wisley is a figment of the filmmaker's imagination, so Jane couldn't have accepted his proposal.

03 Although the image of Jane and Tom bound for Gretna Green is a romantic one, and her rejection of him borne out of principle, it's also entirely fictional. The couple never planned to elope together, and they certainly didn't flee to the border.

04 Jane never met her namesake, Tom's eldest daughter, and she certainly didn't read aloud to her amid a crowd of adoring fans. Not only that, but Jane Lefroy wasn't named after Jane Austen, but in honour of her maternal grandmother, Jane Paul.

05 Tom and Jane didn't meet in middle age and, unlike the film, no poignant looks were exchanged during a reading of *Pride And Prejudice*. In fact, once Tom left Hampshire in 1796, no evidence exists to suggest that the couple ever saw one another again.

Biopic

JOAN OF ARC

Director: Victor Fleming **Starring:** Ingrid Bergman, José Ferrer, George Coulouris **Country:** USA **Year:** 1948

An historical epic from Hollywood's golden age that's surprisingly accurate

Ingrid Bergman stars in the title role of this Golden Age homage to France's patron saint. Set during the Hundred Years War, with England dominating a weakened French throne, a young peasant girl begins hearing voices, claiming that she is sent by God to set her country free.

With the aid of the Dauphin Charles (José Ferrer) - heir to the French crown - Joan rallies an army and marches to Orléans, which is under siege by an English army. Equipped with her own battle standard and bespoke armour, she inspires the French to victory. However, when she is betrayed by the duplicitous Dauphin and captured by the enemy, Joan is put on trial, found guilty of heresy and executed.

Despite being a little old to play a teenager - Joan is supposed to be around 14 when the film is set - Bergman had campaigned studios and producers for years to get the film made. Though the film was nominated for a staggering seven Academy Awards, winning two, it failed to inspire audiences at the box office.

★ VERDICT ★

C+ HOLLYWOOD — Academy Awards aside, a production of its time that shows its age

B+ HISTORY — Accurate armour to please the Medievalist pedant

OVERALL B

Bergman's costume armour was made of aluminium and weighed 20lbs (9kg)

01 Ingrid Bergman was in her early 30s when she played the role of the teenage Joan of Arc. The actress also retained her Swedish accent, however growing up on the German border Joan may well have had a Germanic accent similar to Swedish.

02 The early peasant costumes of the women in the film are more 17th than 15th century, however all the armour was designed by the Metropolitan Museum of Art to guarantee its authenticity. Apparently this was at Bergman's own request.

03 Before breaking the siege of Orleans, Joan gives an impassioned speech for the English to surrender and spare themselves from battle. Much of what she says in this scene is lifted directly from the many letters Joan sent making such requests.

04 Joan goes into battle carrying her standard rather than a weapon and later inspires her troops by charging at the enemy again despite being pierced by an arrow. This is all chronicled extensively in histories and appears to be accurate.

05 In her trial, Joan confesses to save her life, but she later backtracks after promises of improved conditions are not fulfilled, such as being allowed to attend mass. She is condemned as a relapsed heretic, which trial records confirm.

Joan of Arc

Joan was not pursuing peace but rather the defeat of her enemies, which included the Burgundians, who had allied themselves with the English

Dr Helen Castor on the True Joan of Arc

The historian and author delves into the misconceptions behind the Maid of Orléans and the challenges she faced

Dr Castor is an historian of the Medieval period, and has published several books including biography *Joan of Arc: A History*. Her 2010 book *She-Wolves: The Women Who Ruled England Before Elizabeth* was made into a BBC documentary series.

What was it about Joan of Arc's story that drew you into writing about her?
I started thinking about Joan as a direct result of talking about my previous book, *She-Wolves*. 'One of the biggest problems female rulers faced,' I kept saying, 'was that medieval women couldn't lead armies on the battlefield – apart from Joan of Arc, and we all know what happened to her.' Eventually I realised I didn't know what happened to her. Or at least, I knew the outline of her story, as we all do – but I didn't know exactly how and why she came to do the extraordinary things she did. Once I started investigating, I was fascinated.

What would you say are the biggest misconceptions about her life?
That she was 'saintly' in the sense of wanting peace and reconciliation. She didn't: she wanted victory and her enemies' submission. That the cause for which she fought was straightforwardly nationalist resistance to foreign invasion. It wasn't: the conflict was a civil war within France, in which Joan fought for the Armagnacs against not only the English but the Burgundians – the 'false French', in her eyes – who had allied themselves with the invaders. And that she never faltered in her faith in her mission. In the end she faced an appalling death with profound courage, but the last week of her life was filled with fear and doubt.

How did you approach the idea of her hearing voices?
As I did everything else in the story. I was trying to stand in the shoes and see through the eyes of the people who were there – all of which meant starting from their assumption that God and the devil were at work in the world, so that the idea of someone hearing the voices of angels, saints or demons was entirely plausible. For contemporaries listening to her story it remained feasible that Joan was lying, ill or mad, but it was equally likely that she had truly encountered otherworldly beings – in which case the key question was not whether or not the voices existed, but whether they came from heaven or hell. And that framework of faith also helps to explain why Joan – who believed in the reality of her mission, and wasn't otherwise physically sick or intellectually incoherent – interpreted her experiences, whatever they were, in the way that she did.

Are there any particular elements from your research of Joan that really helped to flesh her out as a person for you?
Like everyone else who has worked on it, I think, I found myself endlessly absorbed by the transcript of her trial for heresy in 1431, at which she was the only witness. It's a complex and multilayered document, and Joan's voice is heavily mediated through the process of translation and transcription – but all the same it's unmistakably hers. I see new things in the text every time I look.

Do you have a sense of when the myth-building around Joan's story began?
Immediately. You could argue that Joan started it when she called herself La Pucelle, 'the Maid' – a name that put the unlikely facts of her youth and her sex at the centre of her claim to a unique relationship with God. It was well under way 25 years after her death, when witnesses from both sides of the previous divide in France gave evidence at the hearings held to overturn her conviction for heresy. Of the men who had been with her at Orléans, two remembered a 'miracle' that had allowed her to enter the besieged town: one said the wind had suddenly changed to allow her boat to cross the Loire; the other, that the river had been too low until Joan arrived, and then the waters rose. Of those who'd taken part in her trial and been present at her death, many now claimed to have wept; two said they'd rushed to fetch a crucifix to hold before her eyes as she died; one, that a white dove had fluttered from the flames as she took her last breath, and that her heart wouldn't burn, no matter what the executioner

115

Biopic

Yolande of Aragon, duchess of Aragon and the mother-in-law of the Dauphin, was a powerful woman who likely influenced the decision to recognise Joan's claims

did. These days, the myth is so vast that she's almost become all things to all people.

To what degree did the circumstances of the time create a perfect storm for Joan to make her entrance and be heard by the Dauphin?
A perfect storm is a good way of putting it. Contemporaries believed that God's hand lay behind everything that happened in the world – but, at the same time, that direct intervention from heaven was likely only when all human help had been completely exhausted. By late February 1429, after many years of war and with little hope of stemming the Anglo-Burgundian tide, the Dauphin – who'd always been looking for someone else to lead his armies, because he clearly couldn't do it himself – must have felt he'd reached that point. And, if God were going to work a miracle, a teenage peasant girl might be a particularly miraculous way to do it.

Was there anything particularly unique about her message in an era when messengers from God would have been generally more accepted?
Joan wasn't the first or last person in medieval Europe – not even in 15th-century France – to claim they brought a message from God. But most messengers did just that: brought messages, about what God wanted kings and popes to do. Joan was

> **"Her certainty and clarity of purpose were just what was needed in the political and military stalemate of 1429"**

different because she said God had sent her on a personal mission, to drive the English from France and to lead the Dauphin to his coronation. She brought the message, and wanted to carry it out.

Would Joan have faced prejudice based on her social standing and age on top of being a woman?
Yes. In all three ways she was unqualified, in contemporary eyes, for the role she claimed. To her enemies, that made her a witch. To her own side, it made her a miracle, at least while she was winning apparently miraculous victories. When she stopped winning, it meant she could be cast aside because she'd become too proud – reached too far beyond her station – and God had abandoned her.

How politically savvy was Joan?
I wouldn't say she was savvy. She didn't have the subtlety or experience to be an effective politician – but then she wasn't trying to be a politician. She wanted the politicians to stop politicking and listen to God, through her. Her certainty and clarity of purpose were just what was needed in the political and military stalemate of 1429. But they meant that she was left baffled and sidelined when the politicians took over again after her failure to capture Paris that September – an attack for which they'd allowed her only a single day of fighting. She couldn't understand why they no longer listened to her – nor, when she was captured in 1430, why they didn't seek to ransom her. The truth was that by then, politically, she'd become a problem rather than a solution.

Were there any women of this time that Joan would have sought support from?
One in particular, though I wish we could say more about their relationship: Yolande of Aragon, duchess of Anjou, mother-in-law of the Dauphin Charles. She was – unlike Joan – an extraordinary

Joan of Arc

Seeing the Dauphin crowned in Reims was a big part of Joan's prophecy

Myths surrounding Joan's story emerged during her lifetime and continue to exist to this day

politician, diplomat and powerbroker, and circumstantial evidence strongly suggests that she was instrumental in recognising the potential usefulness of Joan's claims and bringing her all the way from Domrémy to Chinon. But the fact that Yolande's influence - like that of so many powerful women - was exercised behind the scenes means that we can't know for sure exactly what she did or said, or how much she saw of Joan in person. Otherwise, Joan's response to other women wasn't always positive. When a woman named Catherine de la Rochelle came forward to claim she'd been sent by God to make peace between the Dauphin and the Duke of Burgundy, Joan said her visions were false and she should go back to her housework.

Did Joan have any sympathisers on the Burgundian/English side of the war?
Not many, at least while it was going on. The soldiers she fought against called her a whore and a witch, and the theologians who tried her believed her a heretic. But it's clear from the trial transcript that some of the clerics involved were impressed by the blazing certainty of her faith and her courage, even if they weren't won over to her position. So, sympathy if not support. And then, once the war was over and Joan's Dauphin had won, most of the newly reconciled Burgundians fell over themselves to make clear that they had always known she was right about the identity of the true king of France, and that the conflict - and Joan's death - had been entirely the fault of the English. Hindsight's a remarkable thing.

Did you find any common traits between Joan of Arc and the medieval she-wolves you've written about previously?
Charisma. Intelligence. Resourcefulness. Purpose. Bravery. Maybe above all a belief in their own agency, in a world where that wasn't easy for women to claim for themselves.

JOAN OF ARC IS OUT NOW FROM THE FOLIO SOCIETY

Biopic

FIRST MAN

Director: Damien Chazelle **Starring:** Ryan Gosling, Claire Foy, Jason Clarke **Country:** USA **Year:** 2018

A rare period film that seems driven by its pursuit of accuracy

Not long after working together on the Academy Award phenomenon *La La Land*, Damien Chazelle and Ryan Gosling teamed up again in this oddly more grounded retelling of the Apollo 11 Moon landing. Test pilot Neil Armstrong (Gosling) enters into NASA's Gemini program, which faces a string of challenges, accidents and setbacks during the Space Race, including the loss of Apollo 1's crew in a fire. Meanwhile, the Armstrongs face their own heartbreak with the death of their daughter – a tragedy that serves as an emotive through-line for the narrative.

While the successful Apollo 11 landing inevitably serves as the film's triumphant third act - spoiler alert, they land on the Moon - the preceding trials and tragedies faced by the Apollo team are a sobering reminder that the journey to the lunar surface was not easy, but was indeed hard as JFK famously proclaimed years earlier. Gosling brings out his characteristic minimal, reserved performance while depicting the driven yet privately grief-stricken Armstrong, and the film's dedication to accuracy was rewarded in an Academy Award for visual effects.

★ VERDICT ★

B- HOLLYWOOD — Enough human drama threaded between solid setpieces

B+ HISTORY — Plays it close to the record, apart from the odd emotional beat

OVERALL: B

The film was released a year before the 50th anniversary of the Apollo 11 Moon landing

01 The film opens with Neil Armstrong's X-15 crash before he joined NASA. The craft begins bouncing on the atmosphere, unable to descend, and he uses thrusters to return to Earth. The only possible inaccuracy is the clouds, which wouldn't form at that altitude.

02 The film appears to attribute some of Armstrong's stoicism to the death of his daughter Karen from brain cancer. How this affected his outlook is unclear, but the Armstrongs did lose her in 1962 and some colleagues later said they didn't even know he had a daughter.

03 *First Man* depicts protests against the Apollo programme, with many people bemoaning the expense and loss of life. These are all genuine debates from the era and the programme only really gained popularity around the time of Apollo 11.

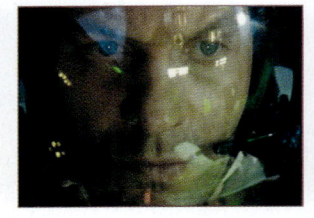

04 There are a couple of small inaccuracies in the Moon landing. It has an audio warning as the landing module approaches the surface, but in truth it was just alarms. And it suggests they only had seconds to spare in their landing, but they had a little time.

05 Armstrong leaves a bracelet with his daughter's name on the Moon, but there's no evidence this happened. That said, he was off comms for ten minutes and later claimed his log of personal items for the mission was lost, despite being fastidious about keeping documents.

The crew of Apollo 1 - Gus Grissom, Edward White and Roger Chaffee - who died in a tragic accident during a launch rehearsal

NASA and the Cold War

NASA's chief historian Brian Odom discusses the agency's role in the space race, the Apollo programme and its impact

What was the 'space race'?
It depends on the period that you're addressing, but most people are really talking about the [John F] Kennedy administration into the [Lyndon B] Johnson administration - the 1960s. I think you have to separate out Sputnik, although the space race resulted from the fear it instilled in the American public, but the space race was really a race to the Moon. Kennedy wanted to get to the Moon first as it would be a great propaganda coup. In the global South, you had a lot of countries becoming independent from former colonial powers. What system would they follow? Would they follow the US liberal democracy or would they follow the Soviet example of communism? These two ideological systems were in conflict with each other and Kennedy saw the race to the Moon as a way to demonstrate American technological power and the benefit of one system over another.

How much was the foundation of NASA a response to the launching of Sputnik by the USSR and, by extension, the space race?
[President Dwight D] Eisenhower's chief problem during this period was which branch of the military would be responsible for developing a launch vehicle. This was problematic because it put the various branches in competition with each other. When Sputnik launched, Eisenhower wasn't that concerned about it, he didn't see it as an existential threat. He saw it for what it was: the Soviet Union launching a transmitter into orbit. But the American public saw it differently because they saw it as part of a larger Cold War

NASA's chief historian, Brian Odom, has worked at NASA for over ten years. Having studied at both the University of Alabama and Middle Tennessee State University, he is a doctor of philosophy and public history. He is the co-editor of NASA and the Long Civil Rights Movement.

competition. When Eisenhower opened NASA for business on 1 October 1958 he was really trying to disentangle all the military branches from being in competition with each other and move space exploration into a government agency dedicated to peaceful, open communication instead of directly responding to Sputnik.

What was NASA like in its early years?
In those early years, particularly 1958-1961, NASA was working to understand what its overall programme would be. What were its priorities? Where would it apply the majority of its funding? There was a goal to put a man in space, which would be achieved with Alan Shepard's flight, but there was also a huge element of NASA that was thinking 'what are the scientific questions that this agency is going to answer'? Questions like 'what can we do with satellites in space?' It was kind of a wild west, it was trying to figure out what it wanted to be. Following Shepard's flight in May 1961, it became very clear that the space race was continuing. President Kennedy committed to the lunar programme, and once that commitment was made the resources came with it. NASA's attention for the next seven or eight years was focused on putting a man on the Moon.

How dangerous were those early years of spaceflight compared to more recent missions?
One thing to stress is that space exploration has not gotten easier. The challenges that were there in the very beginning are still the challenges that we face today. Yes, they were developing new systems and putting human beings at the top of rockets that were built for nuclear delivery systems [the Mercury and Gemini programmes] but what we've learned over the decades of space exploration is that it hasn't gotten easier. Remember the Challenger accident in 1986, the Columbia accident in 2003. Space is still very, very challenging and dangerous. It hasn't gotten easier, but we've learned a lot over the decades

How significant a victory was the Moon landing?
That's a good question, and as historians it's something that we are still debating. I think the Moon landing really resonates more today in terms of the propaganda aspect; it was a huge achievement. The incredible achievement of building the technological systems that could enable you to do this, to land human beings on the Moon and return safely. But did the actual landing on the Moon achieve Kennedy's goal of demonstrating the superiority of one set of institutions over another? I think historians still debate that question. That doesn't lessen the achievement, but the idea of the Moon landing as a victory over the Soviets? That's a great question.

How much can we consider NASA and its achievements to be products of the Cold War?
We can't forget about the Cold War context for all this activity and the seemingly existential threat of the Soviet Union. As an historian looking at this from a contextual standpoint, I can tell you that I don't think Kennedy would've committed to going to the Moon without the race between the US and the Soviet Union. Without the Apollo programme, how far and how quickly would our technology have advanced to the point it is at today? The Cold War made the Moon landing a priority in Kennedy's mind and his commitment to it really did change America and American technology. People who were influenced by the space race went to college to engage in science and mathematics to be part of something like this. They may not all have contributed to the space programme, but they went on to contribute in many other fields. So without the space race and the Apollo programme what's the impact on these fields? It's difficult to say if there had been no Apollo programme, how the world would have changed.

Biopic

COMMAND MODULE COLUMBIA

United States
1969

On 16 July 1969, astronauts Neil Armstrong, Edwin 'Buzz' Aldrin and Michael Collins blasted off from Cape Kennedy in Florida. The Apollo 11 mission aimed to see the first human Moon landing, with the astronauts then returning safely to Earth. The famous space flight not only saw the Americans achieve their aim, but it also became the space mission where humanity first walked on the Moon. A few hours after the successful lunar landing of Apollo 11 on 20 July, Armstrong emerged from the spacecraft with a TV camera, ready to transmit the first Moon walk to an audience of an estimated 650 million people.

"One small step for man, one giant leap for mankind," Armstrong's voice echoed around the world. The Americans had succeeded in putting the first man on the Moon, followed almost immediately by the second, Aldrin, who joined Armstrong on the lunar surface 20 minutes later. While outside the spacecraft, Armstrong and Aldrin placed medallions on the Moon's surface which commemorated three Apollo 1 astronauts and two cosmonauts who had died in accidents during their endeavours to reach space.

The Apollo 11 spacecraft was made up of three modules: the Service Module that contained the main propulsion system, the Lunar Module (nicknamed The Eagle) that landed on the moon, and the Command Module (nicknamed Columbia) that was the only section to return to Earth. The Command Module began its descent on 24 July and carried the three astronauts back to a hero's return, landing in the Pacific Ocean. From there the astronauts were picked up by a ship waiting for them nearby. The Columbia became a highly significant piece of space race history, and was exhibited across the United States until it found its permanent home at the Smithsonian National Air and Space Museum in 1971.

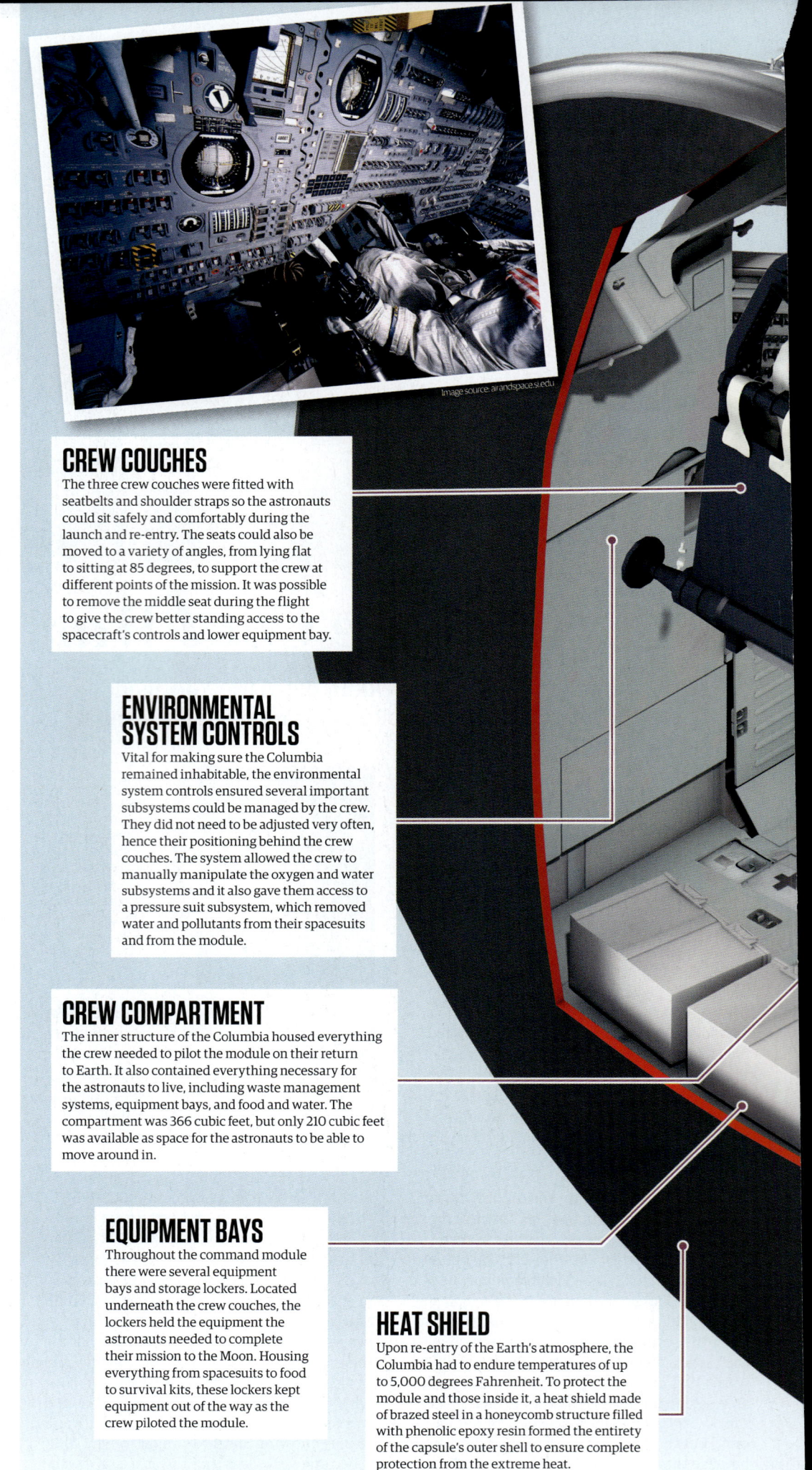

Image source: airandspace.si.edu

CREW COUCHES
The three crew couches were fitted with seatbelts and shoulder straps so the astronauts could sit safely and comfortably during the launch and re-entry. The seats could also be moved to a variety of angles, from lying flat to sitting at 85 degrees, to support the crew at different points of the mission. It was possible to remove the middle seat during the flight to give the crew better standing access to the spacecraft's controls and lower equipment bay.

ENVIRONMENTAL SYSTEM CONTROLS
Vital for making sure the Columbia remained inhabitable, the environmental system controls ensured several important subsystems could be managed by the crew. They did not need to be adjusted very often, hence their positioning behind the crew couches. The system allowed the crew to manually manipulate the oxygen and water subsystems and it also gave them access to a pressure suit subsystem, which removed water and pollutants from their spacesuits and from the module.

CREW COMPARTMENT
The inner structure of the Columbia housed everything the crew needed to pilot the module on their return to Earth. It also contained everything necessary for the astronauts to live, including waste management systems, equipment bays, and food and water. The compartment was 366 cubic feet, but only 210 cubic feet was available as space for the astronauts to be able to move around in.

EQUIPMENT BAYS
Throughout the command module there were several equipment bays and storage lockers. Located underneath the crew couches, the lockers held the equipment the astronauts needed to complete their mission to the Moon. Housing everything from spacesuits to food to survival kits, these lockers kept equipment out of the way as the crew piloted the module.

HEAT SHIELD
Upon re-entry of the Earth's atmosphere, the Columbia had to endure temperatures of up to 5,000 degrees Fahrenheit. To protect the module and those inside it, a heat shield made of brazed steel in a honeycomb structure filled with phenolic epoxy resin formed the entirety of the capsule's outer shell to ensure complete protection from the extreme heat.

First Man

MAIN DISPLAY CONSOLE
One metre high and just over two metres long, the main display console (MDC) was designed to be used by all three crew members, but could also be used by one astronaut when the other two were in the lunar module. The MDC controls were arranged according to where each crew member would sit and what their responsibilities were. On the left of the MDC were the flight controls and on the right were the spacecraft subsystems management controls.

TUNNEL ENTRANCE
The forward docking tunnel entrance provided a route for the crew of Apollo 11 to move between Columbia and the lunar module (the Eagle) when the two modules were docked together. Sealed with a mechanical hatch, the tunnel was used by Armstrong and Aldrin before and after their moonwalk. Another entrance was positioned on the side of Columbia, which was used by the crew to get in and out of the command module.

WINDOW
On the side hatch of the command module there was a small window. Directly facing the crew couches, the Apollo 11 astronauts would be able to see an incredible view from this window as they flew into space and towards the Moon. Michael Collins mentioned the view in a tribute he wrote to Columbia: "How could I be lonely? You have me and I have you (plus the fuel cell), and that view out the window."

COMMANDER'S CONTROLS
As mission commander of Apollo 11, Neil Armstrong was responsible for the commander's controls. These included the flight controls as well as the management controls for some of the spacecraft subsystems such as stabilisation, crew safety, Earth landing and emergency detection. Also situated with the commander's controls were one of the navigation panels and the indicators for the spacecraft's velocity, altitude and attitude.

AN ODE TO COLUMBIA
Michael Collins was the only astronaut of the Apollo 11 mission not to walk on the Moon. While inside Columbia, he took the time to write a message on the wall of the craft which has since become a treasured part of space race history. The message reads: "Spacecraft 107, alias Apollo 11, 'alias Columbia'. The Best Ship to Come Down the Line. God Bless Her. Michael Collins, CMP."

121

Biopic

ELIZABETH: THE GOLDEN AGE

Director: Shekhar Kapur **Starring:** Cate Blanchett, Geoffrey Rush, Clive Owen **Country:** UK **Year:** 2007

Elizabeth I's finest hour against the Spanish Armada wasn't quite Hollywood's

One of the most celebrated monarchs in English history, Elizabeth I's reign has inspired centuries of drama, telling the story of the queen with the 'heart and stomach of a king', who refused to share her throne with a man. This 2007 retelling sees Cate Blanchett return to the throne, nine years after appearing in *Elizabeth* (1998), which focused on the early years of the monarch's reign.

Director Shekhar Kapur's second foray into Tudor history centres around the critical period of England's war with Spain, culminating in the Armada of 1588. Somewhat counter-factually sailing to the rescue is Sir Walter Raleigh (Clive Owen), who leads the English to victory over the grand Spanish fleet. While students of history may also get a sinking feeling at Jordi Mollà's performance as a craven, malevolent Philip II of Spain, it's an entertaining antithesis to the heroic warrior queen, dressed in shining armour, belting out her famed speech. While box office takings and critical reviews fell far short of Kapur's 1998 instalment, *The Golden Age* did receive an Academy Award for its costume design.

Depicted as a child, the Infanta Isabella was actually an adolescent during this period

VERDICT
- **C** HOLLYWOOD — Some fine performances if you can stomach the script
- **E** HISTORY — Not a lot of real history at the heart of the drama

OVERALL D

01 In the film, Elizabeth is confronted on the altar of Old St Paul's Cathedral by Anthony Babington wielding a pistol. While this near-assassination is good for tension, Babington's plot was uncovered during the planning stage and he was hung, drawn and quartered.

02 "We're losing too many ships!" screeches Charles Howard, Earl of Nottingham as the Armada meets the English fleet. No English ships were sunk during the real battle and Howard – Elizabeth's most effective enforcer – wasn't the screeching type.

03 Both English courtiers and Spanish envoys wear swords when they meet Elizabeth I, but in reality the constant threat of assassination meant that only members of the Royal Guard were allowed to carry weapons in the queen's presence.

04 The film depicts the queen being presented with aspiring suitors from across Europe, including Erik of Sweden. In 1588 – the year of the Spanish Armada – the queen was 52, all the wooing had happened when she was around 27 and Erik had actually died in 1577.

05 Sir Walter Raleigh takes a lead role in the on-screen defeat of the Armada. In reality his input was limited to the less-than-blockbuster subject of naval reform, while the defence of the realm was co-ordinated by Sir Francis Drake, Robert Dudley and various others.

Elizabeth: The Golden Age

Royal Rivals

How do the reigns of these two queens compare?

Elizabeth I, Queen of England

Mary, Queen of Scots

RELIGION

By the time Elizabeth ascended the throne, England could no longer cope with being pulled back and forth between Protestantism and Catholicism. Favouring a tolerant approach Elizabeth's Religious Settlement consisted of the Acts of Supremacy and Uniformity passed in 1559, which established a middle ground between the two religions and allowed people to believe in what they wished, with Elizabeth as the Supreme Governor of the Church of England. Although recusants of both religions resisted the new measures, a tentative balance was reached.

While Mary was away in France, Scotland had gone from being a Catholic country to a Protestant one. Consequently, as a Catholic female ruler, the cards were stacked against Mary in a rough and male-dominated realm. However, just like Elizabeth, Mary took a tolerant approach to religion. Mary understood that she was not in a position to fight the powerful Scottish lords and so she did not interfere with religion, even helping to crush a Catholic rebellion in 1562. Mary also wanted to avoid upsetting Elizabeth, in case it risked her chances of being named heir.

POLITICS

It is well known that loyal and close advisors such as Cecil and Walsingham served Elizabeth for the majority of her reign, and she relied on them heavily. The queen was known to comprise and listen to her advisors, for which she has been commended, but could frustrate them with her indecision, often taking months to make a choice. Having said this, Elizabeth could certainly stand her ground with her advisors, even if they did go behind her back.

Unlike her cousin Elizabeth, Mary was not surrounded by men who were loyal to their queen and many of them were suspicious of her as a Catholic. Her attempts to mediate between her advisors often backfired and some of them in particular, namely her half-brother Moray, had designs on her crown. Mary's fate was sealed thanks to her disastrous marriages to Darnley and Bothwell, who both wanted to seize her power, further weakening her position beyond repair.

SECURING THE SUCCESSION

To the frustration of Cecil and her advisors, Elizabeth constantly flirted with the idea of marriage but never committed to it instead choosing to style herself as England's 'Virgin Queen'. In doing so, she never provided England with an heir and she refused to name one until she was lying on her deathbed. Without a child to succeed her, Elizabeth was forced to leave the crown to Mary's son, King James VI, bringing an end to the Tudor dynasty.

Undoubtedly Mary's greatest achievement was successfully producing a male heir for the Scottish throne. It was a triumph over Elizabeth, who remained childless, with Mary able to show that she had the means to continue her dynasty. Although she lost her throne and her head, Mary's son James succeeded her in Scotland and he eventually succeeded Elizabeth in England, joining the two realms in a personal union.

STABILITY

As Queen of England for over four decades, Elizabeth provided England with much needed stability after the short and turbulent reigns of her brother, King Edward VI, and her sister, Queen Mary I. Though Elizabeth's position on throne was threatened while her cousin remained alive and she was targeted by numerous assassination plots, the queen ultimately prevailed to oversee a golden age in English history.

Unfortunately for Mary, her position on the Scottish throne was always far from stable. She was always perceived to be more of a French queen than a Scottish one, and the Scottish lords resented the fact that France had held so much influence in Scotland during the regency of her mother. Trapped in a vicious cycle of political intrigue and poor decisions, Mary lost her throne just six years after her return, which is a testament to how unstable her crown really was.

LEGACY

There is no denying that Elizabeth left an enduring legacy that continues to fascinate us to this very day. She dedicated an extraordinary amount of time to cultivating her image and propaganda, creating some of the most iconic portraits in English history. Elizabeth left behind a stable and secure England for which she is celebrated as 'Gloriana', forever a symbol of English patriotism and success.

If this rating was about infamy, then Mary would score 5/5, no questions asked. Her downfall and execution was one of the most controversial moments in history and to this day, there are constantly new films, books and television series dedicated to examining her complicated life. However, losing her crown permanently damaged Mary's reputation as a queen and consequently tarnished her legacy in the centuries since her death.

Biopic

SELMA

Director: Ava DuVernay **Starring:** David Oyelowo, Oprah Winfrey, Tim Roth **Country:** USA **Year:** 2014

Is this Civil Rights retelling right on the facts?

Set in one of the most volatile periods of the Civil Rights movement in the United States and at the peak of Martin Luther King Jr's powers, Selma is an impactful biopic of the celebrated leader. Directed by Ava DuVernay (although Lee Daniels was originally attached) it was a movie that attracted criticism over historical accuracy, although many of the details are up to interpretation.

The film begins with the shocking murder of four Black girls in Birmingham, Alabama and the resultant campaign for voting rights reform that King and the Southern Christian Leadership Conference leads in Selma. It's an often complex portrayal of the characters and issues involved. King and others debate the nature of their campaign and argue over the tactic being employed in revealing ways. We see the splits between the different factions of the Civil Rights movement, such as between the SCLC and Student Nonviolent Coordinating Committee (SNCC).

Selma ultimately made over $67 million at the boxoffice from a budget of $20 million and picked up an Oscar for Best Original Song for John Legend's 'Glory'.

US Representative John Lewis who is portrayed in the film, defended it from critics over its accuracy

★ VERDICT ★

HOLLYWOOD: A-
A stirring biopic of MLK at the peak of his powers

HISTORY: B
An honest and at times brutal portrayal of King's campaign

OVERALL: B+

01 Most of the film's controversy is around the portrayal of President Johnson. Many working with him at the time dubbed him a champion of civil rights. King's autobiography paints a different picture. We may never know if Johnson was a barrier to King.

02 When King meets with Johnson, the famous Resolute Desk can be seen, but this is inaccurate. Towering at six foot 3.5 inches, Johnson was too large for the historic desk. For comfort, he had a plainer replacement made by the Senate cabinet shop.

03 None of King's speeches that appear in the film are accurate. However, this is for good reason - all of King's speeches are under copyright. Ava DuVernay had no option but to rewrite all of King's famous phrases, but this is cleverly and subtly done.

04 The death of 26-year-old Jimmie Lee Jackson is one of the most harrowing sequences and, unfortunately, almost entirely accurate. The only fact that the film missed is that Jackson died days after the shooting in hospital, not in the café where he was shot.

05 We see a woman trying to earn the right to vote, but is rejected after being unable to name the 67 county judges in Alabama. This was one of the requirements used to restrict African American votes. The woman, Annie Lee Cooper, was real.

Behind The Movement

Some of the figures who helped shape the Civil Rights movement

MARCUS GARVEY
17 Aug 1887 – 10 June 1940

An early proponent of Black Nationalism, Marcus Garvey believed in a pan-African movement that involved global mobilisation of Black people against oppression. He founded the Universal Negro Improvement Association and even launched the Black Star Line to build trade links between Africa and America.

BAYARD RUSTIN
17 March 1912 – 24 Aug 1987

One of Martin Luther King Jr's closest advisors and one of the organisers of the March on Washington in 1963, Rustin grew up in a Quaker family who were heavily involved in the NAACP. As well as fighting for Civil Rights, Rustin was also openly gay and faced further discrimination both within and outside the movement.

ELIJAH MUHAMMAD
7 Oct 1897 – 25 Feb 1975

The man who would become the head of the Nation of Islam was born to former-slave sharecroppers in Georgia. He took over the NOI from its founder Wallace D Fard after he mysteriously disappeared. He was a strong advocate for black separatism and helped develop Malcolm X and his own successor, Louis Farrakhan.

FANNIE LOU HAMER
6 Oct 1917 – 14 March 1977

Joining the movement in 1962 to fight for voting rights, Hamer was fired from her job because of her activism. In 1964 she co-founded the Mississippi Freedom Democratic Party, which challenged for speaking time at the Democratic Convention. Her testimony before the DNC credentials committee garnered national attention.

ELLA BAKER
13 Dec 1903 – 13 Dec 1986

While Baker worked with Martin Luther King as director of the SCLC, her commitment to mobilising black youth in America saw her split from King in 1960 to form the independent Student Nonviolent Coordinating Committee, focused on grassroots organising over the top-down leadership she saw elsewhere.

STOKELY CARMICHAEL
29 June 1941 – 15 Nov 1998

The originator of the rallying cry of 'Black Power', Stokely Carmichael (later known as Kwame Ture) originally joined the SNCC (and became its chairman) before seeking a more militant path closer to that of Malcolm X. He ultimately aligned more with the newly formed Black Panther Party and moved to Guinea.

Biopic

MALCOLM X

Director: Spike Lee **Starring:** Denzel Washington, Angela Bassett, Albert Hall **Country:** USA **Year:** 1992

A sweeping biopic that seemingly leaves no stone unturned

One of the most important figures of the Civil Rights movement, the life of Malcolm X was almost destined to be brought to the big screen. Growing up under attack from white supremacists, before falling into a life of crime, the young Malcolm's life changes when he meets Elijah Muhammed (Al Freeman Jr.), and converts to Islam. He soon grows to become one of the leading voices in the Nation of Islam, advocating for Black nationalism and liberation, by any means. After becoming disillusioned with Elijah Muhammed's leadership, Malcolm breaks away from the Nation of Islam, but becomes a target of the organisation's tactics.

Based on Malcolm X's autobiography, Spike Lee's 1992 epic casts Denzel Washington in one of his early standout roles. An early screenplay adapted by writer and activist James Baldwin underwent several difficult rewrites, and several of Malcolm's contemporaries and his widow Betty Shabazz were consultants during production. Washington's powerful portrayal of Malcolm received particular recognition among critics, and he was nominated in the 1993 Academy Awards for best actor.

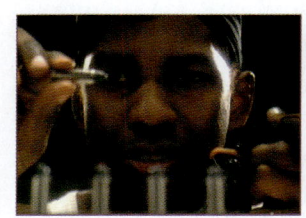

VERDICT

- **Hollywood: A-** — A powerful performance by Denzel Washington
- **History: B-** — Based on an autobiography, so rarely misses the mark
- **Overall: B**

Civil Rights activists Al Sharpton and Bobby Seale both have cameos in the film

01 Just as depicted in the movie, Malcolm lived in Harlem, New York, as a young man and became involved in criminal activities. He was arrested and convicted of larceny and breaking and entering in 1946. It was while in prison that he would find Islam.

02 Contrary to the movie, it was his siblings who introduced him to Islam, not a fellow prisoner. John Elton Bembry got him interested in reading, which later expanded to religion. In the movie a character named Baines takes on this role, merging the two stories.

03 Upon leaving jail Malcolm drops his surname Little and adopts X as his last name, becoming a minister in the Nation of Islam. As shown in the film, he rises up through the ranks as a fiery and sometimes controversial speaker, building a strong base in Harlem.

04 The film accurately depicts Malcolm X's pilgrimage to Mecca (he actually travelled abroad on a number of occasions) and the revelation he experienced of seeing Islam as a multi-ethnic faith. His newfound openness was always through conversion to Islam, though.

05 The assassination of Malcolm X remains a hotly debated event. Spike Lee took his depiction largely from the FBI report, which is disputed. The overall series of events, from scuffle in the Audubon Ballroom to Malcolm X being shot, appear accurate.

Malcolm X

Rise and Fall of X

Key events and defining moments of the Civil Rights hero

1925
Malcolm X born
Born Malcolm Little at University Hospital in Omaha, Nebraska, he is the fourth of seven children. His father, Earle Little, is a baptist lay speaker, while his mother, Louise Norton Little, is a stay-at-home parent.
19 May 1925

1931
Defining moment
Malcolm's father killed 1931
Aged six, a young Malcolm Little enrols at Pleasant Grove Elementary School in Michigan. That same year, his father is killed after being struck by a speeding streetcar. The official report states it was an accident, but Malcolm's mother Louise is convinced it was murder. His father had been an outspoken leader of the local Universal Negro Improvement Association (UNIA), so rumours run rife that members of the Black Legion had organised a hit on Earle to get rid of a black pride activist. His father had taken out life insurance before his murder but the money is never paid out to the family.

1939
Louise Little committed
After dating a local man for a few months, Louise Little becomes pregnant. The man then vanishes once he learns of the pregnancy, causing her to have a nervous breakdown. She's committed to State Mental Hospital in Kalamazoo, Michigan.
1938-1939

1943
Avoids military service
At the age of 18, Malcolm moves to New York. He's drafted to the US Army, but is deemed unsuitable for service. Rumours claim he feigned a mental condition to avoid being drafted into service during WWII.
1943

1952
Defining moment
Freedom at last 1952
After serving six years of his eight to ten-year sentence for larceny, Malcolm is released from prison. Having become a dedicated follower of the Nation Of Islam, Malcolm soon comes to the attention of Elijah Muhammad. He meets with Muhammad in Chicago and few weeks later is appointed an assistant minister for the movement. Around this time he abandons his birth name Little and starts using the surname X. Around this time the FBI also creates a file for him, following a letter he writes to President Truman opposing to the Korean War.

1947
Converts to Nation Of Islam
During the early years of his sentence, Malcolm becomes aware of the Nation Of Islam, a religious movement originating in the US. He converts and finds inspiration from the words of their leader, Elijah Muhammad.
1947

1946
Serving time
After getting involved in the criminal underworld, Malcolm commits a number of burglaries in and around Boston in 1945. In 1946 he's convicted of larceny (unlawful taking of another's property) and is sent to Charlestown State Prison, Boston.
1946

1953
Preaching across the US
Elijah Muhammad elevates Malcolm X to the influential position of minister and sends him to preach at a number of newly opened temples. Over the next two years he spreads the NOI word in Boston, New York and Philadelphia.
1953-1955

1957
Johnson Hinton incident
Four members of the Nation Of Islam are beaten with nightsticks by New York police officers. After the men are arrested, Malcolm arrives with a crowd of some 4,000 NOI followers and force the police to give them medical attention. Covered by national news, it is the first time Malcolm permeates the public eye.
26 April 1957

1958
Malcolm meets Betty
In 1955, Malcolm meets Betty Sanders at one of his lectures. A year later she joins the Nation Of Islam and takes the symbolic surname X as the two continue to court. In January 1958 Malcolm proposes over the phone and they marry two days later.
January 1958

1963
Courting infamy
Following the assassination of John F. Kennedy, reporters approached Malcolm X for a comment on the event and he described it as "chickens coming home to roost". The comments cause national outrage and he is barred from representing the Nation Of Islam.
1 December 1963

1965
Defining moment
Assassinated in Manhattan 21 Feb 1965
Following a pilgrimage to Mecca the year before, Malcolm returns a far less radical man. He begins denouncing any form of violence and urging people of all colours to work together to attain civil rights for all. He receives death threats from a number of more radical Islamic groups, including outspoken members of the Nation Of Islam. His wife Betty even contacts the FBI and tells them her husband is "as good as dead." While preparing to address an Organization of African-American Unity rally in Manhattan, Malcolm is shot dead by angry militants. Three men are arrested and sentenced to life in prison.

1964
Leaving the NOI
Malcolm splits from the NOI and soon converts to Sunni Islam. He meets Martin Luther King Jr for the first and only time at a Senate debate on the Civil Rights Bill. At this time he also urges African-Americans to be prepared to take arms if their voting rights are not protected.
8 March 1964

127

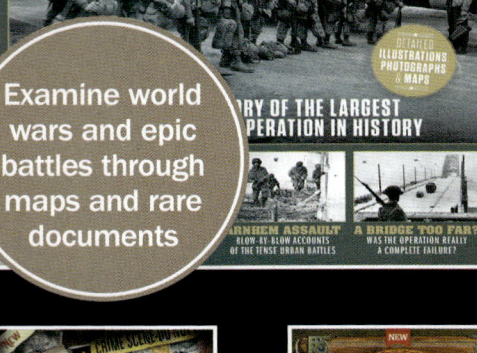

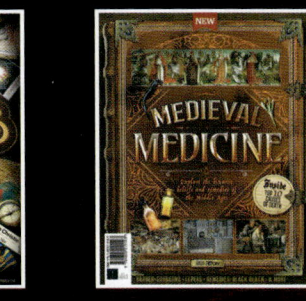

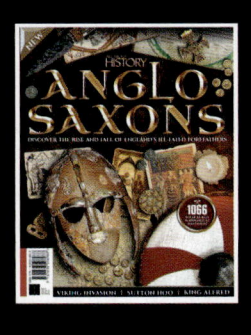

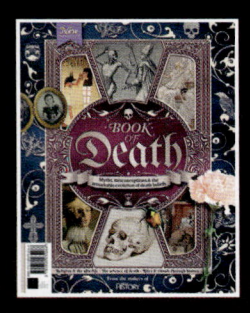

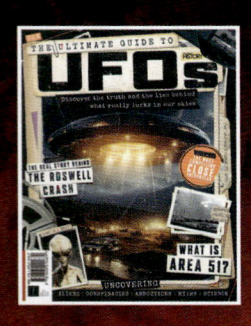

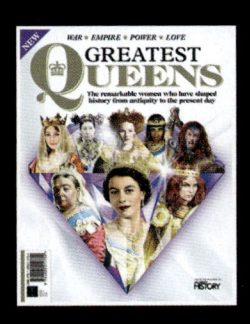

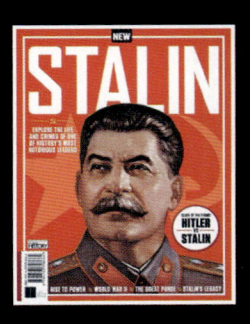

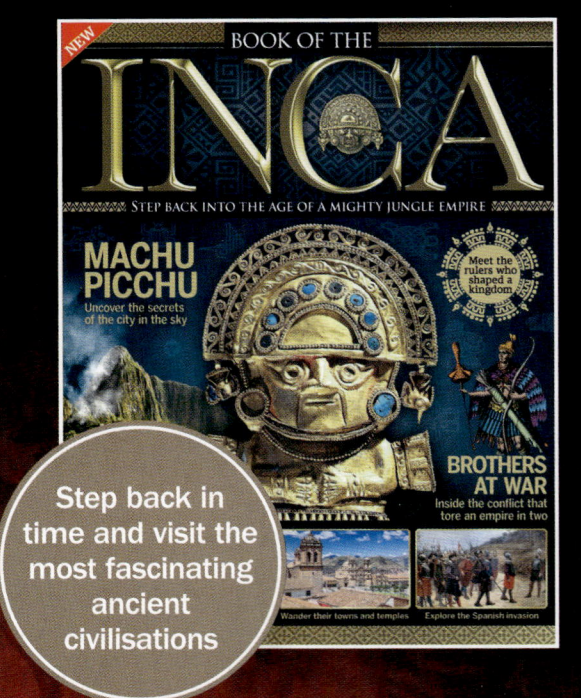

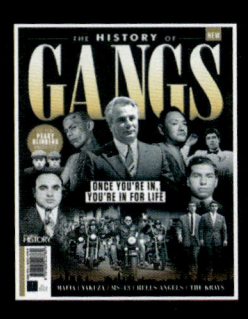

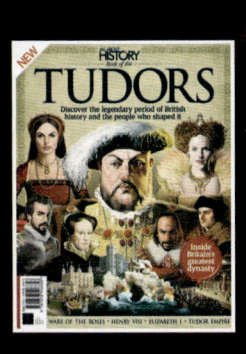

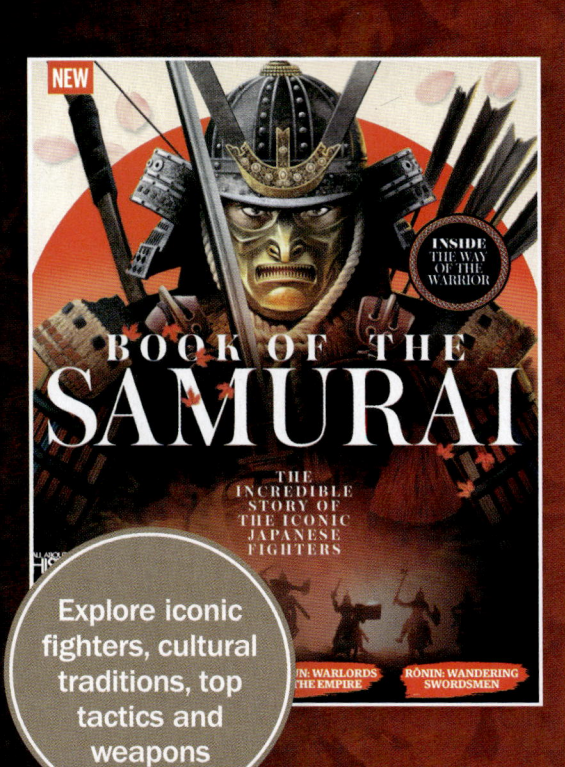

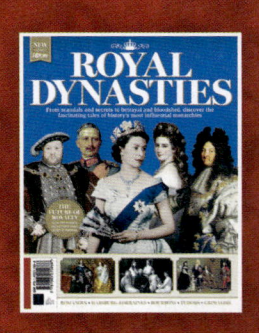

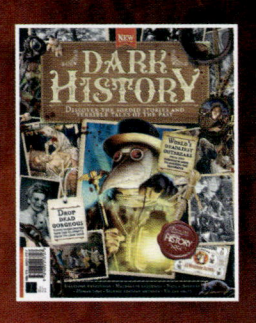

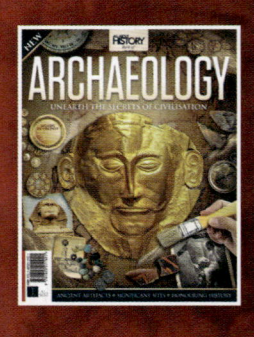

Examine world wars and epic battles through maps and rare documents

Step back in time and visit the most fascinating ancient civilisations

Explore iconic fighters, cultural traditions, top tactics and weapons

✓ Get great savings when you buy direct from us

✓ 1000s of great titles, many not available anywhere else

✓ World-wide delivery and super-safe ordering